SEX AND M,

Unlocking and Restoring the Power of Sex Through Biblical and Psychological Insight

Chris Legg, LPC

Mark Legg

CONTENTS

Praise for *Sex and Marriage*

"Looking for a new way to understand what your spouse is really saying about sex? I heartily recommend Chris Legg's book! Whether you're engaged or have been married a lifetime, like David and me, this one creates lightbulb moments for you both. Practical and yet *thoroughly researched*, this is exactly the kind of book we like to take turns reading out loud to each other. So fun!

If marriage is a parable of God's love, how then are we supposed to live? *Sex and Marriage* has all the good stuff packed into only twelve short chapters. Step by step, Chris Legg applies practical insight as a professional counselor, pastor, and biblical scholar. Set aside a few hours; I bet you'll read it cover to cover without pausing, just like I did!"

—Cathy Krafve, speaker, author of *Marriage Conversations*, and host of Fireside Talk Radio

"Chris and Mark Legg are the real deal. These are wise, fun, brilliant men who have richly blessed me. I am confident they will positively shape you as well. There is deep wisdom here, summarized in approachable and palatable pith like: 'If you pursue a man sexually, he assumes that you are pursuing him. If you pursue a woman sexually, she is likely to interpret that as you pursuing sex, not her.' I know of no place one can find insight so finely distilled that it glides into practical application with ease. This is an important, wonderful book, and I praise God for it."

—Dr. Wayne Braudrick, author, professor, and Lead Pastor of Frisco Bible Church

FORWARD

About a year ago, a friend from graduate school attended a weekend marriage conference where the speaker referenced several of our research studies. Our friend introduced herself to the speaker, mentioned our friendship, and said we would appreciate knowing he found our work useful.

We did! ·

Chris reached out to us, and it was clear he was a man who wanted the same things we did: For each partner in a marriage to better understand themselves and one another. Like us, he wanted each spouse to use that understanding to thrive in their relationships and honor God in the process. We had found a co-laborer and friend.

When Chris later asked us to review a book called *Sex and Marriage* that he was writing with his grown son, Mark, we were intrigued . . . and nervous. We had by now watched some of Chris' presentations and had seen that his teaching was insightful, humble, and sensitive on a topic that has often caused significant pain in people's lives. But a book is different than a talk. Written text—especially on this topic!—can often be misunderstood or taken out of context because of space limitations, and can't provide for all the unique circumstances that couples encounter. We held our collective breath when Chris sent us the manuscript.

We were quickly able to exhale. Reading this book felt like reading Malcom Gladwell. Chris and Mark show an amazing gift for synthesizing big thoughts and research studies into actionable insights. We found ourselves taking notes and saying things like, "I hadn't heard of that study before," or "Ahh, that makes so much sense now," or "That's such a helpful perspective, I'd never thought of framing it that way."

But they also go beyond an author like Gladwell. Chris Legg isn't simply a researcher turned writer. He's a pastor and licensed therapist with twenty-five years of experience. Chris's insights aren't just based on the research others have done; they're based on years of real-life interactions with real-life people with real-life struggles. As a result, he has a genuine heart for women and men who are hurting and who will find both insight and encouragement here. All of that is what sets this book apart.

To get the most from this process, we encourage you to read this book with a curious mind and generous heart. As you see these "aha moments," think about what you can learn, not just what you expect your spouse to learn. Then, we hope both of you will be willing to read and discuss it together.

It takes courage to write a book on such a sensitive topic today. It would have been much easier for Chris to continue to do marriage retreats one at a time and leave this book unwritten. We are so grateful for Chris and Mark's willingness to step out. And by the time you get even a short way into this remarkable book, we think you will feel the same.

Shaunti and Jeff Feldhahn, bestselling authors of *For Women Only, For Men Only,* and *Secrets of Sex and Marriage*

To my best friend and lover, Ginger Legg. Thank you for navigating the rapids, cultivating the garden, unlocking the door, stocking the fridge, and creating a living parable of God's love with me all of these years. You are God's Engedi for me. I thank Him for the good gift of you.

Caution: Generalities Ahead

This book is meant to create understanding that leads to freedom, not put people in boxes. Nevertheless, in every audience, there are people who feel radically misunderstood.

So much has been published from a Christian perspective about marriage that's not about intimacy but transaction (we attack this concept in Chapter 8). This tendency has led wives, especially, to dread books in which their sexuality is merely a commodity for trade. Books that claim men only want you to sexually fulfill him, stay attractive, clean the home, and satisfy basically all his wants are toxic and exhausting. You have every reason to shudder at the thought of risking another marriage book. I pray this is radically different. For men, you can feel overwhelmed by just another Christian marriage book with stuff you can't live up to. They feel fluffy and based in some therapist's (or pastor's) opinions that don't seem worth any more than yours. Again, it is my intention, if you follow the path from beginning to end, to create a practical and emotionally sound strategy for being a world-class husband!

Sadly, there must be generalities in any book about marriage, especially ones about sex. Those generalities sometimes come from anecdotes, which can be misleading, but many come from hard statistics. There's a reason speakers at marriage conferences can get great laughs with broad strokes. Here, I've tried to make the generalities based on evidence.

Here's an example we'll discuss a few times in this book. Around 30 percent of women seem to have a higher sex drive than their husbands. For every joking comment about this difference that lands with the 70 percent or more of the crowd, there are maybe a third who feel like, well, as one woman described it to me, "circus freaks." I unpack this seventy-thirty split more in FAQ 2, reviewing relevant data, studies, and my professional experience. Of all places, I don't want anyone to feel like a freak here, so I want to be crystal clear and up-front about my assumptions in this book.

The patterns that I'll unpack (mainly how most men seem to integrate sex and their identities while most women don't) are not universal. However, even for couples where the wife has a higher sex drive, the patterns I'll discuss often apply to them. My interpretation does not merely correlate to sex drive—it goes deeper than that.

Men have sexual and emotional desires. Women have sexual and emotional desires. In many ways they overlap at the individual levels and at the gender/sex levels; in many ways, they do not overlap at the individual level and sometimes at the gender/sex level. There is no universal way to capture sex differences.

For example, I personally know two or three women who, having heard my teaching about sex and marriage, said they finally felt understood—*but by the insights into how men think!* So, by my best guess, maybe as many as 10 percent of women intuit sex the same way most men do (who intuit things my way around 90 percent of the time). I have to assume that a certain percentage of men would have the reverse, but it is probably even more difficult for them open up about it. Women who want to make love more often or who intuit sex in ways common to

men are not freaks, fiends, or nymphos. They are just women who have a
threshold or intuition that is less common among their sex. A man with
an intuition to not integrate sex and their identity is not less manly—it's
just his intuition. Again, this is something I explore in FAQs 1 and 2.

There's another bias at play here. For all the couples I've seen in therapy,
I only see the ones with problems. Those people whose sex lives are wonderful and running smoothly, I don't see in my office. So if, in any given
marriage, the husband intuits things the same way as the majority of
women (and his wife is in the majority), I won't see them for counseling
because there's no conflict! I genuinely think that in twenty-five years of
counseling, I may have met two examples of couples struggling with sex
who intuited things similarly.

Of course, sometimes the minority will be with the minority and those
marriages will experience the challenge of *both parties* identifying better
with the *opposite sex* stereotype. My wife and I have this in regards to
multitasking. I am in the minority of men who prefer to multitask and
my wife is in the minority of women who prefer to mono-task.

However, much more often, the majority with be mated with the majority. Therefore, most of the examples in this book will cater to that
blending, but I want you to know that this is not out of ignorance or
dismissal for the rest. For all of us, here is my recommendation:

Embrace it. Ladies, if you identify with the common male intuition, use
this book to find the language to talk about it with new comprehension!
Men, if you connect with the more typical female perspective, let your
wife know! This shouldn't be shameful to either of you. Remember,
understanding is the goal. Understanding binds together with intimacy
and love. On that note, remember that around half of this book is a

biblical unpacking of marriage, so it applies to all of us. Exactly how will we live that out in each of our marriages, especially regarding sex? That's what the rest of the book is about.

With this caution out of the way, we can begin.

IT'S ONE OF THOSE DAYS . . .

I t's one of those days. You and your spouse can't seem to get on the same page. You're together but never in sync. Miscommunication abounds. Both of you feel misunderstood. Throughout the day, you get snappier and more short-tempered. A few times, one of you attempts something more harmonious, but it doesn't play.

Man, days like that are exhausting, emotionally and spiritually. In these situations, neither spouse feels loved or even liked very much.

Now, imagine that at the end of a day like this, the husband sidles up to his wife and says, conspiratorially, "Hey . . . you wanna mess around?"

Insert screeching record player sound effect here.

Her response? *What—Is he insane?* She is shocked at his lack of love, compassion, and sensitivity. She makes her "no" to his advance *crystal* clear.

His response? He is blindsided and hurt by her rejection. She didn't just let him down, she shut him out.

At the end of a tension-fraught day, she is *devastated* by his sexual offer, and her dismissal *crushes* him.

Both limp away like emotionally wounded soldiers. Any hope for immediate reconciliation is destroyed. How is this possible?

"How could he?" she thinks.

"Why would she?" he thinks.

It hurts me just to think about it. But it doesn't have to be like this. This moment, and thousands like it, reveal a disconnect—a misinterpretation—undermining the satisfaction of countless marriages. We have all been there. Our gut reactions on how to solve this conundrum are probably contributing to the problem.

A moment like this reveals a rift that this book is all about. In the end, before the FAQs, I will play this scenario out again with a happy ending, but see if you can figure out this marital puzzle as you read along.

INTRODUCTIONS

Before we go any further, howdy. I'm Chris Legg, a licensed professional counselor, founder of Alethia Family Counseling, and lead pastor at South Spring Baptist Church. I've been honeymooning Ginger, my absolutely stunning wife, for about thirty years, and we've got five awesome kids (one of them, my oldest, Mark, is my coauthor). My passion is the truth and teaching it to lead others to freedom. My son's passion is the truth and writing it down. Hence, the team up.

I pick up opportunities to teach everywhere I can—kids, adults, couples, family camps, college students, high school students, or church congregations. Teaching and counseling go hand in hand because, in each case, I'm endeavoring to help others see the truth and let it set them free. I hasten to add that I am *not* the final arbiter of truth. Jesus is. I'm a skeptic, and I think everyone else should be too. That's an invitation—be skeptical of this book!

In my counseling career, I've particularly loved walking alongside married couples. There, I've seen some of the greatest strides and most genuinely heartwarming successes. I've witnessed marriages brought back from the brink of divorce, even rescued from divorce itself.

All marriages are beset by hardship and disagreement. The most common conflicts seem to be about money, in-laws, and sex. It's a shame that sex can become such a matter of contention, given its immense potential for joy and unification.

In addition to being a common source of strife, I've also found this struggle to be healed by a few pivotal understandings. Key insights and corrections of ignorance can go a long way. I teach about sex, romance, and marriage frequently. Given how helpful some of these insights have been for others (and my wife and I), I figured I ought to write them down.

I hope this book differs from others for several reasons.

First, it contrasts other Christian perspectives or, at least, it contrasts many of the well-earned and damaging stereotypes of Christian views on sex (shudder).

Wives, I promise that I will not directly or indirectly claim that you exist for your husband's pleasure. This is not another "Christian" book in which sex is a commodity you're supposed to give (or trade) to your aroused husband because sometimes you just need to "take one for the team." That suggestion is rotten and thoroughly unbiblical. A client once told me, after reading a Christian book on marriage, "So . . . men want a prostitute who cleans his house?" Yikes, huh?

Husbands, this is also not another "shame on men for wanting sex" script. I'll help you find the words you've been trying to find to talk about sex since year two or three of marriage. This material will finally give you the personal insight and language to communicate to your wife how much you desire *her*. Equipped with the right communication and understanding of her feelings, you open up the way to more unified, enjoyable sex.

Second, though I am a pastor, I am also a professionally trained psychologist and a licensed counselor with almost three decades of experience. I've seen an unfortunate pattern that many well-meaning Christian authors damage marriages, especially in the realm of sex, because they don't have the proper training. I don't want to sound combative, but I've seen hundreds of couples' vulnerable lives damaged by untrained or poorly researched teaching.

Third, I've counseled hundreds of wives and been blessed with an amazing thirty-year marriage and best friendship with my wife. I wrote this book, in part, because I've noticed men and women tend to experience sex differently in some ways. We should strive to understand and empathize with those differences. This book is not just directed to men or women, but both.

Fourth, I don't intend to water down Scripture or undermine how *both* spouses must sacrifice in service to God and each other. I won't sell you a fake magic bullet and I won't downplay how hard marriage can be. There will be a few simple understandings that will immensely help (I hope), but hard work is ahead. Like learning to use a new tool, the greater the skill, the less the effort. But no matter how skillful we become at loving our spouses, a great marriage still takes time and effort.

Another caveat. Because I broadly hold to the historical evangelical process of the interpretation of the Bible, I'll strictly be referring to heterosexual marriages and working with the assumption that sex is for married couples (I have a short FAQ on mixed-orientation marriages). Perhaps the principles here could help all kinds of secular unions, although I doubt it (for reasons discussed later). If you're not a Christian and want to continue, I hope you see the beauty of the gospel and come into contact with the blessing of God's wisdom!

Finally, Mark and I researched extensively in preparation. We sifted through thousands of pages of books, research papers, articles, podcasts, and blog entries to make sure my insights as a therapist are factual and sound. While many prominent therapists, self-help gurus, or megachurch pastors speak from some experience, too many works are based on anecdotes alone. Don't be intimidated by the footnotes! They're there to keep us accountable. This book was workshopped through dozens of counseling and speaking sessions, but I needed to find out if what I was seeing was just my limited perspective or if others were seeing the same patterns (even if they interpreted them differently).

It is a great thing for theologians, using good hermeneutical techniques, to unpack the biblical insights into marriage. The authors who stick with biblical insights are immeasurably valuable. Recently, I have enjoyed and recommended Francis Chan's *You and Me Forever* and Timothy Keller's *The Meaning of Marriage*. The only danger is when theologians break off into therapeutic advice rather than biblical insight. For these questions, direct research from the likes of Shaunti Feldhahn, George Barna, John Gottman, and countless others seems best.

If you're committed, like I am, to the idea that "all truth is God's truth," there must be a way to integrate psychology and biblical truth. This integration represents one of my central missions and life's work. Hopefully that integration shines in this book. Instead of creating a sociological or psychological study or merely writing a biblical exegesis on marriage, I've tried to present a third path, hopefully drawing on both backgrounds in an illuminating way. In that sense, I've attempted to make research on marriage and sex accessible, diving into studies to see how and when the current research could lend insight into my experience in counseling and the church. In that sense, it's an interpretation of research—a way of understanding it—that I think will make sense to many.

Introduction from Mark Legg, Coauthor (but Mostly Ghostwriter)

It's an honor to work with my dad. He's a steadfast father and faithful friend. It's a privilege to write for him and with him because I believe in his teachings. I've separated long enough from his household to know my family is no common one. It's too shallow to say Dad's teachings "work," although I suppose that's fair to say. There's depth to his teachings, apparent to everyone who discusses his ideas with him.

Not only are his teachings thoroughly thought-out, but he lives by his own principles at home. Thankfully, I never experienced the scarring trauma some children face when they walk in on their parents having sex. I did, however, witness my parent's *marriage*. My mom is wise, exceedingly kind, gracious, gentle, generally exuberant, nurturing, and wholly special to me. Their marriage is not in any sense one-sided. Rather, it is one that represents the reciprocal love of God and His people, as marriage should (spoilers). My parents, like any others, had conflicts and disagreements, but their marriage always became stronger for it. I can genuinely say I'd like my marriage to look like theirs. Do you need any more proof of this book's validity?

Though it's been a joy to work on this book, and my dad has been generous given my relative inexperience, I would not have written it alongside him with such vigor if not for its smooth and blessed application into my own marriage, which happened in the middle of this book's formation. (I married in 2022 my lovely, astonishingly wonderful wife, Shannon). I'm overwhelmed at the privilege to work on this work, which I hope will change lives.

Now, back to the main body of the book, in my dad's voice.

Regardless of all the research, applicability, depth of teaching, and anecdotes, at the end of the day, *you* must get to know your spouse; I can't, even if I were your marriage therapist. Neither can I replace a personal marriage counselor through words on a page. Not surprisingly, I am a big fan of counseling; you might consider it as you seek to integrate what is applicable to you in this book. The book's premise is that you must get to know your spouse and yourself better. The better that's achieved, the better sex becomes.

By the end, I hope both of you will gladly receive each other with greater understanding, which will lead to freedom. Let's make the labor of lovemaking more gracious and enjoyable. I'll do this by setting up the foundation for sex by unpacking Marriage (Part I), helping you interpret one another (Part II), and giving application to these principles (Part III).

How do we get unstuck and on the path of freedom, improved sex, and more unified marriages? We'll need to start with marriage. In order to recreate the Garden of Eden in our marriages, we have to start at the beginning.

PART I

A FOUNDATION IN MARRIAGE

I remember as a child when we stayed at my grandparents' house. We would get up early in the morning, run to their bedroom, and knock on their door. They would call us in and we would scramble into their double bed (they owned both king- and queen-sized beds that they kept in their guest rooms) and snuggle together. Hop (my grandfather's nickname) would pretend to keep sleeping ("just resting my eyes") and Grandmama would giggle at our attempts to wake him up.

Years later as a young man, after Hop died, I asked Grandmama something that had never stood out to me until then. "Why did we have to knock on your door when we were kids?"

She told me about how my grandfather had shipped out to fly bombers in the Pacific theater in World War II soon after they married. The time they saw each other in the next four years measured just a few weeks in total. She said that ever since he had come home almost sixty years earlier, they "were making up for lost time."

I do not doubt it.

My father's parents were an exemplar of marriage. Like all couples, I'm sure they faced their conflicts. I had the privilege of examining their marriage through the innocent lens of a grandchild. But these two hard-working, humble Alabama teachers modeled something fantastically: They genuinely loved and enjoyed one another, on display for everyone to see.

For all sixty-two years of their marriage, or at least while I was around, they snuggled, laughed, flirted, tickled, and (now I know) engaged in a lifetime of seducing one another. I remember the warm, safe feeling it gave me to see how they loved and enjoyed one another. I believe the sex they experienced helped make that love and flowed from that love. They became a major inspiration for my wife and I. In their marriage, I got a unique glimpse of what God's love for us looks like, which brings us to an important question:

What is marriage anyway? Maybe it's been a while since you've said those vows, and perhaps some of you haven't said them at all yet, in which case this section is perfect for you. Like me and everyone else, maybe you jumped into marriage having a less-than-perfect understanding of what you were getting yourself into. My experience is that very few people understand even the basics of marriage psychologically, biologically, or theologically.

For example, I thought my marriage was the establishment of the Chris Legg Fan Club and I was marrying the new president of the CLFC. Of course, I wouldn't or couldn't have described that then, but if I'm honest, I didn't realize that we were creating a new story together, not merely adding my wife to mine. I don't know how many wives feel that, but I am aware of several husbands who have later admitted to doing just that. What was I thinking? Honestly, I don't know if I could have told you, but we got married anyway!

Couples like my grandparents mastered tending the garden of marriage. They intuited that seduction, lovemaking, and romance are integrated with work, kindness, patience, and folding the laundry.

Sex and relational flourishing go hand in hand. Clinical psychologist Dr. Ron Welch put it this way, "During my years in clinical practice, I have come to realize that most sexual problems couples describe to me are not about sex. They are usually problems with intimacy that are based in communication, relationship, or conflict issues. The sexual relationship is just the place where these problems are most noticeable."[1]

See why I want to lay down a good foundation?

Let's go back to the drawing board on marriage; then, we can work on the sex problem.

---

1. Ron Welch, *10 Choices Successful Couples Make: The Secret to Love That Lasts a Lifetime* (Grand Rapids, MI: Revell, 2019), 167.

One

COMING UP WITH MARRIAGE "FROM SCRATCH"

When Ginger, my wife, and I were dating (an undisclosed number of years ago), I distinctly remember one Sunday when we went to church. At this point in our relationship, I was completely, utterly smitten with her (as I still am). Naturally, I struggled to keep my distractible brain focused on the sermon and not on my stunning girlfriend sitting an inch away, close enough to feel her warmth.

I do remember with *crystal* clarity how she began scratching my back. Reality fell to pieces, and you better believe I remembered zero percent of the preacher's point. Why did something this small affect me so much that I remember it to this day? I only remember one out of a hundred sermons, but this became a core memory. The answer will establish our first principle for a good marriage.

Imagine you want a back scratch—sorry if you started itching. What is the *best* way to experience it? You have four options.

Option one is sinister. You can *manipulate*, *threaten*, or *demand* to get one. This might include throwing a biting remark, an emotional dagger, an adult fit, or an ultimatum. Using the Jedi mind trick falls into this category.

Unless you're a psychopath, this method does not feel gratifying. And, of course, it's flat-out wrong and hurtful to manipulate like this, especially if it's a loved one.

Option two: You could offer someone five dollars to scratch your back. Before you object that the idea is ridiculous, there are a few companies that render professional snuggling. Yes, that's real, Google it. It only costs eighty dollars an hour—what a bargain! Okay, maybe you'll keep your money. Still, hypothetically, you could pay someone to scratch your back. Purchasing one is still not particularly satisfying, but it's definitely better than option one.

The third option is less strange than options one or two. You might kindly *ask* someone for the back scratch. This is probably pretty normal if you have a significant other. If you're a lady, you probably wouldn't hesitate to ask any one of a dozen of your girlfriends to scratch your back. Though a man might struggle a bit more, all in all, requesting a back scratch is healthy and pleasant.

You can probably guess the fourth option: someone might *give* you one unprompted. This is precisely what my wife did back when we were dating, and still does.

And *wow*. Assuming it's an appropriate person to be touching you, the back scratch feels even better than if you asked for it, right? Ginger probably didn't think much about it, but it signaled to me that she knew and loved me. I remember feeling "claimed." At that moment, she declared to the world, at least to the people sitting behind us in the pews: "He's mine, and I'm proud that he's mine." She *wanted* to scratch my back. That remains my interpretation to this day.

Don't get me wrong, asking is alright, but the *meaning* behind her freely given action provides me with more than the physical relief of a good itching. It implies that Ginger knows me enough to know I like scratches, wants to own me in front of everyone, and that her attention is on me. Those subtle things make a huge impact.

In each of the four choices, the final option clearly provides the most enjoyment and fulfillment. The manner in which we receive things makes a difference. Sometimes the heart behind an action means more than the action itself.

I call this the gift principle.

Principle: The Gift

People prefer receiving freely given gifts over requesting them and prefer requesting them over purchasing or demanding them.

Here's another quick example to show it's not limited to back scratches.

I've just finished mowing the lawn. I'm bummed when I remember we've run out of my favorite Propel drinks (water flavored with a hint of synthetic-tasting grapes). When this happens, I venture into the garage, looking for stray bottles. Maybe one rolled under the car? I know it sounds ridiculous, but in that moment, I'm parched. I'm desperate. But instead of needing to scrounge around, I found a brand-new case of them—Ginger had picked some up the day before!

That "gift principle" moment feels fantastic for so many reasons. I didn't need to drive to the store and pick up more. I got to quench my thirst right after hot yard work. Those positive responses are around the Propel itself.

More subtly but more powerfully, I feel known by Ginger. It's something simple: cheap, flavored water. It means more to me that my wife actively thinks about me, knows exactly what I like, and wants to take the extra time to benefit me.

I was willing to purchase them myself, and I would have asked Ginger to pick some up if she happened to be shopping. Instead, when I saw them in the garage unannounced and unexpected, I knew Ginger had lovingly considered me the day before.

The gift principle, then, refers to actions done for another person that make them feel known and cared for.

To the Drawing Board

Based on this gift principle, I went to the mental drawing board and tried to come up with a system that could reproduce it. Think of how incredible it would be if we could access this kind of experience daily!

I failed. Any way you look at it, if the goal is to secure the gift principle for yourself, you miss the point. A friendship that says, "I want *you* to be friends with *me* so that I can get back scratches from *you*" implies either a request or worse—manipulation.

Some kind of contract that constantly evaluates each person's performance doesn't quite work either. Constantly keeping a tally to balance the scales doesn't sound pleasant or free. It's something like the request or even buying.

It's simply impossible to guarantee it for yourself.

However, you could guarantee that gift experience for *someone else*. I could guarantee it because I control what I do. Now, if this relationship is about your partner, and the *two* people choose to do that for *each other* . . . Houston, we have liftoff. The gift principle suddenly becomes the center of the relationship in an underlying way.

So what if, bear with me here, we set up an institution where two individuals are committed to *giving*, to live out that gift principle for each other, a relationship unified by selflessness?

Heck, while we're dreaming, let's have these partners commit to it for their entire lives so, in addition to their mutual commitment to self-sacrifice, the relationship solidifies. This to-be-named institution becomes consistent and secure without the need for keeping score. This would allow them the space to improve their selflessness and learn what the "Propel" and "back scratches" are for the other. Then, they could know in hundreds of situations what the best gift-giving response is. I said it was crazy, right?

If one person fell into a slump or got grumpy, their partner would go ahead and love them anyway. The non-grumpy one can pick up the emotional slack. Why does this work? Because the gift principle isn't built on a transaction, keeping score, or performance. It's based on doing what you can do in the moment. Additionally, we hope that the grumpy party will make an effort to act selflessly despite their mood. Indeed, most people's bad moods break pretty quickly if someone's actively showing them love.

If both people get in a bad mood, it's good they established their commitment for the long haul. They know they'll need to make up because they're "stuck with each other." But notice, in this context, that anchor encourages growth; it's not negative at all. When they're both feeling great, this gift principle setup is easy! They spend all day trying to outdo each other in their selflessness.

Of course, we're talking about people here, so this setup couldn't ensure perfect bliss and harmony. Not all moments would be full of freely given self-sacrifice, and kindness wouldn't always be received as such. Even after decades of close friendship, no one can know anyone exactly. But, at least in this arrangement, they could fail forward.

Man, I should patent that or something!

Full disclosure. I didn't come up with this system. God did. It's called marriage.

In fact, everything I just laid out is, in essence, devoted friendship. Indeed, *I think marriage is God's most refined and defined version of friendship.* God, in his brilliance, created marriage with the gift principle built in.

Most experiences in life can be bought or manipulated, but that reduces the purity of the experience and leads to long-term dissatisfaction. When two people commit themselves to self-sacrifice, it leads to a lifetime of true, deep fulfillment.

Was it challenging to recognize what I described as marriage? Your marriage may look wildly different from the picture I painted. I get it; that's okay. We can start with broad brushstrokes together, painting over the old, ugly picture to start fresh, or we can fill in the finer details if your marriage already looks pretty close to the ideal. Either way, let's keep God's picture in mind.

At this point, I want to warn of two dangers.

First, don't read too much of the gift principle into sex yet. I need to clear out a lot of junk before we discuss sex.

Second, I'm going to predict that your brain just jumped to something like this: "If only my spouse would've gotten the memo about self-sacrifice *before* we got married!" Or "When did they last give *me* an unsolicited back scratch? I certainly can't remember when they bought a case of *my* favorite drinks!"

Unfortunately, if you just caught yourself thinking that, you've missed the point (gosh, maybe you just made it!). My argument showed that we need to aim at loving one another selflessly, and in response, you thought, "Why don't *they* do that for *me?*"

This leads us to the next foundational principle.

Principle: Start with Me

We only have one magnifying glass. We can keep it focused on our spouse's behavior and what they can do to improve the marriage or we can train it on ourselves—where we have the real power to change things.

Since this book addresses both spouses, you will be tempted to study the application for your spouse rather than yourself. I predict a good deal of cognitive dissonance in your future. Prepare to catch yourself when you revert to this oh-so-natural condition.

Here's how you *should* react to my description of marriage:

"Man, *I* bet *I'm* pretty terrible at doing that for *my* spouse! *I* bet *I* could do better at that! *I* really wish *I* would have known this better before getting married." Or "When was the last time I gave them a back scratch?"

I struggle with this tendency too. I've been married for decades (happily), and I often miss the point of marriage. Everyone does. The leap from the gift principle to "that means *they* should give *me* . . ." is easy to make.

If you're thinking, "Chris, I love my husband/wife, and they love me! In fact, in every area except for our sex life, our marriage is fantastic!" If that's the case, praise God, that's good news. That means your issues stem from misunderstandings rather than a lack of a good foundation.

Still, these principles are a good reminder to discuss with your partner and rededicate yourself to.

If we observe any problem in life, like "my marriage is falling apart," we tend to blame anyone but ourselves. To fix it, we tend to put the responsibility onto anyone but ourselves (see Jesus's teaching on the speck and the log in Matthew 7:1–5).

Dr. Timothy E. Clinton, an expert in the psychology of relationships, points out that most people will have the overriding desire to "fix" their spouse in failing marriages. In his experience, the desire to "solve" the marriage often originates from pure intentions, but it doesn't work.[1]

Dr. Clinton delves into common problems that eroding marriages face. First, he believes you can turn your marriage around; so do I. But change needs to start with someone. Fundamentally, since you can only control *yourself*, the change must therefore begin with you. (If you're doing relatively well in your marriage but still struggle with your sex life, these principles still apply.) He writes:

> Step One: Be the First to Change. "Why should I change first?" we hear you ask. "I'm tired of giving and never getting anything back." These are words we often hear from husbands and wives the instant we suggest this course of action. They ask this question because they know that change equals vulnerability, and vulnerability equals risk. And taking risks is what got them hurt in the first place.[2]

I completely understand. I also agree with Dr. Clinton when he says,

> Why should you risk change? Because you are the only one you have control over. And your relationship is too important to simply abandon. The marital commitment you made before God is too binding to let anything, least of all pride, resentfulness, and fear, prevent you from making every effort you can to fulfill it.[3]

The prominent psychiatrist Dr. William Glasser developed a counseling philosophy called "choice theory" and an approach to therapy he termed "reality therapy." In this style, he hammers one central point: you cannot change anyone else's behavior. At best, you can only provide information to others.[4] He had the rare skill of condensing complex truths into simple, tight sayings. One of his ten axioms says, "The only person whose behavior we can control is our own."[5]

Remember, you are not directly responsible for your partner, nor can you force them to do anything. That's not your duty, although you can give them helpful information. We'll talk about that next chapter.

The "start with me" principle is a helpful tool that applies to all relationships. Opening our hands and letting go of control over someone else's decisions will lead to freedom. It's incredibly difficult to do because it takes defeating your pride and taking serious emotional risks. I'm not saying if you start improving yourself, your spouse will likewise improve. I refuse to make false promises. You may put your heart out there to get stomped on again. If this persists in your marriage, it's time for professional counseling. (Of course, if it's *abusive*, you need to do all you can to make yourself safe—create space, stay with family, get the police involved, etc.)

All of that said, if you start showing affection and selflessness toward your spouse, you'd be surprised how often they want to reciprocate and change their behavior.

Recently, I created a teaching video explaining much of the material in the second half of this book. I've encouraged some clients to watch it and then debrief it with me as a couple. Just this week, a husband came in with a letter to his wife indicating that he had mastered, *mastered*, the aspects of the video that are meant to help wives understand their husbands. After watching the video, he felt understood and relieved to finally feel known! Not usually an emotional person, he nonetheless choked up with tears as he read it to her.

I followed everything he said and could relate to his every word. However, I inwardly cringed. Everything in the letter, as sincere as it was, indicated that he completely missed the parts of the video that were meant to help *men understand their wives.* I was confident of how his wife would experience hearing this letter—and it wouldn't be good.

It wasn't.

We salvaged the conversation, and I sent him back to the video with a new assignment: Pay attention to the other message of the video! When it came to understanding himself and being able to put it into words? Score. *Nothing but net.* When it came to gaining new skills to communicate with his wife and understanding her perspective and interpretations? *Air ball.* (For those ignorant of basketball terms, "air ball" means bad, and "nothing but net" means good.)

Understanding oneself and putting emotion into the correct words is critical but not the final step. I also want to protect us from a transactional mindset early on and we will unpack it more later; a transactional mindset is defined by determining what I need to *give* in order to get what I *want.*

In a transactional marriage, there will be a list of assets that each spouse has that the other one wants (often the word "need" is used) and each must trade the resources back and forth, and so long as they faithfully make these transactions, no one feels the need to go visit another market for those needs. I presume that this has most often been introduced into Christian marriage material unintentionally. This is not what God designed in the Garden. I think He wanted us to invest in one another as an act of grace because we are free to do so. Naive? I don't think so. Miraculous? Certainly.

From beginning to end, this book should have a feel similar to Phil Connors's (Bill Murray's) experiences in *Groundhog Day.* In this classic rom-com, Phil gets stuck on the same day that replays repeatedly. In this eternal prison, Phil tries to manipulate his coworker Rita to sleep with him, but he's got to do it in one day. All of his early efforts are transactional in nature. What perfect series of moments, gifts, and insights will get him what he wants? Eventually, he really begins to care about her more than himself. After hundreds (or thousands?) of rejections as recurring days pass by, he grows in his character and starts selflessly loving her and others. He learns more and more about caring for and loving Rita in the terms that mean the most to her. By the end, he knows everything about Rita's heart and every tiny preference. He is no longer trying to just get his selfish desires met (the movie carefully and expressly communicates this). So by the end of the movie, in only one day (though countless for him), she is inspired by a selfless, kind, and considerate man and falls in love with him.

This gift principle and its straightforward application in marriage will lead to greater fulfillment and enjoyment for both of your lives. Though receiving gifts is terrific, giving leads to even deeper and longer-term satisfaction. The man who understood humans best, Jesus, memorably said that "it is more blessed to give than to receive" (Acts 20:35). Though selflessness may be impossible to live out perfectly due to our sin, we are wired to enjoy selflessness regardless because of God's first intention for us. Selfish people aren't normally happy in any meaningful way.[6]

The right way may be challenging, but it sure beats the crappy alternatives.

I know that a certain percentage of you are married to someone with a personality disorder like narcissism, a deeply entrenched addiction like alcoholism, or some other kind of unhealthy codependency. That makes the application of these principles much more difficult and complicated. The "start with me" principle still works, but putting it into practice has to be highly strategic and thought-out. The deeply unhealthy party probably won't appreciate selflessness. You'll need help from a professional who can adapt these principles to your specific conditions. For that, I recommend mental health therapy.

Marriage consists of entering into a lifelong committed relationship, which is fundamentally about selflessly considering the other person. It's about the grace of sacrificing your preferences and supporting your spouse when feasible. It is the Christian life (Philippians 2, Ephesians 4, etc.) lived in the most intensive Christian community: two people bound together.

Someday, I will answer to God for whether I sought to live out my role as husband His way—selflessly and sacrificially. I do not answer for my spouse; her heart and success in this ministry are between Him and her.

To sum up, we covered two principles:

The Gift Principle:

Humans prefer receiving freely given gifts over requesting, and we prefer requesting over purchasing or demanding.

The Start with Me Principle:

We can't control the actions of others, only our own.

My job is to serve my wife in His name. In marriage, your job is to do the same for your spouse in His name. And the reward is a lifetime of joy and running the race well. If we're lucky, the reward is to look back on life like Hop and Grandmama.

1. Timothy E. Clinton, *Attachments: Why You Love, Feel, and Act the Way You Do* (London: Waterstones, 2009), 209. One general pattern is that the wife tries to "fix" her husband, who inevitably responds with defensiveness. I'll talk more about this phenomenon in Chapter 12. As you can imagine, this approach does little to save one's marriage.

2. Clinton, *Attachments*, 224.

3. Clinton, *Attachments*, 224.

4. William Glasser, *Choice Theory: A New Psychology of Personal Freedom* (New York: Harper Perennial, 1999).

5. Glasser Institute for Choice Theory, "Quickstart Guide to Choice Theory," accessed October 31, 2023, https://wglasser.com/quickstart-guide-to-choice-theory.

6. Stephen G. Post, "Altruism, Happiness, and Health: It's Good to Be Good," *International Journal of Behavioral Medicine* 12, no. 2 (June 2005): 66–77, https://doi.org/10.1207/s15327558ijbm1202_4.

Two

BUILDING MARRIAGE OUT

F or a while, my eldest son, Mark (the coauthor of this book), and I would regularly camp on the Buffalo River in Arkansas. We rented canoes with a handful of other dads and sons and struck out with our food and gear in dry bags. We traveled downstream, intermittently paddling or allowing the river to carry us for miles. In the afternoon, we would go ashore and set up camp.

One year, we were about to go down the worst of the rapids on our route. The most vital rule is to keep the nose of your canoe pointed downstream. You can usually glide over rocks if you're facing forward, but a sideways canoe is sure to tump. Near the beginning of this stretch of rapids was a green canoe flattened and wrapped around a tree sticking out of the river. It was bleached from the sun and warped by the constant barrage of millions of gallons of water. The aged monument served as an eternal warning and reminder: Do *not* let your canoe get sideways.

This particular morning, I packed my pipe with tobacco as we approached and started puffing. Apparently, I had grown cocky after our past successes. My ten-year-old son and I drifted toward the rapids. I calmly pointed out the route we would take. I was sitting pretty, confident as a peacock, with my pipe alight, expertly guiding from the back of the canoe when, just as we entered the rapids, I felt it shift.

We started to rotate. My superior rudder skills, which are usually plenty in rapids like these, accomplished nothing. I dug in, but some unseen current forced us sideways in the water. Realizing that I couldn't fight it, I chose to use the momentum to spin the canoe 180 degrees.

My son remembers me shouting, "Well, guess we're going down backward!" I looked over my shoulder, trying to mentally reverse my paddling, and I caught a glimpse of Mark's eyes, now bigger than sauce plates. I may have been choking on my pipe smoke, which was still clenched between my teeth (it bears teeth marks from that day), but if I pulled it off, I wouldn't have to face my wife with her firstborn son bruised up or worse.

The rapids shot us out the back, and we were triumphant. The rest of the fathers and sons watched in stunned disbelief. Of course, I strongly implied it was intentional. ("We veterans needed a challenge. Figured we would try it out backward!")

Life will try to throw your marriage off. Like the proverbial boxer, everyone has a plan until they get hit. Everyone has a plan until they face the rapids. If you are passive, life will flip you to the side and tump your marriage over.

Marriage is not merely coasting along the river in a canoe, though it may have felt that way in the first year or while dating. Marriage requires hard work and adjusting to life's white waters with serious effort. Sometimes, it's more tranquil, but other times, it's like trying to keep two canoes close together while paddling them through rapids!

If you're not prepared to paddle hard for your marriage, it will end up turned sideways, broken up, or drowned.

Principle: OJ and Chocolate Milk (or the Sleuthing Principle)

Actively learn your partner's wants and preferences.

When I sit down with a couple for premarital counseling, I usually start the conference with some harmless chitchat, asking questions about their lives and how they met. Then, I'll kick the session into gear by springing this on 'em: "If you're trying to get your wants and needs met, marriage is terrible for that." Then I wait and see if they bolt from the room or if they just blink at me like I spoke Greek.

I also say this line at weddings. Without fail, I get chuckles and nods of agreement from the longtime married people in the room.

In both cases, I press on, "Marriage is a great way to sacrifice your wants and needs for *someone else's*." Of course, this is another way of phrasing the "start with me" and "gift principle." As a refresher, here are Dr. Glasser's rules for the "start with me" principle.

1. The only person whose behavior we can control is our own.

Here's his second axiom to kick this chapter off:

2. All we can give another person is information.[1]

From our gift principle, we know marriage is built around selflessness. Combining these two ideas leads to what I call the "sleuthing principle":

3. Focus on learning information about others (e.g., your spouse) to love them better.

If you're going to live out the gift principle, you have to know what your spouse wants for a gift!

My wife loves a made bed. It took me a while to figure this out. I didn't make the bed growing up; I'm simply not a bed-maker kind of guy. I didn't have the habit and don't see the point to this day. I'm personally an "uncluttered floor" kind of fellow. The more cleared-out the floor space, the better. Of course, my wife loves that too, but over the years, I noticed that she seemed pretty content when the bed was made, even if there was stuff scattered everywhere else.

Early on, this confused and annoyed me, but my mindset eventually changed. Now, I see this as an opportunity to show love to her in a way that I know she will appreciate most. I'm leveraging this information to love her best with limited time. Of course, she would love for me to clean the whole room, but when I only have a few minutes (who has time to clean the entire room?) I can easily make our space feel 60 percent clean (to her) by making the bed instead of clearing the floor. Sure, the piles of clothes, books, essential oils, containers, board games, and everything may remain, but *she* feels much more at ease when walking into our bedroom.

Watch and listen—play detective. Sometimes, to guys, it can feel like a fully-fledged Sherlock Holmes mystery to uncover what your wife wants. Sometimes, to girls, it feels the same way to get even a basic idea of how their man feels. Worse, men can take valuable information from their wives and easily interpret it as criticism.

Let's say I come home from a trip and bring my wife roses. My wife graciously accepts and says she's grateful for them. As she prunes them and finds a vase, maybe she comments, "Actually, I love these flowers;

they're beautiful. But I think tulips may be my favorite now. In fact, I really love white tulips if you ever find those!"

Later, I will investigate why some of us, especially men, hear this response and react like this: "Wow, did she just criticize how I bought her flowers? I cannot believe how ungrateful she is!"

Many men respond to feedback as criticism. Instead, we should view these comments as "insider information" about how to love our wives better with fewer resources. This insider information will be vital to our understanding of the art of "Whole Life Seduction" in Part III. To get there, we need to understand the skill of listening, receiving, and accepting what the Gottmans call "bids."

Bids are "the fundamental unit of emotional communication." Bids can be small or big, verbal or nonverbal. They're requests to connect. They might take the form of an expression, question, or physical outreach. They can be funny, serious, or sexual in nature.[2]

Men often need more training in recognition of these bids. Wives make "bids" that intend to guide their husbands into loving them better, but we hear the bids as criticism, or we don't hear them at all. When husbands and wives pay attention and listen to these bids as positive, we'll be in a place to love our spouse better and more efficiently.

In addition to helping us get gifts and serve each other well, it also applies to emotions.

Emotional safety, like emotional connection, is built through the process of attuning. When a woman makes a bid for your attention, when she reaches out to you emotionally and you meet her reach, this demonstrates your trustworthiness and emotional safety. If you shut her down, ignore her, or otherwise don't attune (especially when she is upset), she will not feel safe with you emotionally, nor will she feel safe to be herself with you.[3]

So, if you crack a joke to your friends about your marriage completely innocently and light-heartedly, but your husband later communicates that he felt belittled by the joke, accept that information. Husbands, you must communicate that information and not just fall into a bad mood. Wives, you, too, must communicate your feelings. Don't give the excuse, "He should know just by reading me!" Maybe, but he needs to learn.

When our partner gives insider information, we can be defensive or oblivious, or we can say to ourselves, "I'll file this away for next time." If your spouse doesn't communicate openly like this, *ask*. If you tend to forget details, write them in your phone notes immediately after they drop the hint. It seems obvious that guys especially should ask their wives what their favorite flowers (candy, drinks, snacks, animals, books, movies, songs, jewels, etc.) are, but you'd be surprised how few do. If you are reading this and realize you've never asked these questions, start somewhere. Don't feel ashamed of missed opportunities; start now!

As a quiz to test the sleuthing principle in premarital counseling, I'll ask the couple what each of them likes to keep stocked in the fridge.

"Imagine you've just been working on the lawn. It's June in Texas, and it is 100 degrees outside. You're sweating and a bit dirty from gardening. You come back inside for refreshments. When you open the fridge, what is your favorite drink to have there?"

One guy responded that it was chocolate milk, and the girl said orange juice. On to the next question: "Let's say you only had money to buy one, and you're on your way home from work, and you stop by the gas station to pick up a drink. Given what I've discussed, which one do you pick up?"

I've prepared them for it, so the guy knows to say orange juice, and the girl knows to say chocolate milk. They picked the other person's favorite drink. Ding—success!

When you put this into practice, you often satisfy both partners' preferences simultaneously. You can buy OJ and chocolate milk from the gas station. Or maybe you both like OJ, so certainly get that. Any time these align, we celebrate, but we certainly mustn't assume that they do.[4] These principles reflect what our attitudes and approaches should be in marriage (not in a legalistic sense; we all fail, after all). Often, of course, shared interests and preferences helped bring you together as a couple in the first place.

However, as emotional energy, time, and money fluctuate and become restricted at certain points in marriage, practicing these sleuthing principles becomes critical to weave through currents and rapids.

At the core of marriage is selflessness. The better informed our selflessness, the easier and higher quality our actions become.

By the time we're sixty years married, we should have multiple PhDs in our spouses.

Now, what word connects to the idea of selflessness? What drives us to act without consideration for our well-being? What causes men and women to leave behind careers, family, habits, pride, and self-centeredness? Love, of course.

Five Greek Words for Love

Have you ever noticed the strange phenomenon in English that we have one word for "mild preference in taste" and "undying loyalty"? That all-elusive, one-size-fits-all word is *love*.

With a straight face, we say, "I love donuts," "I love the Dallas Cowboys," "I love my country," "I love my girlfriend," and "I love my eighty-year-old grandmother."

That is *incredibly* unhelpful.

Other languages often use multiple words for love. Since I spend a lot of time in the Bible, and Greek is the language of the New Testament, I'll use it to illustrate my point.

Greek utilizes five words for love.

1. *Mania*—Manic love is not really a "love" at all. However, in today's world, when people say they "love" something in English, they sometimes refer to this concept. The word "lust" is close but probably not strong enough—"obsession" and possession is more accurate.

I "mania" that which I madly desire to own and have all to myself.

Mania is generally seen as taking over the "lover" like insanity—thus the connection to modern concepts of madness (klepto*mania*, pyro*mania*). It is the opposite of a phobia (an obsessive need to avoid something). "Mania" is translated as "madness" and "beside yourself" in Acts 26:24.[5]

This unquenchable desire for possession of someone is unhealthy in any relationship.

2. *Storgy* (or "storge")—Storgy is defined by dependence and is commonly called "motherly love."

When your dependent is no longer reliant on you—when your beloved daughter, your precious flower, goes off to college and eventually marries—this love remains only in its emotional remnants. It's one of the more vital loves because it rests on the commitment of one trait of the receiver: that he or she is *dependent*. When a child grows up and becomes an adult, they are no longer dependent. The love of a mother never fades, of course, but as the child gains independence, this kind of love should blossom into agape and philia.

However, under normal circumstances, this type of love is toxic to a marriage. As strange as it sounds, the tendencies of how mothers treat their sons or how fathers treat their daughters can creep into marital relationships. If one partner relies like a child on their spouse or one partner constantly parents their spouse, something is amiss.

3. *Eros*—Eros is the root word for "erotic," but it does not merely describe pleasurable sexual love. Eros describes all emotional love, the *feeling* of love, the desire to be near a person. Eros is the exciting, passionate, nervous butterflies that sweep over us in the right circumstances.

Eros says, "I enjoy how you make me feel." As an emotion, eros changes, sometimes suddenly. It's based on circumstances, the interpretation of those circumstances, and the target of its emotion. As an emotion alone, it is morally neutral. However, it can just as easily lead to lust (sinful desire) as well-placed passion, romance, or sexual magnetism.

Modern culture prizes this love most. After reading the definition of eros, did you think, "Well, that's what love is, right? Why define another kind of love for marriage?"

If this is your only foundation for love, your marriage will fail. Period. Full stop.

Think of eros as the fruit and flowers of a new relationship. Eventually, as a new season arrives, the fruit will die away, but it will produce later in the next season. Eros is in constant flux (like all human emotions), and understanding this variability will help create healthy, sturdy, long-term marriages. The word *eros* does not appear in the New Testament, but we see it play out in the Old Testament book the Song of Solomon.

4. *Philia*—Philia[6] love refers to brotherly, friendship love. Philia describes the love between two people who have common interests and experiences. *Phila*delphia is the city of brotherly love. It also denotes "fondness for."[7] Hemo*philia*cs seemed to ancient doctors to have a "fondness" for bleeding. In Aristotle's *Nicomachean Ethics*, this word is translated as affection and, most commonly, friendship.[8] Philia's love generally grows over time except in the case of some kind of betrayal or some other reason for intense dislike. Many New Testament passages employ it, including Matthew 10:37, John 12:25, and Revelation 3:19.

Unlike eros, which pulses up and down like waves, philia grows steadily, like a building constructed brick by brick. For this reason, when close friends reunite after years of separation, they say, "It's like we picked up exactly where we left off."

Philia is half about the circumstances and half about the commitment of two people to one another; it says, "I love who we are together," or in the case of a nonperson: "I am fond of this." So philia refers to both fondness in a more general way (as in, "I am fond of playing poker") and to the development of fondness in fellowship ("I am fond of spending time with John playing poker").

This kind of friendship should mark marriages. It's not the only love required in a marriage, but it provides good pillars for your marriage to stand on. Philia makes marriage far more enjoyable, but it's unnecessary for every single area of your marriage. I may bond with my friends over my collection of *Detective* comic books, and my wife may connect over a new Christian fiction series she's reading. Usually, we don't bond over those particular interests. Don't feel any pressure that *all* your likes need to overlap; they won't.

"Marry your best friend." True enough. Or, better yet, "make your spouse your best friend."

5. *Agape*—Agape love is entirely about the lover and their virtue and has nothing to do with the one loved.[9] In its purest form, agape love requires no payment or favor in response. In the Bible, we are commanded to agape our enemies, whom we don't have philia for. We may vehemently dislike (feel strongly unfriendly or anti-philia), but we are called to agape such people anyway.[10] Why? Because we understand their inherent value in the eyes of God.

The most common word for God's love for us is *agape* (1 John, John 3:16). Jesus commanded us to have agape for one another (Matt. 5:44, 1 Cor. 13). This lack of input from the recipient makes it possible for us to love our enemies because agape love is not dependent on circumstances; it says "I love you because I choose/commit to." You can see why the translators of the King James Version of the Bible used "charity" for this Greek word. Agape is love freely given and freely committed to.

Unlike eros or philia, agape creates a straight line that neither fades nor grows in its ideal form (which only exists perfectly from God outward). Oddly enough, even though many people marry because of eros's love, they make vows that speak of commitment despite any circumstance: "For richer or poorer, better or worse, in sickness and in health." That's agape love, a commitment to the best for another, no matter what emotions or feelings exist.

I "Love You"

Is philia central to marriage? What about agape? Since Christ calls us to agape our enemies, Christian spouses should certainly "desire God's best" for one another. Maybe eros? Of course, couples feel that kind of love on and off, even if we wish that existed all the time (more on that later). Eros is like a shifting sandbank, not a good foundation, but romance *is* clearly important to a healthy marriage.

Let me demonstrate a core issue that arises from the misplacement and misuse of love.

When someone comes to me for divorce counseling, what do you think they lead with?

Fill in the blanks: "I've _____ out of _____."

The answer: "I've <u>fallen</u> out of <u>love</u>."

What do they mean exactly? Notice that "falling" implies passivity. This phrase indicates *eros* love, meaning they're discussing divorce based on their lack of emotional, romantic attraction in that moment or season. You can cease agape loving someone, but that is a decision, and it takes *responsibility*—and it's the wrong choice.

It's easy to say, "Well, it's not my fault I'm not in love with my spouse anymore. I don't feel these 'authentic' emotions. Let me follow my feelings and try someone else."

It's harder to own the lack of agape love and use the "start with me" principle: "I haven't been showing agape love for some time now. My marriage is down and out because of me. Maybe my spouse too, but I'll at least take responsibility."

The eros obsession underlies most modern divorces and permeates our Disney princess culture.

Since Jesus commands us to agape everyone, what makes our spouses special? Ahh . . . that's the question, isn't it? Why not marry more than one person? That's a conceptual problem we will tackle in the next chapter.

Suffice it to say, for now, let's think of marriage as focusing agape toward your spouse. Sure, you're concerned for others, but your spouse takes priority.

That is true love.

Eros, though emotional, can be cultivated (cf. Part III). *Eros* isn't the core of marriage but plays an important role. Something else to note: You should only cultivate eros with your spouse. If any fruits of eros start budding in another friendship, uproot them as quickly as possible.

The greatest marriages depend on agape, which stands firm in the fiercest storms. Most marriages depend on eros, which goes in and out like a low and high tide.

Consider C. S. Lewis's "law of undulation." This law indicates the rising and falling nature of our emotions. Humans can create space for emotions one way or another, and emotions are built on circumstances. We have a great deal of control over those circumstances, but in the end, emotions act unpredictably.

We often don't have control over the emotional ups and downs: hard financial times, a death in the family, a good job, a raise, poor health, a bad case of melancholy, or even chemical imbalances leading to depression.

If you devote yourself to your spouse, you give your marriage the best chance of lasting happiness. This holds regardless of whether you feel strong eros love for your husband or wife in any given season.

True devotional love will touch at a deeper level than the emotional, pleasurable eros. This principle applied to sex will require harder work and sacrifice but with a greater payoff. Philia grows well in the soil of agape; the fruit of eros grows most dependably on the tree of good philia.

Principle: The Garden

My family has a garden in our backyard where we cycle through seasonal plants, often planting from seeds. It's one of my prides and joys. There is something very satisfying about growing, tending, and eventually enjoying the fruit of a garden. Not surprisingly (given the Eden account), a garden provides a beautiful analogy for marriage. But by *beautiful*, I also mean potentially tragic.

Consider this: What is the natural state of a garden? You might be tempted to say growth and life. Wrong. The natural state of a garden is a lot of weeds, brown plants wilting away, and, in my case, wild animals tearing it up. Death, weeds, and disappointment are the default state of a garden (especially in the 110-degree summers in Texas).

If you inherit a garden from a family member and they have tended it well, you will enjoy many good things from it, even without tending it, for a little while. Year one is pretty good. Year two is less abundant. In year three, you probably find mostly rotten plants. It will revert to its natural state unless you invest time and energy. Entropy is working against your garden.

Similarly, the natural state of marriage is divorce.

If you allow it to go on without intentional efforts, its natural state is overgrown with resentment, regret, disappointment, entitlement, and pent-up hurt feelings. If you've allowed your marriage to become overgrown already, there will be an intense, hot afternoon of pulling up weeds, putting in new soil, and planting new seeds. And by afternoon, you may be looking at months or more of mentoring, counseling, and recalibrating.

What is the fruit of this garden? Many things, but one that we deeply desire, is eros.

The garden principle is this, then: *Marriage naturally deteriorates but, when tended, bears fruit in season.*

If your garden has deteriorated from neglect, you likely won't see the fruit of your labor for a while. We can go to the produce aisle in the grocery store and buy a tomato more easily. Pornography is free. Hookup sites are usually free as well. Divorce sounds a lot easier—and it might be. In a consumerist society, we expect things we want now. But trust me, planting and tending leads to so many richer, sweeter things.

This idea that marriage deteriorates over time without effort is backed by research. *Battles of the Sexes* references Dr. David Buss's research: "While dating, 25 percent of women complain that men ignore their feelings and it increases to 30 percent by the first year of marriage. By the fourth year of marriage, 59 percent of women say their husbands ignore their feelings."[11]

It's great, in theory, to say, "I'm ready to replant my garden! I'm ready to work hard, Chris!" But when weeding metaphorically means changing a few diapers or cleaning the room a certain way, we'll need to draw on something else to be so gracious to our spouses. We can't agape all the time, and we especially can't muster it up because we're such good people. We need a higher reason, a higher calling.

Principle: Love (*agape*) because He First Loved Us

We need a higher reason to agape our spouse because they can't earn your sacrificial love. Neither can you earn theirs.

The most robust demonstrations of love from stories and movies as well as real life include great sacrifice. A screenwriter named Randall Wallace told a story that, for its myriad historical inaccuracies, was brilliant: *Braveheart*. Wallace says good action movies move people to emotion because they reveal the things worth fighting for. Men, doesn't that ring true? These movies of glory stir us to want to pick up arms because something else is important enough to die for or even to live for.

It's not the wars themselves that get our blood stirring; wars are terrible. It's the willingness of men to sacrifice everything for what they value. In a speech in Detroit in June of 1963, Dr. Martin Luther King Jr. stated his belief that "if a man hasn't discovered something he will die for, he isn't fit to live." He said this about five years before his assassination.

Though we think of this kind of sacrifice as manly (and it certainly is), we are just as drawn to stories of women. In *A Quiet Place*, a postapocalyptic thriller where monsters and people hunt by sound, Emily Blunt portrays Evelyn Abbott, perhaps the strongest female character in any recent movie. Black Widow and Captain Marvel's best moments pale next to her grit and strength. In *A Quiet Place*, she's pregnant. In one scene, she steps on a nail and can't cry out; otherwise, the terrifying creature will kill her and her child. She goes into labor with the beast in the next room and must remain completely quiet, alone in a dirty bathtub. I won't spoil any further, but the point remains: We are inspired by sacrifice because we know in our hearts that sacrifice reveals what we treasure most.

While each of us hopes we would be willing to sacrifice like William Wallace or a strong mother in crisis, most sacrifice comes in ordinary, everyday ways that are rarely made into movies.

We don't sacrifice for fun; we need a motivator (freedom in the case of *Braveheart*; children in the case of *A Quiet Place*). Personally, I can't just quit eating donuts after one or two without a compelling reason. I don't work out because I want to. Although I've heard that "some people" do enjoy it, I need some kind of external motivation.

The more immediate the motivation, the more likely I am to do it. The more directly connected the motivation is to my sacrifice, the better.

So if acting on the gift principle means that you have no guarantee that your spouse will repay you or love you in return, how in the world do we find the motivation? Especially since they (and we) are often not particularly lovable.

On our own merit, I don't think we deserve other people's sacrifice. I don't deserve it, and I'm pretty confident you don't, either. We need an example of what it is to love someone who often doesn't love us back very well if we are to keep paddling the canoes, tending the garden, or filling the fridge with a drink we do not like.

There must be someone or something worth living and dying for, even when it isn't glamorous.

For the Christian, it is Christ.

One of Jesus's closest followers, John, thus writes, "We love because He first loved us" (1 John 4:19). Christian marriages should center around sacrificial love by choosing someone and not expecting a perfect return on our efforts. That kind of love is how Jesus loved us. It is not transactional. This is not a quid pro quo.

We could rename the "gift principle" the "grace principle," for God extended us grace, giving us what we didn't earn. The Greek word for grace, *karis*, means gift. Remember, when you do the dishes, God first loved you and gave you the example of loving. Dying on the cross pretty well outweighs the suffering of changing a diaper, though it does not diminish it. It rather elevates the love shown through the menial and humdrum tasks.

You love your spouse because Christ ordained dignity and value for them, a value worth sacrificing for. He calls you to love based on His merit, not theirs.

This leads to our fifth principle: *Love (agape) because he first loved us.*

In this chapter, we've mixed the concrete to pour the foundation for our marriage.

To love someone by sacrificing for their preferences and needs, we must first know them. Imagine if I bought my wife a bunch of camping supplies for her birthday because I like camping. If she bought me flowers or candles (especially cinnamon candles), that probably won't do the trick either.

Focus on learning about your spouse so that your love focuses on what means the most to them. Then, we covered the importance of distinguishing romantic or emotional love, eros; friendship love, philia; and self-giving love, agape. All three are important. However, eros cannot be the foundation for our marriages; agape must take that position. To agape, we need an example. Jesus provides that example.

This kind of love moves us to the next aspect of our foundation—the definition.

---

1. "Quickstart Guide to Choice Theory."

2. Logan Ury, "Want to Improve Your Relationship? Start Paying More Attention to Bids," *The Gottman Institute*, June 16, 2023, accessed Oct. 30, 2023, https://www.gottman.com/blog/want-to-improve-your-relationship-start-paying-more-attention-to-bids/.

3. John Gottman, Julie Schwartz Gottman, Douglas Abrams, and Rachel Carlton Abrams, *The Man's Guide to Women: Scientifically Proven Secrets from the Love Lab About What Women Really Want* (Emmaus, PA: Rodale Books, 2016), 11.

4. I've created an entire course on premarital counseling for our church, and I have training videos for my therapists that go over what I call "life rules." We don't have time to go down the rabbit hole this chapter, but basically, everyone has different life rules going into marriage. Conflict usually arises because of conflicting life rules.

5. "G3130—mania—Strong's Greek Lexicon (KJV)," Blue Letter Bible, accessed December 19, 2023, https://www.blueletterbible.org/lexicon/g3130/kjv/tr/ss1/rl1/0-1/.

6. Kenneth S. Wuest, *Wuest's Word Studies from the Greek New Testament for the English Reader* (Grand Rapids, MI: Eerdmans, 2019), 3:62. "Phileo (Φιλεο)" is a love that consists of the glow of the heart kindled by the perception of the object that affords us pleasure. It is the response of the human spirit to what appeals to it as pleasurable. The Greeks made much of friendship. The word was used to speak of friendly affection. It is a love called out of one in response to a feeling of pleasure or delight that one experiences from an apprehension of qualities in another that furnish such pleasure or delight. "Agapao (Ἀγαπαο)" on the other hand speaks of a love that is awakened by a sense of value in the object loved, an apprehension of its preciousness.

7. There are contextual exceptions to this definition of philia, but this explanation helps me illustrate my point.

8. Henry George Liddell et al., *A Greek-English Lexicon: A New Edition Revised and Augmented Throughout by Sir Henry Stuart Jones, with the Assistance of Roderick McKenzie, 2 Vols*, Online, 1940, accessed through the Persus Digital Library, Tufts University, https://www.perseus.tufts.edu/hopper/.

9. Again, there may be a few textual cases where agape refers to friendship.

10. Wuest, *Wuest's Word Studies*, 62.

11. Joe Malone and Sarah Achelpohl Harris, *Battles of the Sexes: Raising Sexual IQ to Lower Sexual Conflict and Empower Lasting Love* (New York: Morgan James Publishing, 2018), 119.

Three

WHAT MARRIAGE IS

I believe that God exists in three persons as the Father, Son, and Holy Spirit while being one being. Because of this, one of my stranger musings went along these lines: Why not *three* distinct and necessary sexes and *three* people in one marriage? If I were God, that would make the most sense. God hypothetically could have created three different sexes and instituted marriages between three sexes. So why do *two* people "become one" in marriage?

My assumption is that God designed and created marriage the way He wanted. There must be some reason. While the broadness of the last chapter is helpful because we covered everyday things like devotion, service, and friendship, it's not enough. There must be more to the reasoning behind His design.

Pseudo-Marriages

When I first started professional counseling, I ran into dozens of couples headed toward divorce. I expected this, of course. I also ran into dozens of couples who weren't technically married but lived together, were sexually active, and, in almost every practical way, were married. Some even had children. They were cohabiting and living in a strange mixture of states, like a pseudo-marriage. These couples were also struggling in their relationships, maybe headed toward breaking up. This created a quandary. I use specific techniques for counseling married couples versus dating couples. I asked the pseudo-married couples whether they wanted me to treat them like they were dating or married. They always wanted me to treat them as married.

So, to the best of my ability, I rendered professional counseling to those clients as though they were married. I know it sounds bad, but I sometimes forgot whether they were actually married because, in my brain, I genuinely tried to treat them the same.

After about three years of counseling, my younger self noticed a pattern. On the one hand, I hadn't lost even one married couple to divorce. Not one. They were all on their way to restoration and healthier marriages.

First of all: Not bad! This was a massive achievement. Marriage problems? Come to see the up-and-coming Chris Legg, who boasts a one-hundred-percent success rate. (Tragically, this record has since been broken, but it lasted for a while.)

On the flip side, however, *every single one* of the pseudo-married couples ended up breaking up. Not a *single* one could be called a success—unless breaking up was a success. I tried to help them work through that process, of course, but at the end of the day, I had a one-hundred-percent breakup rate with them.

That trend has mostly stayed the same in my twenty-five years of counseling. Couples who, while cohabiting, received the same counseling as my married clients typically broke up. Research backs the trend that cohabiting couples don't as often end up married to the end of life.[1]

Notice that the pseudo-married couples came to therapy because, at that moment, they wanted to fight for their relationship and presumably spend the rest of their lives together. It's not as though they were jumping ship at the first sight of hardship. The only difference was that they didn't *call* their relationship marriage. They lacked marriage's essence, if you will.

At this point in our culture, cohabiting is more common in adults aged eighteen to forty-four than marriage. The reasons people cohabit rather than marry are wide and varied. Sadly, but perhaps predictably, four in ten cohabiting adults cite finances and convenience as primary reasons for moving in.[2] They aren't *practicing* marriage in an effort to *be* married. They do so because it is more convenient, expedient, or financially advantageous.

Another common reason is to give marriage a trial run. "Well, you wouldn't buy a pair of shoes without trying them on, would you? You don't buy a car without test-driving it, do you?" No, I don't, in either case. The car logic made sense to me. However, the research in the 1990s, when I was getting started as a therapist, flew starkly in the face of this logic. Couples who lived together were much more likely to get divorced later if they did get married than couples who did not cohabit.

However, many thought there was some kind of cultural pressure back then. How about now? The findings persist. A report about how cohabitation impacts women discovered that women who cohabit before marriage are about a third more likely to see that marriage end in divorce than those who do not.[3]

The clue may come in the shoe and car analogy. The purchase of shoes and cars is not about mutual sacrifice. The transaction is, well, transactional. So long as the shoes perform well for me, I keep them.

So long as the car keeps running, I am committed to it. But what do we do when they don't?

We trade them in.

Our commitment isn't to the shoes or the car but *only to what the shoes or the car can do for us*. I am not trying to oversimplify something that I know perfectly well isn't simple, but that's where the logic breaks down.

Even though the pseudo-married couples were practically married, they weren't *actually*. At least one of them, and maybe both, weren't willing to take the vows aloud and in community. As trivial as this seems, it apparently has a massive effect on the end result.

By the way, don't feel doomed if you were one of those people who bought in to the cohabitation error and sin. Devote yourself to something more profound—the decision to honor God by sacrificing in His name for your spouse. Cancel the selfish mindset, confess that you've been viewing marriage as something for your personal comfort, repent, and take a new path. I am glad you are here. Keep reading.

Marriage in One Sentence

Marriage is many things. For example, marriage is a ministry partnership, investing in the next generation, expanding the kingdom of God, and usually involves raising children. Teaming up with someone in marriage creates a space of security and fortitude, making life's unbearable challenges more bearable. Marriage helps a couple tackle life in sections, accomplishing different tasks, like a system of specialized parts. Also, marriage provides counsel to both partners and tempers the extremes and flaws of each spouse that might be present. Learning to accept your spouse's differences as potential strengths to offset your weaknesses rather than merely irritants is vital for a powerful marriage. So there are many ways to describe what marriage can accomplish: security, multiplication, procreation, and more.

Only God gets to define His creation and invention. Our question is not one of effect, recognition, or pragmatics. I mean the research, design, and creation purpose of marriage. In one sense, God defines marriage in Genesis 2. The covenant is when two people commit to forsake (leave) all others and commit to be faithful (cleave, become one) to their spouse until one of them is dead. We could say marriage is two people committing exclusively to be together in the sight of God.

That's good, but we can do better. That thesis doesn't explain why men and women need to be distinct. Men and women possess different instincts, brain development, interpretations, hormones, life cycles, and come from Mars versus Venus. In other words, why are men and women asymmetrical? Why not marriage between androgynous people? I mean, think how easy marriage could have been if we all felt, thought, and experienced the same things! While our instinct is to think of these differences as a "bug," they aren't; they're a feature.

The Hebrew Scriptures

First, let's examine some key passages in the Old Testament, especially from the prophets.

We humans love to tell stories. We connect to narratives and analogies much better than cold, hard facts. It is part of our psychology. We are big-brained pack animals, always trying to clarify facts and truth to one another. Accounts, narratives, stories, and lessons are our best tools of understanding.[4]

We have various names for more significant versions of these, from the more invented (wives' tales, myths, fairy tales, legends) to the more real-life and pragmatic (teachable moments, biographies, object lessons, and "morals of the stories").

I grew up out in the woods, and these important lessons sometimes come as simple little rhymes. If you want to stay alive in East Texas, you need to remember that "red and yeller, kill a feller." That includes East Texas pronunciations. If you want to not catch an itchy rash, I strongly recommend "leaves of three, leave it be."

Biblically, narratives take the form of parables, prophecies, visions, and the like. Particularly in prophecies, God often uses object lessons played out in real life to teach powerful truths.

The prophets of the Old Testament were people who received messages from God and then communicated them to the people of Israel. These messages generally consisted of intense conviction and warnings of judgment. As you can imagine, they weren't very popular. Instead of receiving a warm welcome for their messages that called their whole culture to repentance, they were often ostracized or killed. But God didn't only command them to give extremely unpopular sermons; that would be bad enough. Instead, He also commanded them to act these messages out in dramatic performances.

For instance, God directly tells Jeremiah to make a five-hundred-mile round-trip trek to bury his undergarments (probably something like long briefs) under a rock, hike all the way back to Judea, and wait. Later, he's told to make the twenty-five-day walk again, dig them *back* up, and bring them to the Judeans so that God could compare them to rotten underwear.[5] Pretty eccentric.

"God's prophet" is the most demanding job description out there.

One of the most profound examples of these object lessons is found in Hosea. We don't know much about Hosea's life other than a timestamp of when his ministry began. When Hosea was first called by God, God told him to marry a "promiscuous woman" (possibly prostitute).[6]

How did that conversation go?

God: "Listen, man . . . um . . . you've been a faithful prophet and everything. So the good news is you get to marry! The bad news: she is *for sure* going to commit adultery and sell herself into sexual slavery."

Hosea: ". . ."

We get essentially no details about how this went down. We know nothing about Hosea's life; how he found this woman, Gomer; or how Hosea felt about God commanding him to marry a promiscuous woman. (As a professional therapist, I can tell you he wasn't happy.)

So Hosea married Gomer and had three children with her, giving them some cute baby names: "No Mercy," "Not My People," and Jezreel—the site of many battles and slaughters. Then, Gomer betrayed Hosea and turned to a life of sexual sin. (It is the beautiful message of the rest of the passage that God promises to rename the children with names brimming with grace—check out Hosea chapters one and two).

Hosea's anguish at the betrayal of his wife is compared to God's anguish at the betrayal of Israel. Just like Hosea pursued Gomer with foreknowledge of her adultery, God pursued Israel knowing full well that Israel would be "unfaithful" or "promiscuous" by worshiping other gods. Gomer leaves Hosea in an act of infidelity (which literally, from Latin, means "unfaithful") just like Israel is unfaithful to God.

After Gomer leaves Hosea, God commands Hosea to pursue her in an act of pure grace. He tells Hosea to win her back—to woo her. The Hebrew language here even suggests seduction.[7] The text says Hosea must pay a fee as a part of winning her back. The amount he pays is not enough for a dowry, but it is about the price of a slave. This means Hosea found her as a sexual slave of some kind. Metaphorically, this low price expresses Israel's unworthiness as they sold themselves into sexual slavery to idols.[8]

Here's what I want us to take away: The gut-wrenching poetry of Hosea harshly condemns Israel for what sin? Well, actually, a host of sins. Social injustice, sexual failure, lack of trust in God, putting on a false show, that women can be sold into sex slavery (yikes!), and ultimately, idolatry. But the revealing part is how God refers to Israel's idolatry and worship of other gods as "adultery."[9] They have broken their covenant with God.

There are several covenants made between God and Israel, but the main one referred to by the prophets is from Deuteronomy 28. If Israel follows God, God will bless them. If they follow other gods, he will curse them. (Ultimately, praise Him, Yahweh will restore His chosen people no matter how imperfect we are.)

I can't even imagine the sadness and anger that would swirl together in the abject betrayal of an unfaithful spouse. Even the fear of adultery can cause intense emotional responses. God feels something similar when His people betray Him. This also gives insight into God's perfect, sinless form of "jealousy."

When God's people betray Him in preference to the love of themselves or other gods, He sends His prophets to condemn the sin of "adultery," or, more intensely, prostitution (Ezekiel 6 and 16, Jeremiah 3–5, Lamentations 1, Hosea 1–2, Amos 3, Isaiah 57, and many other places). These hard-hitting passages give us a deep insight into God's relationship with His people.

Consider these two examples from Jeremiah 3:6–9 and Ezekiel 23:37. They aren't very subtle.

The LORD said to me in the days of King Josiah:

> "Have you seen what she did, that faithless one, Israel, how she went up on every high hill and under every green tree, and there played the whore? And I thought, 'After she has done all this she will return to me,' but she did not return, and her treacherous sister Judah saw it. She saw that for all the adulteries of that faithless one, Israel, I had sent her away with a decree of divorce. Yet her treacherous sister Judah did not fear, but she too went and played the whore. Because she took her whoredom lightly, she polluted the land, committing adultery with stone and tree. For they have committed adultery, and blood is on their hands. With their idols they have committed adultery, and

they have even offered up to them for food the children whom they had borne to me.

Does this language sound familiar? A promise of love between two parties that lasts forever? Is this ringing any bells (no pun intended)?

If you're not putting the pieces together yet: You can't commit adultery with someone unless at least one party is married to someone else. So who is married in the minds of the prophets?

Surely not Israel and the idols, so it must be God and Israel. This traces back to God's agreement with Abraham, the beginning of the Hebrew people. Such an agreement is called a covenant. Marriage between God and His people.

The New Testament Scriptures

Even though the apostle Paul was a bachelor and lamented married people's "divided attention" between their spouse and God,[10] he still highly praises marriage as a gift from God. He also sees deep meaning in it. In his case, the meaning is clearly theological, even more than practical!

The main passage quoted on marriage is found in Ephesians 5.

Paul begins in 5:21 by stating that all believers, regardless of gender or status, should submit to each other.

"Let every one of us submit to one another. Wives also to your husbands" (5:21–22). The word "submit" does not appear in the verse directed toward the wives. It is implied by reference to the previous verse, quite possibly Paul's ever so subtle way of calling out the wives of Ephesus:

"Wives, this means you. You have to submit to your husbands." (Also, Paul *never* commands women to submit to men in general.)

Submission is challenging, no doubt, and submitting to a spouse is sometimes the hardest expression of submission! But Paul doesn't shy away from it.

Even when my role places someone in submission to me from an authority perspective, I ought to look for chances to *sub*ordinate my "mission" (*sub*mission) in order to achieve someone else's vision.

"Wives submit to your husbands" is maybe *some* guys' favorite verse on marriage—but remember, Paul is talking to wives here, not you, men. Never hold this over her head. When we examine Ephesians 5, we need to practice the "start with me" principle. In fact, I wish guys could be entirely blind to what their wives are "supposed" to do according to Paul.

Paul might be setting husbands up by starting with wives. It's like he's getting men to agree with the first premise of equating wives to the church before he points out what that means for husbands, who he links to Christ.

"Husbands, love your wives, as Christ loved the church and gave himself up for her" (Eph. 5:25).

So we're supposed to love our wives to the point of torturous death? I don't hear guys quoting that one very often. Again, wives, don't hold this over your husband's head; it's directed at them, not at you.

In the final verse of the section, he writes, "This mystery is profound, and I am saying that it refers to Christ and the church." (Eph. 5:32)

In other words, talking about the mystery of marriage *is* talking about Christ and the church!

This analogy continues through eternity, by the way. In the new Jerusalem under the new heaven, the celebration will be the wedding feast of the Lamb! "'Let us rejoice and exult and give him the glory, for the marriage of the Lamb has come, and his Bride has made herself ready; it was granted her to clothe herself with fine linen, bright and pure'—for the fine linen is the righteous deeds of the saints" (Rev. 19:7–8).

Jesus calls Himself the bridegroom in Matthew 9:15; He is the one who fulfills the role of husband to the church because He will not break His promise to love and cherish us forever. Our attempts at marriage are the analogy. His covenant love is the reality. In marriage, we are seeking to mimic Him.

Finally, we can arrive at the one-sentence definition of marriage.

Principle: Marriage Is a Living Parable

Marriage was designed, created, and instituted to serve as a living parable of God's love for His people.

At this point, you might ask, "Is it a living parable of God's love for His people, or is it about OJ and chocolate milk, loving your spouse with devotion so that your lives become enriched together? *Which one is it?*"

Hopefully, you see by now: It's both. They're inseparable.

If marriage is a living parable of God's love for His people, then consider what His love is like. Jesus emptied Himself; experienced life as a human, filled with frailty, exhaustion, and pain; took on the role of a servant;

and served to the point of death on the cross. Who does that? What god shows their power through personal sacrifice?

If God wants marriage to be a parable of His love for His people and His love is so exemplified through sacrifice, then it makes sense that He would hardwire sacrifice into marriage.

Why are men and women so different? In part so that we have ample opportunity to sacrifice for one another.

In the same way that God created human fatherhood because he is the Father, God created marriage because he wants to be married to His people. It's not as though humans invented marriage, then God, as an afterthought, said to Himself, "You know what? Marriages are kind of like how I love my people! Maybe I should borrow that idea from humans."

No. It's the opposite. God's love for His people came before marriage.

When other people look at our marriages, we hope they would say, "God's love for the church and the church's love for God looks like that. Maybe God could love me the way that man loves his wife; maybe I could be loved by God the way that woman loves her husband."

Will it be clumsy when we try it? Yes.

Will it be imperfect? Absolutely.

Will we hurt each other, miss the mark, and mess up daily? Of course.

And this answers the other question about the three sexes. No need exists for a third human person or gender in marriage. Our limitations and flaws mean that a third Person is required in a marriage union—God

Himself. Only by His power can we live in God-honoring marriages. He did not just call us into an impossible lifelong sacrificial covenant and abandon us. We are only a hazy picture of God's selfless love, but if we trust Him, obey Him, and double down by making a habit of loving with vulnerability, respect, and intimate sacrifice, even in the often boring work of everyday love, we will be that much closer to mirroring God's perfect love.

In Christian marriage seminars, a commonly used picture is a triangle with God, husband, and wife at each of the three corners. When the husband and wife grow closer to God, they grow closer to each other. Here is the triune marriage I was wondering about. And, my friend, this kind of marriage will shine like a bright city in a dark world.

Principle: Your Marriage Is a City on the Hill. So Shine.

Look around. People wander in a dark wilderness of ruined marriages, devastated relationships, divorce fallout, bland passivity, and pitiful complacency. I fear that, for many reasons, too few Christian marriages are acting as lamps on stands.

I believe the main reason the church loses so many young people is the poor marriages of their families. I don't think sex, drugs, rock and roll, or activist professors are the main issue. The fact that so many Christian parents' marriages are dull, uninspiring, passionless, and lifeless leaves students looking for something other than their parents' faith to inspire them! If our Christian marriages were significantly more impressive than the world's marriages, our pews would be packed.

In premarital counseling, I ask couples: "Is there a marriage that you are aware of that you would want your marriage to be like?" In the nearly three decades of my experience, only a handful of times has a bride or groom answered, "My parents," and two of those were from the same family.[11]

Can it be that almost no Christian marriages are worth emulating? No wonder we have silenced our own voices when it comes to society and marriage. A 2010 article written by two journalists for *Newsweek* damningly wrote: "When conservatives argue that same-sex couples are going to 'destroy' the sanctity of marriage, we wonder, *wait, didn't we already do that?*"[12] Ouch.

Bad marriages absolutely wreck our witnesses.

In decades past, statistics were skewed by people like Elizabeth Taylor and Johnny Carson, who were married many times. Each new marriage wrecked the curve for the rest of the world—for everyone who has been married eight times, there must be sixteen people married only once to get the average back down to something reasonable.

A new statistic, though, accounts for this by measuring the number of first-time marriages. According to this, a painful 30 to 40 percent of first-time marriages end in divorce.[13]

And this doesn't include broken, painful, and even abusive relationships that stay together, and it certainly doesn't include the number of couples cohabiting without ever marrying (which has skyrocketed). There's a good chance the percentage will rise as the younger generations get older and start to marry (since they're marrying later and later, if at all).

There's good news with all this bad news.

If you've ever been in a deep cavern at a state park, at some point on the tour, your guide might have told you to turn off your flashlights. That kind of pitch-black darkness is terrifying—suffocating. When the light comes back on—what a relief! Even a candle would illuminate the whole place!

It may not have been quite that dark at night in the first century (when the New Testament was written), but there were no iPhones and no light pollution. To this day, when our Israel guides turn off the lights at our nighttime Galilee boat tour, we viscerally feel the darkness. In the first century, a myriad of dangers lurked about in the dark. If you got stuck on the road from Galilee to Jerusalem as dusk fell, you're thinking about wild animals, the bitter cold, and bandits.

So imagine traveling with your family for dozens of miles on rocky, dusty terrain, and dusk starts to fall. You're thinking all the time about their safety and hoping you make it before night falls. Did you calculate the route correctly? Blackness starts to cover the sky, and doubt sets in. Night falls, and the city is nowhere in sight. Every sound echoes as paranoia. The Mediterranean cold is causing your family to wrap clothing tighter. Should you stop to see if you can make a fire and set up camp and risk being beset by bandits? Or should you press on?

Then, suddenly, you see a light on the hill ahead. Safety. It means a warm place to stay with your relatives, hot food, and a good foot washing after a hard day's journey.

That is what a city on a hill means to the audience of the Sermon on the Mount (Matt. 5).

That is what a good marriage will look like to a weary generation exhausted by countless divorces.

Imagine a young couple, Robert and Julia. They are five years into marriage with two kids. Their marriage is rocky. They've both seen their parents' marriages fall apart, and even though they swore they would never make the same mistakes, it seems they are. Maybe one night, though, after some incessant nagging, Julia gets her hubby to go bowling with her. They meet another young couple while on their date. After some casual conversation, they strike up a friendship.

Eventually, they have them over for dinner, and Robert and Julia notice something strange. These new friends don't seem to be faking their affection! Their life has all the same stressors: kids, work, money issues, and other run-of-the-mill challenges. But the way they talk about each other and look at each other, they seem authentically content and secure in their relationship, even in those moments when they are a little edgy. Hanging out with them seems strange but also refreshing, even inspiring.

This glimmer of hope eventually causes the struggling Julia and Robert to break down and just outright ask: "What is your secret?"

Their secret is that they accept what marriage is, a living parable of God's love for His people, and it is expressed in sacrificial love—on display for all! They don't get to say they're perfect—they're definitely not, but they can share how their love reflects Christ's love for them.

What an invaluable witness!

Remember Ephesians 5. Marriage is supposed to represent Christ's love for the church. For Christian teens, if mom didn't submit and love dad well, and if dad didn't love and serve mom well, then the whole Jesus thing seems like a big joke. A witness can work both ways.

Nowadays, we seem less likely to believe that marriage can help make for happier lives. (Even though statistically married people seem to be happier than unmarried people.[14]) The number of people getting married continues to decline, and the marriages that are failing in divorce continue to be around 40 percent and are increasing across many age groups (especially people fifty and older).[15]

It's not just that our parents get into an argument over whether the toilet paper should be over or under. Marriages in America are failing at a staggering rate. Even beyond official divorce, an alarming number of marriages have unofficially disintegrated, even when still sharing an address.

This may all seem trivial to you. You came to this book for help in your sex life and it's hard to think about the state of America or even the church's witness when you just want some sanity. However, these patterns reveal that the issue is systemic as well as personal. If we change the personal, then, in time, we also may change the culture.

I cannot wait to get to the sections of this book about sex. The insights there are my favorite.

"Enough with the idealistic stuff, Chris. Marital problems happen buried in mountains of laundry amid shattered career dreams. Get to the nitty-gritty stuff," you might respond.

Okay, fair enough.

Hope for All

I got marriage counseling early in my marriage with Ginger (we were consistently in conflict over finances), and simple tips helped us—sometimes ridiculously simple. The rest of this book will give you insights to help solve some of those superficial roadblocks in sex that you're probably completely unaware of.

This book's most significant frustration for me is how I can only hope to increase your understanding. Unless I spend hours on therapy with you, I can't determine the specific application for you, but I can lead you to hope. If both spouses are committed to the marriage, and you're reading this book for tips to smooth out friction from issues like sex, good news! A few lessons often clear that friction since we're all on the same team.

Here's another note (warning, it's based on anecdotal evidence). I've found in my career that, *almost without exception*, if the husband fights for their marriage by adopting the principles I've talked about, then the marriage *not only heals, it thrives*. I rarely see a husband willing to make an effort to create a great marriage and the marriage fail. The main exceptions generally involve severe mental illness; even then, we usually make great strides. I do sometimes see wives make a lone, noble attempt to save their marriage, but they can't manage it. When both partners are on board, with teaching and counseling, their marriage succeeds.

When the husband tries, it almost always succeeds. I don't know why this is or if it is common to marriages, but it is certainly my experience. Barring mental illness, it seems to me that most men have the marriage culture they create! To the degree this is accurate and not merely my experience, we men need to step it up.

An extreme example involved a couple I worked with many years ago. The wife had patiently asked the husband for basic trust requests like healthier boundaries with work and other women, for example. As he put it, he had "gotten busy, and she had gotten lonely." After months of work in which he would not make even the most superficial efforts, she got fed up and moved out. No explosion. No bang. He just came home to an empty house and a note. He disputed the proceeding, but he couldn't stop it. They soon divorced.

The end?

Not so much. Months later, he reached out to and challenged me, "So you're telling me, and have been telling me, that if I would make these small adaptations and then pursue her well, the way we talked about, that she might come back?"

I said, "Several dozen times, she and I said that, yes."

"Do you mean it?" he asked.

"Has she given her heart to another man?" I asked. My experience is that until someone, especially a woman, has given their heart to another, they are open to their past significant other. (This can be healthy or toxic, by the way.)

"I don't think so," he said.

"Then yes, I mean it."

He took me up on the challenge. A few months later, they were re-married. They kept working hard, and he worked on listening well and seeking to love as a man, not as an adolescent in an adult's body. In other words, he grew up. The last I heard, they still were married well.

When they both step up and get to work, the results will always be inspiring. Man, I *love* those redemption stories.

I had worked with a couple in which the husband had broken trust at every level within a short period of time—infidelity, dishonesty, gaslighting, and even lying about paying their bills. When they came to see me, they were days from losing their house and their marriage. We started the process of rebuilding trust; the husband learned to tell the truth even when he was afraid of rejection. They both began to push back against the "overbearing mother–adolescent son" marriage that they had unintentionally created. He learned to invest his energy into her rather than taking the easy path of getting the attention and affection from others. It wasn't easy for either of them; he had to break a lifetime of bad habits and unhealthy coping mechanisms. She had to leave some space in her heart to forgive and to keep trying. Now, years later, they are not only doing well, but they have even just survived some serious family traumas without losing their willingness to invest in and love each other.

As Kathleen Norris is quoted as saying, "There was never a marriage that could not be made a success, nor a marriage that could not have ended in bitterness and failure."

We have hope. Jesus redeems the worst of us.

I say all that to say if your marriage is at *that* point, you probably need professional counseling, but do not give up hope.

If you're in an abusive situation, that possibly can still be redeemed (Jesus does crazy stuff), but you absolutely *must* get help. That will probably require rigid boundaries, the police, going to a therapist, or separation. If that's you—get help. Without some help in a cyclically abusive relationship, some of these ideas of sacrifice can backfire and create a codependency that can be hard to recover from.

With that warning and hope for redemption out of the way, we're just about ready to talk about sex.

As a recap: Marriage is a living parable of God's love for His people. Just as, in my understanding, fatherhood reflects God's nature as the Father, marriage should reflect Christ's love for the church, His bride.

I'm with C. S. Lewis on the idea of Christian hedonism (in case you didn't notice, I'm a big Lewis fan).[16] That idea runs like this: God desires the best for us. We will receive the greatest fulfillment and happiness if we follow His plan. If we settle for sexual flings, divorce to find greener grass on the other side, or manipulate our spouse for things we want, we're doing just that: settling. We're settling for garbage, second-rate love, and certainly no true happiness.

If we reflect on the best things in life, we realize they are usually difficult. I hate to harp on kids so much, but while they are one of the truest joys of life, they're also expensive and ornery. So, as one of the greatest joys of life, it's no surprise that marriage is hard.

However, one of the brightest lights in the human experience is sex. I believe that God intends sex to be the significant advantage of marriage over all other relationships. God's plan was for sex to be a unique source of power and protection and comfort.

And yet, in so many of our marriages, sex is the primary source of pain, stress, hurt, and disappointment. So imagine how the potential can swing toward the good! It may not feel like sex gives that right now, and it may not for you, but hopefully with better understanding, the following insights will help you work through them.

They've certainly helped me and my wife and dozens of other couples who have gotten a handle on these principles.

---

1. Nikki Graf, "Key Findings on Marriage and Cohabitation in the US," Pew Research Center, November 6, 2019, https://www.pewresearch.org/fact-tank/2019/11/06/key-finding s-on-marriage-and-cohabitation-in-the-u-s/. Though studies have shown that cohabiting before marriage (and this only looks at those who eventually *did* marry—most don't) can lead to short-term strength because the couple is used to each other, in the long term it still statistically leads to a higher chance of divorce and significantly less marital satisfaction. These studies are tough to measure because they take so long to get good data on, but what's available points to it; Michael Rosenfeld and Katharina Roesler, "Cohabitation Experience and Cohabitation's Association with Marital Dissolution," *Journal of Marriage and Family* 81, no. 1 (September 24, 2018): 42–58, https://doi.org/10.1111/jomf.12530; Galena K. Rhoades, Scott M. Stanley, and Howard J. Markman, "The Pre-Engagement Cohabitation Effect: A Replication and Extension of Previous Findings," *Journal of Family Psychology* 23, no. 1 (January 2009): 107–111, https://doi.org/10.1037/a0014358.

2. Nikki Graf, "Key Findings."

3. Theresa E. DiDonato, "Are Couples That Live Together before Marriage More Likely to Divorce?" *Psychology Today*, January 27, 2021, accessed January 6, 2024, https://www.psychologytoday.com/us/blog/meet-catch-and-keep/202101/are-couples-that-live-together-before-marriage-more-likely-to.

4. John E. Hummel, John Licato, and Selmer Bringsjord, "Analogy, Explanation, and Proof," *Frontiers in Human Neuroscience* 8, no. 1 (November 6, 2014), https://doi.org/10.3389/fnhum.2014.00867.

5. Elmer A. Martens, *Jeremiah: Believers Church Bible Commentary* (Independence, MO: Herald Press, 1986), 103.

6. Some think she was a prostitute when he married her, and some believe the Bible is predicting that she will act in adultery. Others argue that she was an average Israelite woman who took part in sexual rituals in worship of idols.

7. Robert Chisholm, "Hosea," in *Bible Knowledge Commentary: Old Testament*, eds. John F. Walvoord and Roy B. Zuck, 2nd ed. (Wheaton, IL: Victor Books, 2003), 1385.

8. Robert Jamieson, Andrew Fausset, and David Brown, *Commentary Critical and Explanatory on the Whole Bible: The Old Testament: From Song of Solomon to Malachi* (Scotts Valley, CA: CreateSpace Publishing, 2017), 652, accessed via Logos Bible Software.

9. On page 1385, Chisolm summarizes: "[Hosea] compared Israel's covenant relationship to the Lord with marriage and accused Israel (the Lord's "wife") of spiritual adultery. She had turned to Baal, the Canaanite storm and fertility god (cf. 2:8, 13; 11:2; 13:1), in an effort to promote agricultural and human fertility."

10. 1 Corinthians 7:34.

11. Since writing this paragraph, I shepherded my son and his wife through premarital counseling; he mentioned our marriage, and she mentioned her parents. Wow. How proud can a couple be? Here come the waterworks!

12. Jessica Bennett and Jesse Ellison, "The Case against Marriage," *Newsweek*, June 11, 2020, https://www.newsweek.com/case-against-marriage-73045.

13. CDC, "FastStats," Marriage and Divorce, updated April 24, 2023, https://www.cdc.gov/nchs/fastats/marriage-divorce.htm. The statistics are actually difficult to boil down to one number. Some articles report it's 40 percent, but the CDC seems to report it's closer to 40-ish percent if you boil down the rates of new marriages and new divorces. (Marriage rate, 6.0. Divorce rate, 2.5. Number of divorces, 689,308, and number of marriages, 1,985,072).

14. Lyman Stone, "Does Getting Married Really Make You Happier?" Institute for Family Studies, February 7, 2022, https://ifstudies.org/blog/does-getting-married-really-make-you-happier.

15. US Census Bureau, "Census Bureau Releases New Estimates on America's Families and Living Arrangements," November 29, 2021, https://www.census.gov/newsroom/press-releases/2021/families-and-living-arrangements.html;
Beti Prosheva Gavrilovska, "How Many Marriages End in Divorce," Review42.com, July 26, 2023, https://review42.com/resources/how-many-marriages-end-in-divorce/.

16. You can find this idea of "Christian hedonism" in a couple of places. In *Screwtape Letters*, a high-ranking demon named Underwood is speaking to his understudy. The demon says about God, "He's a hedonist at heart. All those fasts and vigils and stakes and crosses are only a façade. Or only like foam on the seashore. Out at sea, out in His sea, there is pleasure, and more pleasure. He makes no secret of it . . . He has a bourgeois mind. He has filled His world full of pleasures." C. S. Lewis, chap. 22 in *The Screwtape Letters* (Uhrichsville, OH: Barbour Publishing, 1989); Lewis's autobiography is titled *Surprised by Joy*, and it explores his finding ultimate satisfaction and happiness in God at such a greater weight than anything else; C. S. Lewis, *Surprised by Joy: The Shape of My Early Life* (New York: HarperCollins, 2017).

PART II

INTERPRETING SEX

If you skipped to this section, I totally understand. I am selling this book with insights to heal and empower your sex life, so it makes sense to jump ahead. God knows that in the past, I skipped to the sex chapter of marriage books. When we were struggling, when I seemed utterly unable to explain my heart and soul to my wife, when *my best efforts* seemed only to make things worse, the topic always seemed to be sex.

However, I strongly encourage you to start at the beginning. Much of this could get you into trouble without the correct mindset. Plus, we now need to get to the same kind of deep theological understanding of sex that we did for marriage.

On another note, if you came to this book because the husband has a lower sex drive than the wife in your marriage, you're not alone. Chapter 4 may feel like it doesn't address you because you're not the target audience, but the themes, topics, and language I discuss will nevertheless be rewarding and profitable for your marriage. Plus, it may help you get the vocabulary to discuss it, even if it is reversed. If at any point you get discouraged or confused, go to FAQ 1. There, I address a few specific reasons why you might find your sex drive imbalanced.

Everything I talk about in Part II (and the whole book, actually) can at least be used as a handbook by which you can say, "It's not like this for me, but . . ." Husband, you might discuss with your wife, "Well, I personally don't interpret things like Chris said, but I *do* think about it in terms of . . ." You, wife, might say, "Even though Chris is talking about men, this section of the chapter actually resonates with me!"

Here's the crux of Part II: "Men expect women to see things sexually the way they do, and women expect men to see things sexually the way they do."[1]

So we need to talk about identity.

Crash Course in Identity

One of the movie theaters in my town came up with a creative response to the COVID-19 shutdown. They began offering their theaters to be rented by any private group for a discounted price. You could bring your own movies and watch them on the big screen! As a huge movie buff, this experience was a dream come true. I took my kids to watch movies I loved as a kid. I took my wife and daughter on a date to see our favorites. I even took my church staff and counseling team. One movie I wanted to take our church staff to see was the 1978 edition of *Superman: The Movie* with Christopher Reeve and Gene Hackman. There were a lot of things about this movie that I loved and wanted to share, but there was one scene I had in mind for this team of disciple-makers.

Right before his death, Jonathan Kent, Superman's adopted earthly father, catches teenage Clark Kent showing off some of his power by running a bit too fast to score a touchdown. As father and son walk up the driveway to their house, Jonathan puts his arm over Clark's shoulder and encourages him, ending the talk with this: "And one thing I do know, son, and that is that you are here for a reason. I don't know whose reason or whatever the reason is . . . but I do know one thing: it's not to score touchdowns."

The power is already in Clark, but he needs someone to help him interpret it. His father helps him see that his power is for a higher purpose than serving himself. More than his power, this understanding makes him Superman.

We all need people to speak identity into us or at least to help us understand what the things that are true about us *mean*, to interpret them for us. There are many aspects of human identity—our genetics, our history, our character decisions, and beyond. What does it mean that I am frail or strong? What does it mean to be male or female? What does it mean that I come from a certain family, community, state, or country? What does my ethnicity mean? Well, sexuality is a part of human identity—so we need help interpreting this, too.

I'm considering writing another book on identity as its own topic. It's been central to my life's study and work as a pastor and counselor, so this introduction will barely cover the tip of the iceberg. It is painful for me to try just barely to skip across this topic, but I'll manage (and maybe write another book soon).

This section will specifically cover the idea of *foundational identity*. Most of what we will discuss in this book will have to do with your own intuitive experience of your identity—what feels more or less like something is about *you*.

Everyone has foundational identities. These foundations serve to provide ultimate purpose and meaning. Identity acts as an underlying motivation, and if it's removed, then our lives will tumble down in shambles. Undoubtedly, there will be multiple layers and "building materials" that will vie for our attention and multiple foundations we'll try to build on as we go through life.

For some parents, their children serve as their foundation (talk about pressure), or people pleasing and being a socialite (see how long that lasts). For some, their foundation rests in their career and their salary (can you say "burnout"?). For others, it's radical self-service and charity work (what, are you tryna prove something?).

Whatever your primary foundation, you'll probably die for it. Everyone has that kind of foundation, but many are unintentional, not carefully considered, and most are unstable.

As humans, we need something to define us. We need to look for something to guide our definition of our identity and what we live for. It needs to be external.

"What? External? Shouldn't I create this thing called 'identity' for myself, Chris?" Well, a personal and internal aspect of this process does exist. Our internal job is to choose and devote ourselves to an external source of value. However, the foundation, the value itself, can't merely refer to something inside of us. Pause for a second and think. Do you honestly trust yourself to define your own life identity—especially a stable one?

As I often ask when teaching with a facetious tone, "Have you met you?" My congregation knows the phrase well.

I can predict with one-hundred-percent accuracy that you, reading this book, fail frequently and miserably. How many times have you sworn to yourself or God, "I will lose (insert number here) pounds by (insert date here)," "I will never talk to (insert romantic ex's name here)," "I will never abuse (insert addictive chemical or behavior here)," and others?

I wouldn't trust myself as far as I could throw me with something as important as supporting my own identity—and you shouldn't either.

For that matter, you should not place your foundation in other people, no matter how great they appear, no matter how eloquent or trendy. Don't put existential trust in your father, children, professor, husband, wife, or, God forbid, your pastor. They will fail you, no matter how awesome. And if your ultimate faith is in yourself, you will fail you just as certainly as any other human being.

There are aspects of our identity that need to be founded on something stronger than ourselves. Certainly something as transitory as determinations, roles, tasks, or mere activities cannot safely or consistently lead to identity, even though that is a common misunderstanding in our culture.

As Christians, our theology must determine our identity. God defines value and purpose, and we have to work to trust in His ideas about who we are.

So since God is the fundamental determiner of meaning (whether we want Him to or not), our identity should look like this:

Theology → Identity

A. W. Tozer famously stated, "What comes into our minds when we think about God is the most important thing about us."[2]

Bachelor or married, saved or lost, pastor or unholy (that's a joke), male or female, redhead or inferior (also a joke), our identity exists. Whether our identity includes roles like mother, father, son, daughter, missionary, president, writer, or others, you must establish those categories *on top* of something that, unlike them, cannot be taken away. Identity must never be, "You do this, so you become this." Instead, we act on the reality of our identity. We should think, "I am this, so therefore I should act like this."

If you trust Jesus with your life, He bestows on you a new identity. God's power entirely changes you, then you act from that new identity. The Bible constantly makes statements about who we are. Consider a commonly taught passage, which we discussed in Chapter 3:

> You are the light of the world. A city set on a hill cannot be hidden. Nor do people light a lamp and put it under a basket, but on a stand, and it gives light to all in the house. In the same way, let your light shine before others, so that they may see your good works and give glory to your Father who is in heaven (Matt. 5:14–16).

There's a graphic T-shirt that beautifully represents a common misunderstanding.

It says, "B [salt shaker image] + [lamp image]."

Pretty innocent, right? This subtle difference between the passage and the teaching carries enormous consequences.

Jesus teaches to his disciples, "You *are* the light of the world." He does not begin by teaching them to "act like the light of the world" or even "be the light of the world." He says, "You *are* the light of the world."

What's the big deal? Isn't that semantics? It is semantics, and yes, it's a big deal. The real message is to behave according to what you are, not that you are according to how you behave.

If you want to see this pattern in the teachings of the New Testament, here's a quick survey for His followers:

- 1 Corinthians 6:9–11

- 1 John 3

- Romans 8

- Galatians 3:26

- Galatians 4:6–7

- Philippians 3:12

- 1 Peter 2:9–12

- Philippians 3:20–4:1

- Ephesians 2:19–22

- John 15:1–17

- 2 Corinthians 5:17–6:1

- James 2:12

- Colossians 3:12–17

- Ephesians 2:10

- Philippians 1:27

- 1 Thessalonians 2:12

- Ephesians 4:1

Those are just to get you started. Seriously, take some time to go look those up. You'll be encouraged by how the Creator of the universe sees you.

Once you wear the proper lenses, you will see how constant this message is in the Old and New Testaments. In Jesus's kingdom, identity, or "calling," precedes action. Where do we receive our identity? From God and His Word. Knowing God and hearing from Him, we can call "theology" for now.

Otherwise, everything depends on how we perform. If performance leads God to grant us grace or identity as new people, then it's not really grace. So here's the pattern we observe in holy Scripture:

Theology → Identity → Activity

The correct order of identity also applies to concepts like marriage.

God, as Creator and Sustainer, defines marriage (theology). We choose to accept the identity of husband or wife in alignment with how He defines those identities via marriage (identity). What should follow? The suitable activities of a married person (activity). This entire process is founded on God, not our behavior.

Remember, it's *not* "acts like a perfect wife" equals "wife" or "acts like a perfect husband" equals "husband." It's instead:

"I *am* a husband; let me act like one to my wife."

"I *am* a wife; let me act like one to my husband."

It's also not "I feel like being a wife or husband today," but "I am a wife or husband today, as I will be until death do us part." Over time, that perspective will make you feel more secure, happier, and freer anyway because it reflects the truth.

One main principle of the rest of this book will be how men and women seem to see their relationship to sex regarding our egos. Our selves. Our identities.

What is our intuitive understanding of sex in relation to our identity? How linked are they, and how deeply?

All kinds of things shape how we perceive our identity. Our parents calling us trash as children will certainly affect how we view ourselves, but the objective truth is that God treasures us, which means we are valuable. That'll preach, won't it?

What I found is that men and women statistically perceive their own identity differently in regard to sex, which leads to many, or even most, of our misunderstandings.

Reminder: The first and most important goal is understanding your spouse (the sleuthing and "start with me" principles). You need to understand your spouse's instincts, especially when they differ from yours at the identity level! Paying attention to these distinctions will allow you to serve them well in the effort to live out His living parable for His people.

---

1. Malone and Harris, *Battles of the Sexes*, 116.

2. A. W. Tozer, *The Knowledge of the Holy: The Attributes of God. Their Meaning in the Christian Life* (Cambridge, England: Lutterworth Press, 2022), 1.

Four

MEN WANT MORE THAN JUST SEX

Church camp was a formative part of my faith. The hot sun, creaky bunk beds, worn-out furnishings, sweaty middle schoolers, questionable college-age role models, ridiculous activities (usually involving whipped cream and dodgeballs), emotional worship, and air-conditioned speaker nights. I loved them. I still love going to our church's summer camp. I loved it as a youth minister, and I loved going as a kid. At their best, church camps inspire young men and women to learn and grow in their faith while having a ton of fun.

However, I shudder to think about when the girls and guys inevitably split off on the fateful night of all youth camps. The return campers snicker because they know what's coming—the sex talk.

As a kid, I had what I suspect is a typical experience. In order to be cool or maybe to try and genuinely explain the difference between boys and girls, the camp speaker taught a monstrous, horrid, *secular* lie about sex. I remember vividly from one fateful summer: "Girls, you have to watch out for the boys because boys play at love, which they do not understand, in order to get sex, which is what they really want. Girls, you play at sex, which you do not understand, in order to get love, which is what you really want."

I am working hard not to use foul language. Look at the destructive division created in those words: "Girls, who will someday become wives, know that all men care about is sex (not love), and you have to watch out for the 'predators in heat' you are surrounded by. Good luck developing an intimate relationship with one of them someday."

Here's the lie: Men only want sex. Their desire for sex is independent of who they're having sex with, independent of context, and independent of how they get it. As the crass comedian Billy Crystal once said, "Women need a reason for sex. Men just need a place."

This accepted truism can only create feelings of dismissal, replaceability, and disgust in women. Movies, comedians, and advertisements build around this stereotype. If you're a woman reading this, your personal experience probably seems to back this up. There's a reason why most women, some men, and the culture at large believe this lie.

This message has persisted for years and often infects the church. Somewhere along the line, it became, "Sure, it is too bad this is the truth, but we need to get real, right?" Some perceive pastors as cool and edgy when they give the "honest" fact about how men just need sex, and God gave them women to provide it. For the girls (and the boys), this becomes the interpretation tool for virtually every sexual encounter, which probably haunts them for the rest of their lives—unless they learn the truth. Dear reader, keep reading!

As they grow up, women think they need to woo men with sex and "trick" them into emotional commitment because they wouldn't otherwise. Without sexual activity, they can't get a boy and keep him. Given these messages, it makes sense that boys understand their role as helpless animals whose only hope of sexual purity is the strength of the girl fighting them off.

That sounds like a healthy, biblical understanding of holiness and a solid foundation for fifty years of marriage, right? (Sarcasm.)

Practically everything a Christian wife hears or reads about sex revolves around the message "Your husband needs sex, so give it up." After a hefty dose of guilt, she resolves to make sex more of a priority in her marriage. Her resolve lasts a while, but eventually, she becomes resentful. She and her husband may be having sex more often, but it's not getting any better.[1]

In the first lines of this book, I mentioned a client who read a Christian book in which men's top needs were sexual fulfillment, an attractive spouse, and domestic support, among others. These were the things that women were supposed to fulfill. She came into my office and, as I referenced earlier, said, "So basically he wants a prostitute who cleans his house."

If it is true that all men care about is sex, then true intimacy is not possible, and God has set us up somehow to live in merely transactional contracts, not intimate partnerships.

Hmm . . . this "got me to thinking" again. I wondered: Why *don't* men hire prostitutes who clean their houses?[2] I assume it would be cheaper, simpler, and less stressful than trying to have an intimate, loving relationship with a woman who wants me and who wants me to want her.

Even as a young man, I was dubious about this sex lie. I knew that as much as I was interested in sex and female sexuality, there was something much more profound that I wanted to experience within sex someday. I didn't fantasize merely about sex but a *connection*.

I assumed I was the strange one since I was being taught, just like everyone else, that all men thought about, longed for, and wanted was sex. Years later, several things made me reconsider whether I was the only guy feeling this way.

One was the ancient Hebrew story of Esther.

Esther's determination to save her people reflected incredible courage, wit, and intelligence. The phenomenal woman, placed in an unthinkable situation, was chosen by God to save her people. I highly recommend the whole story, but I'll narrow our focus on one small moment that caught my attention: Her sex with Xerxes.

Esther and Xerxes

Xerxes ruled Persia about five hundred years before the birth of Christ and was one of the most powerful men who ever lived. He is most famous for marching a massive army, of as many as two million men, from all parts of the Persian Empire against the Greeks. It remains one of the largest armies to have ever walked the face of the earth.[3]

Xerxes was essentially a god and king over a vast percentage of "civilization" at that time, with authority over life and death for whole people groups. His word was law. As was the custom of all ancient kings, he possessed a large harem of concubines. Concubines were essentially full-time prostitutes, sub-wives, on hand for him at all times. He certainly owned dozens, but he may have housed hundreds or thousands.

The scene is set: Xerxes throws a massive celebration for everyone in his capital. For seven days, everyone drinks as much as they want and does whatever they please. This party would literally go down in history.

The Bible says that by the seventh day, he was "merry with wine." You think?

So he decides to command his wife, or at least his top wife, Queen Vashti, to come up in front of his party and "show the peoples and the princes her beauty" (Est. 1:11). The implication here is pretty obvious: he wants her to strip tease. She refuses.

He is dumbfounded. For some reason, he can't remember the law about the queen refusing the king. (It could have something to do with him being hammered.) The wise men say that Xerxes should fire her. The reason? "For the queen's behavior will be made known to all women, causing them to look at their husbands with contempt, since they will say, 'King Ahasuerus commanded Queen Vashti to be brought before him, and she did not come'" (Est. 1:17).

In other words, wives around the nation may get the idea that they need not slavishly obey the whims of their husbands. That would be disastrous. So Xerxes fires her.

Time for a new wife, the head of his harem.

Xerxes is in charge of half the world, a diagnosable megalomaniac, a sex addict with possibly a harem of hundreds, and essentially a living, breathing definition of misogyny (almost comically so). Keep that picture in your head for the next part.

Enter stage left: Esther. Esther was a Jewish woman of stunning beauty, an orphan raised by Mordecai. She's caught in a strange time of history. The Persian and Median empires had swept the Jewish people into their ever-expanding empire after defeating Babylon. At this point, the Jewish people are scattered across the empire, and their homeland in Israel is a wasteland.

Because of her good looks, Esther is yanked off of the street to become a candidate for Xerxes's palace. Esther then spends a year getting ready to have one night with Xerxes. Over that year, she receives beauty treatments and training to become as attractive as possible, preparing to give him the best night imaginable when she gets her shot. (Comically enough, I've heard some people preach Esther like it's some kind of Prince Charming story. In a word: *no*.) This story reminds us how twisted the mindset of these cultures was, with basically no sense of consensual sex. The brokenness of the power structure, Xerxes, and the whole nightmarish situation for Esther only speaks to the surprising nature of the coming insight as well as Esther's unthinkable strength and bravery.

After a year, she finally had her one night of sex, and he falls head over heels. After one night, Xerxes was so impressed, he gave her the title of queen (Est. 2:17).

Simultaneously, Haman, Xerxes's confidant, suggests to Xerxes he should kill all the Jews (because Mordecai, a Jew, offended him). Xerxes agrees, adding anti-Semitism to his list of upstanding qualities. Esther has not revealed her Jewish heritage up to this point.

The tension builds.

Esther, with Mordecai, formulates a plan to save her people. She's already gained Xerxes's favor via her one-night stand, but he hasn't communicated with her for a while. Now, she must figure out a way to please him so highly that he would revoke the royal order of killing all Jews for her sake.

Esther approaches the king without being invited, even though she could die for doing so, and suggests that she throw a feast. She prepares the meal for Xerxes and Haman; in my reading, she is quite flirtatious and seductive. The king is pleased again by the banquet. Xerxes says he will give her up to half of his kingdom, but instead of asking for the Jews to be saved, Esther plays the smart game and asks him to return the next night.

This stands out to me. At the end of a sumptuous meal with a stunning, exotic woman—after she reminds him of their night of passion together—she essentially tells him to go away and come back tomorrow night.

Is sex all men want?

If so, I expect him to say, "Yeah, right, that's a nice thought, Esther, but nah. Haman, take a hike. We need some alone time."

Remember, Xerxes is the most toxic and damaged man you could imagine, especially sexually, with all the power in the world.

Yet he agrees!

Xerxes is *intrigued* by Esther and her offer. *Why?*

Men, I bet that many of you reading intuitively get his decision, but the story flies in the face of the culture's narrative that men equal sex-driven animals. Xerxes had all of the power in the situation and had no external motivation to walk away from the opportunity to have sex, and yet, it seems like he did just that. What was the internal motivation, then? If all men think about, want, and are motivated by is sex, it makes no sense.

What if men want something else, really, besides sex? Could even Xerxes have been more intrigued by the *connection* she was offering than by mere sex? Esther craftily uses his emotions and curiosity against him, revealing something deep in the hearts of even the worst men.

Men may already intuitively know the answer but can't put it into words. I'm going to do my best to explain this phenomenon. I will be referencing Shaunti Feldhahn's books a good deal. Her research helped me understand that much of what we have been taught about male (and female) sexuality is wrong. Feldhahn helped reveal, for example, "Although popular opinion portrays males as one giant sex gland with no emotions attached, that is the furthest thing from the truth. But because men don't tend to describe their sexual needs in emotional terms, we women may not realize that."[4]

Meet the Newlyweds

Let me illustrate this point by referencing a story about a newlywed couple named Bride and Groom. First, a caveat. My wife once pointed out to me that everyone assumes the following story is about us when we were younger. I disagreed, but she was right, of course. Since then, I have provided this disclaimer: Although our marriage faced similar moments and challenges, *the following story is not autobiographical.*

So let me introduce Groom and Bride. They are recently married. Not only were they virgins, but neither of them had any meaningful sexual trauma in their past. Neither had experience with adolescent flings (which are often traumatic even in average experiences), no encounters with pornography, and not even any really bad breakups.

I know this makes Bride and Groom difficult to relate to since most of us have that junk in our past, but it simplifies and clarifies the dynamics at work. Giving Bride and Groom the best possible start just simplifies the rest of the story and shows how, even under perfect conditions, sex can become divisive for a couple.

After a few weeks of marriage, Groom's new job sends him away for weekend training. Bride and Groom text and call about their romantic, erotic longing for one another. For the newlyweds, sex is still pretty much a novelty. It's free and fun and still feels a little "naughty" to think about. Bride also revels in how sex appeals to her man—especially how it connects him to her so potently. Determined to seduce him when he comes home from his trip, she buys something slinky, spreads rose petals to the bed, sets the lighting just right, and waits.

He comes home to find the rose petal path and follows them to their bedroom, where she waits. She welcomes him into her bed, and they enjoy each other.

Your Husband, Shakespeare

When I give talks about sex, I often stop the story here and ask the men in the audience how this would feel. How does being welcomed into her bed and her body feel? I'm not asking about the primal feelings of intercourse or an orgasm. I'm asking about seeing her there, inviting them in amid rose petals, clad in lingerie, in the dim glow of their bedroom lamp.

Unfortunately, men often struggle with communicating, shall we say, *nuanced* emotions, but not in this situation.

I get intense and profound responses like "welcomed," "wanted," "desired," "loved," "awesome," "amazing," and even more dramatic, "like everything is right with the world," "I am the king of the world," and "everything is perfect."

At some point, if it is a coed group, I will notice the women start looking at each other as if to ask, "We are still just talking about sex, right?"

Years ago, in my efforts to explain to my wife how this moment felt to me, I wrote her a poem entitled "Home." I thought I was unique, or at least uncommon, in my feelings after reading all those garbage transactional marriage books. It described what I experienced when I felt wanted by her. For her sake, I will not publish it here. Married sex may not be shameful, but it is private, after all.

Imagine my shock when, years later, a man in such a group shouted out "home" in response to my question. In fact, in about one-third of the groups that I teach this material to, a man will describe the feeling of being welcomed by his wife into sex as "coming home." Later I discovered that Billy Joel wrote a song by the same name about *his* wife (I guess I'm in good company there).

When someone approves of us, wants us, and desires us sexually, it feels much like being chosen.

Many psychologists pick up on how deeply men experience being sexually chosen.

Shaunti Feldhahn notes, "A man really does feel isolated, [often] even with his wife. But in making love, there is one other person in this world that you can be completely vulnerable and be totally accepted and not judged. It is a solace that goes very deep into the heart of a man."[5]

Stephen Snyder writes, "With good lovemaking, we have a feeling of 'Yes, that's me. Here I am. You found me.' We feel in touch with our deepest, most authentic selves. It's a grateful feeling. 'Yes, you found me. The me of me. Thank you for finding me. Thank you for bringing me home to where I really live.'"[6]

Look at the depth of identity described in that quote. Read it again. It's common for men to feel truly known and discovered when experiencing sexual intimacy with their wives. Feldhahn's research supports the weight of sex in men's feelings.

> A man can be having a horrible time at work, rejection in his industry, and every other area can be going rotten—but if his wife wants him physically and affirms him in bed, he can handle the rest of the world, no problem. Conversely, if he gets the same impostor message at home ("You don't measure up. Don't touch me"), it will devastate him far worse than any career blow [. . .]. Your sexual desire for your husband profoundly affects his sense of well-being and confidence in all areas of his life.[7]

One man responded to the survey query, "I wish that my wife understood that making a priority of meeting my [sexual desires] is the loudest and clearest way she can say, 'You are more important to me than anything else in the world.'"[8]

Every corner I turn, I find that sex makes men feel at home, especially in a healthy relationship. Dr. Laurie Watson describes this in *Psychology Today*:

> Sexual release makes men feel like they are finally home. After the world's hurts and challenges, sex embodies love and care and provides soothing and support. While he may be accused of "only wanting sex," most men want and feel a much more emotional connection than a simple bodily release. Making love literally creates a deep feeling of attachment to his partner and spurs relational generosity, faith, and optimism. Being desired by his partner can be the single most reassuring part of his relationship.[9]

Though I think a lot of what *Psychology Today* puts out now is dubious or worse, I found that word again, "home." At this point, I'm no longer surprised.

Who knew Shakespeare hid in the hearts of so many men?

Bride and Groom Again

Back to Bride and Groom. After the rose petal welcome, Bride seduces him, and they enjoy the good gift of one another in sex—no strings attached, no complications—just free and fun. They snuggle and fall asleep, happy to be reunited after his trip. So far, so good. It is easy to see how this kind of bonding agent is precisely what God had in mind for sex in marriage.

His company sends him away for another business trip a few months later.

This time, for whatever reason, a friend in need, a request from a parent, not feeling great, being tired, almost any stressor, or no particular reason at all, sex doesn't cross Bride's mind. She happily anticipates his return, but seducing him isn't on her radar.

You can bet your bottom dollar he's thinking about it—or rather, about *her*. So many assume that, as a male, of course he's thinking about sex. He is always thinking about sex. It's all men care about, right? But think back a few paragraphs and consider the list of men's emotions connected to being seduced: connected, wanted, loved, desired, and at home. What kind of idiot wouldn't want to experience those feelings again?

The authors of *The Man's Guide to Women* again show that men are drawn to attention more than even "objective" attractiveness. They write, "Whether or not men are interested in a woman is not strongly related to her objective attractiveness, but instead to the nonverbal signals she sends out."[10] In other words, he is looking for meaning in her actions. What do her touches and responses mean to me? What motivates men to seek so much meaning in sexuality and sexual arousal?

Here's my hypothesis: *Men intuitively integrate sexuality into their identity.*

Men experience sexual desire for us as bestowed identity. If a woman pursues us sexually, we interpret that as being about *us*, not merely *sex*.

Men think, "It isn't that she wants *sex*; she wants *me*." It is one of the most potent ways most men experience being chosen.

When someone shows interest in men sexually—when someone gets aroused because of us—most men accept it as a statement of all of the things listed above: home, safety, love, affirmation, and more.

Women often miss this phenomenon of their husband's experience (sometimes because he doesn't communicate his feelings to this effect), but even if they do see it, they don't know why it's there.

One of my roles in marriage counseling is to serve as a translator. For some reason, I'm often able to "speak" the language of other individuals and groups. After so many years of doing counseling with women, I have learned to sometimes speak "women" to men and "men" to women in a way that helps them understand each other. Thus, a translator. However, I have struggled to find ways to explain how men experience sex in a way that communicates to women just how integrated sexuality commonly is into our identity. Even people who live in the reversal of the typical patterns can relate to this. In fact, a man whose wife has a higher sex drive than him may be very much so at peace in this!

Fortunately, I recently read an anecdote that might help.

In her book *Marriage Conversations*, Cathy Krafve relates this story. In the midst of a serious conflict with her husband at the lowest point in their marriage, she tossed what she considered a grenade: "I am only staying in this marriage for the sex!" In the book, she confides that her message was, "There's nothing left for me in this marriage but the physical satisfaction of sex. In my mind, quite a low blow." Imagine her shock when her husband "took my insult as a compliment. It inspired him. What man doesn't want to believe that he's such a powerhouse that his wife would hang around just for the sex?"[11]

In my experience, most men, though obviously bummed (to say the least) that their wife was considering divorce, would still feel a sense of pride at this "low blow." On the other hand, most wives would be deeply hurt and enraged at the thought that the only thing keeping them around is sex. Many wives already fear that exact thing.

So I have now asked several women (including Cathy) if there is a wifely equivalent. "If it weren't for _____, I would divorce you." Is there one? Our first efforts led to several ideas that didn't work. Each value turned into "If it weren't for *all the ways that you are amazing*, I would divorce you."

I think this provides further insight. For many men, our sexuality is so deeply integrated into our identity that *being extraordinary in regard to sex* is kind of like being *extraordinary overall*. Of course, we know *rationally* they aren't the same, but it can feel true. (It also *shouldn't* be true—that's something we'll discuss frequently.)

For Women Only by Feldhahn helps women understand their differences from men and how to love their significant others well. *For Men Only* helps men understand their wives and their inner workings. Both books are life-changing, and I highly recommend them.

In the former book, she writes,

> Isn't sex just a biological urge that he really should be able to do without? Well . . . no . . . Lack of sex is as emotionally serious to him as, say, his sudden silence would be

to you, were he simply to stop communicating with you. It is just as wounding to him, just as much a legitimate grievance—and just as dangerous to your marriage.[12]

I'm going to highlight one particular portion of Feldhahn's research that delves into how men think about sex, and I'm going to quote the question from it at length. This was taken from four hundred respondents.[13]

> With regard to sex, for some men it is sufficient to be sexually gratified whenever they want. For other men it is also important to feel wanted and desired by their wife. How important is it to you to also feel sexually wanted and desired by your wife? (Choose one answer.)

- Very important: 66 percent

- Somewhat important: 31 percent

- Not very important as long as I get enough sex: 2 percent

- Irrelevant, as long as I get enough sex: 1 percent

Women: take a sigh of relief before puzzling over this. Men want more than just sex. *They want to feel desired by you.* Men want the gratification that comes with sex, yes, but they want it from *you* in particular. When men communicate that they want to make love, they're communicating a desire for you *and only you*.

Who are those 3 percent that don't care whether you desire them? Personality disorders like narcissism and psychopathy could cover those 3 percent.[14]

Here's another statistic:

> Imagine that your wife offers all the sex that you want but does it reluctantly or simply to accommodate your sexual needs. Will you be sexually satisfied? (Choose one answer.)

- Yes: 26 percent

- No: 74 percent

Notice, it doesn't say, "Would you generally be satisfied with your experience with your wife?" No, it says *sexual* needs. In other words, sex alone does *not* satisfy three-fourths of men sexually! In this case study, men consider their strictly sexual satisfaction linked to their attitude toward it. If they had said, "Will you be satisfied in your marriage?" I believe the yeses would have been even lower.

Many women will already have newfound understanding and freedom from learning this, but so will many men. The sex deception teaches guys they are lowlives who only want intercourse whenever they can get it. Many men feel pigeonholed by that lie. In reality, men possess profound emotions accompanying sex with their wives.

Even if, by "objective" standards, the wives of husbands aren't supermodel quality, it may not matter much. Men do want their wives to care about their bodies, but men mostly *want to be wanted*, and sex communicates that better than anything else. Again, Feldhahn writes, "Making love with you assures him that you find him desirable, salves a deep sense of loneliness, and gives him the strength and well-being necessary to face the world with confidence."[15] Again, notice the depth of identity-level experience!

In regards to sex, we refer to the state of wanting to have sex as "arousal." There are things that lock or unlock these feelings, but in the case of arousal, men seem more likely to think these emotions are about us at the identity level. If I experience arousal around a woman, I naturally assume she knows that this is about *her* at the identity level. But, as we will soon see, many women seem to interpret sexual arousal as being about *sex*, not about *her*.

Remember, when something is linked or integrated into identity, we interpret that thing as being about us. If something is part of your identity, it means you think of it as an integral part of you. If something is part of your identity, you would feel that if you lost that thing, you wouldn't be *you*.

Put another way: Feeling loved, accepted, desired, chosen, and good enough gives us confidence that we *are* lovable, acceptable, desirable, chosen, and enough.

Aspects of our identity are like Play-Doh. If a kid gets free rein with Play-Doh, the colors will end up mixed beyond recognition. Each color would eventually become brown. The red, blue, and green all become indistinguishable. For men, sex and sexual arousal are *mixed into* who we are, so if you talk about sexuality, you're talking about *us*. Immature, childish men may boast of sexual "conquests." Men commonly refer to their sexual anatomy as their "manhood."

This is why men seem "only" interested in sex. We are deeply interested in what sex *means* to us and intuitively assume sex means the same thing to others, too.

So you may be starting to see some of what's coming, but let's go back to Bride and Groom.

Head-to-Toe Flannels

So possibly stressed and certainly tired (and with sex not on *her* mind), Bride climbs into her head-to-toe flannels. She warmly and eagerly awaits Groom's return from his business trip, then begins to drift off to sleep. Undoubtedly, Groom is thinking about seduction as he drives home.

Groom, understandably, hopes for rose petals. Groom arranges the flowers he bought in his hand so he can get his keys. He unlocks the door and pushes it in.

There aren't any petals . . . That's okay, she must have some other new seduction in mind. His heart racing, Groom heads for the bedroom. The night somehow feels like their first date. Am I setting this up too much? Am I being too dramatic? Ask your husband if I am.

All this anticipation, and he finds her 99 percent asleep, comforter pulled up to her neck, in head-to-toe flannels.

He gets ready for bed and slips under the covers, still anticipating some kind of sexual surprise, but doubt starts to creep in. Warmly, with a contented sigh, she rolls over, gives him a peck, whispers, "Welcome home," snuggles up against him, and promptly falls the last 2 percent asleep.

I ask the men how this moment feels at conferences and talks. This next section may be hard to read, ladies, but please press on.

The answers follow the opposite pattern from before: "unloved," "unwanted," "rejected," "alone," and "hurt" . . . you catch the drift. Though men only sometimes volunteer this answer, I am confident that "confused" should sit prominently on that list. Men do not like being confused and *hate* admitting to it.

Groom is confused that his wife didn't want to repeat the petal seduction since, for him, it was a highlight of his life, and he assumes it was for her, too. Now, even if it *was* a highlight of her life, she likely doesn't interpret it the same way he did.

I'm going to interject here and explain these differences. Both of you are likely nodding along to this story, seeing the split, and even anticipating the train wreck. What's going on?

A few years ago, I began asking women in the audiences of my sex talks, "In which of these two reunifications was Bride *happier* that he was home? The rose petal night or the flannel exhaustion? The satisfying sexual intimacy or the warm snuggle and sleep?"

I get confused looks as they all shrug and say, "The same" or "No difference."

"What?" exclaim the men. Those two experiences are nearly emotionally identical? How is that possible?

Bride has essentially the same emotional responses in both cases—

relieved, appreciative, proud, and loved, whereas he simultaneously had an emotional swing from "all is right in the world" to "unloved."

To her, he's home when he gets home.

To him, it's like he isn't quite *fully* home yet.

Here is a simple way to say it: If you pursue a man sexually, he assumes that you are pursuing him. If you pursue a woman sexually, she is likely to interpret that as you pursuing sex, *not her.*

In *For Women Only*, the Feldhahns discovered a fascinating quote from one man that encapsulates my point: "'No' is not no to sex—as she might feel. It is no to me as I am."[16]

However, the title of their chapter about sex in *For Men Only* is "With Sex, Her "No" Doesn't Mean You!" Thanks again to the Feldhahns.[17]

The research doesn't indicate that women generally don't want or enjoy sex, aren't aroused by their husbands, or even that they fail to get turned on. However, without realizing it, women tend to view sex as an *activity* rather than connected closely with their identity as their husbands do.

Testing My Hypothesis

A classic psychological study sent a group of relatively attractive young men and women to a college campus. The researchers told the men and women to start a conversation with someone randomly, and nearly right off the bat, the study participants asked to go to bed with strangers that night. They recorded the results.[18]

Not a *single* woman accepted; 100 percent declined.

On the other hand, 75 percent of the college guys *agreed* while only 25 percent refused.

There are a few ways to explain this study. Let's start with the woman's perspective. Maybe women declined to have a one-night stand with a stranger because they value sex too much to throw it around. Maybe more of them had a more robust moral inclination than their male counterparts. Maybe. They almost certainly felt unsafe about the idea of sleeping with a total stranger—and rightly so.

What about the guys? In my view, if men naturally integrate sexuality with who they are, then a stranger soliciting sex with them is nothing more than a stranger paying them a massive compliment.

Here's an illustration to demonstrate my point. Imagine that you're an artist. You've dedicated your entire life to this craft, and you pour numerous afternoons into completing one canvas. Naturally, with something so integrated into your identity, you take great pride in it; who you are is wrapped up in your art.

So when you have an exhibition with your painting, you're nervous and self-conscious. If people reject your art, they're rejecting you.

A stranger dressed up in appropriate art critic attire walks up to your painting. He stares for a while and looks at you. "Did you paint this, ma'am? I'm not sure if it's for sale, but this piece sincerely moves me! It's fantastic!"

Would you say, "Well, you're just a stranger, so how can I trust your opinion?"

No! Indeed, in some ways, there's no "bias" with strangers, so you can take that much more pride in your work.

This affirmation of identity is how men think about an unsolicited offer of sex from a stranger. Men often fantasize about this exact scenario if they're not careful. So it's no surprise that, on average, men would more likely accept the stranger's offer of sex.[19]

When a man knows that a woman is aroused with him, he typically takes it as a compliment. When a woman knows that a man is aroused with her, she *might* take it as a compliment, but she also may just assume that this is an example of "men want sex" and not personally about her at all.

So are men willing to have sex with strangers because "you know, who cares so long as it's sex," while women are pickier? My identity theory provides a better explanation.

Here's another study conducted more recently that surveyed casual workplace sex. I'll quote the conclusion from *Battles of the Sexes*:

> When women were asked how they would feel if a coworker asked them to have sex, 63 percent said they would take it as an insult, and 17 percent said they would be flattered. Men's attitudes were the polar opposite. Only 15 percent of men were insulted, while 67 percent said they would be flattered. Clearly, when it comes to casual sex in the workplace, men and women once again see through vastly different lenses.[20]

This study, which looked at workplace sexual harassment, noted that this attitude is part of the problem. If men give unwanted advances to a coworker, in their minds, they probably think of it as flattery—a compliment. Over and over, we see that men view it as identity-affirming when they receive sexual advances, so when they give sexual advances, they often mean it as a compliment.

This can obviously become a twisted, shallow, and illegal version of what sexual relationships should be, i.e., sexual harassment, but the misunderstanding proves my point once again. It may be inexcusable and evil, but there's still some explanatory insight here.

I hear hundreds of women divide their identity from their sexuality in unintuitive ways for men. Notably, women categorize themselves into sexual and nonsexual parts. Wives often complain, "I wish he touched me more nonsexually rather than just grabbing my boobs or swatting my butt." Notice the "just." These women interpret their husbands touching their breasts as touching not them as a person but merely "breasts," as though their breasts were detached! This understanding always makes my wife giggle a little since it's so accurate to her intuition and yet so inaccurate to mine!

This division doesn't exist for men nearly as intuitively. Men will usually touch their wives as sexually as the situation allows. He probably rarely "cops a feel" in church (unless he is sure no one will see) or in front of her parents, but when they are alone in the house, he would need a reason *not* to touch her sexually (more on this in a couple of paragraphs). He doesn't need any special reason *to* touch her in the ways she thinks of as "sexual."

For every woman confused or annoyed at their husband's proclivity to touch, grab, grind, or fondle any time they're in private, there exists a man who is confused or annoyed that she doesn't do the same to him.

The first time I heard this complaint from a wife, I wasn't even sure of what she meant. Granted, I realized pretty quickly that she apparently divided her body into parts covered by underwear and parts that weren't. For some reason, she sought some kind of comfort from "nonsexual" touching. What comfort was she seeking? I think it was the comfort of believing that he loved and wanted her, not merely sex, as she suspects.

Imagine. Your husband wakes up, stretches, yawns, and immediately thinks, "Y'know, I'd love to touch some breasts today," putting intense effort into thinking, "But where can I find some breasts to touch?" Lightbulb, "Oh, I know! My wife has breasts! I'll touch those."

Because it is so natural for many women to divide their sexuality from their identity, they have spent years feeling in competition with their own bodies and their own sexuality. More on this in a few pages. Remember the principle of being a detective about our spouse's preferences and desires so we can serve each other, "starting with me"? Husbands and wives, keep this in mind.

Does this mean women don't enjoy sex? Of course not. Women are designed, created, and wired to enjoy sex. The clitoris seems to serve no other purpose except pleasure. The vast majority of women authors I've read or worked with report they love sex with their husbands, or at least originally did, and experience powerful sexual feelings, arousal, and orgasms.

Freedom, joy, and arousal are so easily stolen by unhealthy understanding. The world's narrative, the sex lie, robs us of the free, joyful, and innocent sex. Joy doesn't have to be gone; it doesn't have to stay gone.

This is what leads to the disconnect in the making for our young married couple. Bride is equally satisfied with Groom—flannels and sleep or seduction and sex. She feels intimate and close to him and assumes he feels the same way in both scenarios. Women intuit sex as one of a list of fun, intimate, warm, passionate experiences they can have together and choose from daily, but not a *privileged* experience. (Unless, of course, you're part of the minority of women who do see it that way, in which case, I hope this helps you understand how to talk with your husband about it!)

The night without sex, Bride didn't choose the activity of lovemaking for whatever reason, but he was home, and they were together; she snuggled up, and they shared a kiss. Sex wasn't in the cards for this particular night—neither was badminton! Just because they didn't engage in sex doesn't mean she feels any differently toward him. But how would he know that? He doesn't intuitively divide out the person, the act, or the feelings; he just knows he is eager to experience rose petals, lingerie, and sex again with his sweet Bride.

This reveals Bride and Groom's misunderstanding. She doesn't understand how deeply he feels about sex; he assumes she feels the same way he does. This misunderstanding is fairly innocent initially, but it can spiral into a much deeper issue. We'll return to their story soon, but first, a brief response to an objection many will raise.

What About the Sex Industry?

Let's examine a taboo subject—the sex industry. If reading about this is too uncomfortable due to trauma, temptation, or other reasons, I completely understand. Please skip this section.

The realities of the sex industry are heartbreaking and dark. When I teach my children about sex, I break the teaching into three headings: the spiritual aspects of sex, the biological aspects of sex, and the broken aspects of sex.[21] This stems from a biblical principle that sin is the twisting of good things and mutilating God-given desires. Or, as C. S. Lewis put it, "Wickedness, when you examine it, turns out to be the pursuit of some good in the wrong way."[22] Satan is not creative—he cannot create new things. He can only take good things God has made and good desires God has given us and offer us twisted counterfeits.

You might naturally think that since men are by far more likely to engage prostitutes and go to strip clubs, it proves many men really do only want sex. But rather than denying my thesis, insights from the sex trade actually support my point. Tragically, the broken aspects of sex are very real and prey on the identity distinction I've been arguing for.

When you start as a professional counselor, especially in a big city, you tend to get groups of friends who refer one another to therapy over time. For instance, once, I had a firefighter come for therapy. He invited his friends and told them how awesome counseling is (I don't take credit for that. Counseling from any well-trained therapist is awesome.) Who are his friends? Well, they tend to be firefighters. So a surprising number of firefighters came through my doors for the next couple of months.

Once, a stripper came to my office for counseling. Partially, she was trying to understand herself as more than just a sex object. She wanted freedom from a career she couldn't figure out how to replace. As was the trend, I provided counseling for her friends for the next few months, who also tended to be strippers. As sex workers, I figured they had a great deal of insight into sex, and they did—especially the broken, addictive, and delusional aspects.

Surprisingly, a large percentage of the strippers were married, sometimes to other sex professionals, and nearly every one of their marriages had serious sexual dysfunctions. If sex were primarily about skill, looks, or just the act of intercourse, they should have the greatest sex lives of us all. Not so; their sex lives were significantly worse—but I digress.

At some point in the therapy process, the original client encouraged me to ask all of the other sex professionals a question in order to understand the industry. Her question for me to ask them was: "What qualities make the best, most successful strippers?"

So I surveyed them. Now remember, alongside pornography and prostitution, going to a strip club ("gentlemen's club" is an unforgivable slander to the word "gentlemen," so I refuse to use it) falls under the heading of other base, superficial, and objectifying sexual practices. They are truly heartbreaking, pitiful, and immoral.

With that in mind, what makes successful strippers? Who gets the most tips? Like me, you may expect them to talk about the size or shape of certain body parts, general attractiveness, athleticism or skill, how well they dance, or any qualities along those lines.

Instead, these women, and some men, gave surprisingly similar answers across the board. In essence, it was this: "The one who can make the most men in the room think that she (or he) is on stage just for him."

In other words, it wasn't about physical attractiveness but about who could form an emotional attachment with the most men, *who could make them feel the most wanted* while she danced. One of them said that the goal was to make as many men in the room think that the only reason she came to dance tonight was the thought that he might be there, and so she could dance for him.

That is mind-boggling to me, but I got this basic answer across the board. This insight shows just how delusional sin can make us (Hebrews 3:13)!

A few years ago, *The Guardian* ran a piece attempting to uncover why men engage prostitutes. Though these men gave several reasons, a common one was for the relationship. Many indicated that it was important that the prostitute "get to know him and like him." Another noted his "ideal prostitute [would] not . . . behave like one." He needed them "to role-play to be a pretend girlfriend, a casual date, not businesslike or mechanical. To a third person, it looks like we're in love."[23] An article from *Scientific American* summarizes, "Researchers have identified emotional and psychological motivations among the men who purchase sex."[24]

You might wonder, "How on Earth could any man think these women are on the stage just for him?" or "How can a man think it is meaningful for a woman to pretend to be his girlfriend?" I will explain this further, but sadly, this shows how much men crave this kind of sexual approval and connectedness, even in their most broken forms.

I want to engage with this gently, but it bears noting. I've learned in trauma counseling that even rapists are often under the delusion of emotionally engaging with the women they rape. In their horrific self-deceit, the power, anger, hatred, and control that they express somehow feel like it connects them to the woman.[25]

In the modern epidemic of pornography, there exists a way to bring these horrible, wretched ideas together: violent abuse by men that women seem to desire. The idea in these pornographic videos is that women enjoy violence or harm done to them. Physical aggression is included in as much as 88 percent of pornographic content.[26] (FAQ 6 deals with porn more in-depth.) This is a tough section to write because I am looking for explanatory value, but I never want to offer an excuse for the destructive evil of these industries. I'm gratified when I see so many ministries working to help boys, girls, women, and men to escape the clutches of this twisted world.

Let's take a moment and examine how patterns of adultery are explanatory as well. You would expect that women who fall into this destructive sin do it more for emotional than sexual reasons. In my experience, an emotional connection is just as important to men, maybe even more so. Men and women almost always cheat because of dissatisfaction with intimacy and feeling underappreciated (not merely because of sex), although the evidence remains murky given the complexity of the topic.[27]

I nevertheless submit that men (and women) usually commit adultery because whoever they cheat with *shows them attention and makes them feel wanted.*

There are "dating" websites that are meant specifically for married people to commit adultery, with opportunities for men or women to commit infidelity. Those sites are clearly horrendous, but it's not surprising they exist.

One site ran a fascinating study on its cheating users. They found that only 30 percent of men cheated with women younger than their wives, and only 25 percent found them more in shape or more interesting.[28] The number was actually higher with women, of whom 50 percent were more in shape than their spouses. This led one writer to say that women seemed *more* "superficial" than men!

Okay, so why do men generally cheat? The same article reports the men found their mistresses "to be more passionate, better listeners, and more caring than their significant others."

The site's founder says, "The tired old idea that cheaters just want a pretty young thing to show off is just not true anymore if it ever was," he said. "In fact, it is our experience . . . that men turn to affairs to fulfill their emotional desires, not some shallow desire for good looks or a hot body."

This confirms what I had discovered in my discussion with strippers and the research done on most men who patronize prostitutes.

This finding does not excuse the completely inappropriate and sinful behavior of adult males who cheat on their wives. Instead, it shows something deeply true about a man's heart: He wants to be wanted. In the case of a healthy married man, he wants his *wife* to want him.

Notice how even in the most broken, stupid, or wretchedly wicked expressions of sexuality, these "men" are still looking for a sense of connection, importance, approval, and desire . . . not *just* sex. Obviously, this is no excuse for abusive and criminal behavior, but it still offers insight into what sex means, generally speaking, to even the most broken, wicked men.

Of course, some only view women as objects, but it's a small, small percentage of men who, deep down, think that way.[29] All of us are prone to sinful feelings of possession or demanding sex and *treating* women *like* objects, but men will find freedom when they realize their heart's deepest desire is to be loved through sex—a natural and God-given desire. For women, knowing that men feel wanted when you show your desire by having free and joyful sex with them helps you understand why your husband has a higher sex drive. He may not be as shallow as you think. Sex is deeply linked to men's emotions.

Men experiencing sex deeply and emotionally is precisely the reason that they turn to cheap counterfeits in the sex industry. It is not hard to see how these feelings can be so impacted by broken and delusional thinking. It's not because men intuitively think of sex as common that they turn to cheap, damaging alternatives to real sex, but because they think of it as important and deeply meaningful. Even in the most based and pitiful expression of sexuality, it is fundamentally about feeling wanted, not only about physical, orgasmic pleasure.

The Disunity Spiral

Let's return once again to Bride and Groom. Groom returned from the business trip to find his wife 99 percent asleep and in flannel pj's rather than lingerie.

Even if Groom didn't consciously "expect" the same rose petal welcome, he feels anticipation. Given the emotional power and the strength of the identity spoken into him at their previous encounter, who wouldn't feel disappointed? Worse, if he isn't mature, he might feel a sense of *entitlement* for the rose petal welcome (even more damaging than expectations). Entitlement can get pretty dark pretty quickly, and many women have experienced not merely the innocent misunderstanding but the narcissistic and abusive controlling-ego response from men who depend on their approval through sex.

Entitlement, expectations, and demands can turn the misunderstanding into a more immediate disaster. Controlling and abusive men are so filled with entrenched insecurities and fear that they lash out when someone causes them to feel negative emotions. If this disappointment brings out the "narcissistic adolescent" in him, the misunderstanding could become detrimental.

Add to this the high likelihood that many women in this situation would have experienced sexual trauma, ignorant and manipulative sexual messages from previous relationships, thousands of hours of agenda-driven media indoctrination, foolish and often unbiblical messages from church leaders, and, in a huge percentage of cases, outright rape and sexual abuse—it's no wonder she guards herself against being hurt or taken advantage of again.[30]

This marriage's sex death knell may be about to sound without either of them knowing it.

Keep reading; we have a lot to learn, and we all have a lot of room to grow.

Thankfully, in the case of Bride and Groom, no trauma or detriment will overtake them. However, it will introduce a confusing dynamic that can grow into something more sinister.

So Groom is lying in bed awake, confused and feeling rejected next to his content, snuggly, happy, and asleep wife. When something is well-integrated into our identity, we need a reason *not* to engage in it. This concept will come up again in the next chapter. The *natural* thing is to engage in things that come *naturally* to us! However, if something is *not* well-integrated into our identity, we need a reason *to* engage. Notice here the couple is *not* engaging sexually.

Groom assumes his wife thinks as he does, and his thinking is that *there needs to be a reason not to engage sexually*. They aren't, so there must be a reason. Therefore, he thinks something is wrong. He is incorrect in that assumption but holds to it subconsciously and quite strongly. The internal questions begin. What did he do wrong to receive such a different homecoming? Did he fail somehow? Did he not communicate enough? Does she not feel in love with him anymore? Does she feel this way about someone else? Is there no tenderness like before in her fingertips? (Apologies to the Righteous Brothers.)

Groom's misled conclusion: She doesn't feel the same about him as she did last time.

He has now embarked on the quixotical fool's errand to figure out the "reason" why his wife didn't want to have sex when the truth is there's no particular deep-down reason at all.

Of course, though there may be no specific reason this time, there might be things that negatively affected her arousal. In other words, there might be what he would call "reasons" for why she's not ready for sex. That's a conversation for later, but for now, note that she doesn't need any *special* reason not to engage sexually. Meaning she is not less in love or anything of the sort.

A man can perseverate (mulling over the same action or thought repeatedly) on this for a long time. He may still hold out hope that this is another, sneakier seduction technique and that as soon as he falls asleep, she will zip out of those flannels and attack him. The poor guy might spend a few minutes trying to lay very still, hoping for her to suddenly and passionately make love to him. Seriously, this sneaky seduction fantasy may make more sense to him than the other options, such as, "She's tired and just fell asleep." When a sexual ambush doesn't happen, his confusion endures and deepens.

As soon as it becomes clear she really is asleep, the rejection and hurt creep in.

The next day, Groom is likely to be uncertain and confused and a little short on sleep from his bewilderment. He probably feels a little like the stupid kid who doesn't know how to feel. He wasn't picked for the team, couldn't work the math problem on the board, and didn't know the difference between a wrench and pliers. Groom knows this feeling of embarrassed confusion, and he hates it.

At first, she notices nothing different, but he can't hide his feelings. Women everywhere know how these "hurt little boy" emotions come out—grumpy, irritable, distant. They often come out even if he's actively fighting them.

So does he sit down over coffee and talk about his emotional confusion, engaging intimately about what's going on in his heart? Probably not. He might not have experience in that kind of conversation, but would she know how to correctly interpret his feelings even if he did? I doubt it. And if Groom's feelings are the darker ones I referenced above (expectations, entitlements, demands), then he may become angry and condemning, like she owes him a debt and failed to pay up. This sinful, demanding attitude is usually rooted in insecurity and confusion. It's ugly. But even our mature and upstanding Groom is at least showing milder emotions—grouchiness, irritability, distance. And she picks up on them.

Now, it's her turn to be confused. She asks questions, trying to pry some emotional feedback:

"Was it a bad trip?"

"Were the speakers boring?"

"Did you get enough sleep?"

"Was your boss a jerk?"

He gives short, negative responses. He wants to communicate with her about his feelings but feels afraid or needs more vocabulary. Finally, Groom says everything was fine *until he came home.* To Bride, this is even more confusing because she experienced nothing but warm feelings for him last night.

What "resolves" this? Typically one of two things, and both of them lead the wrong direction.

Most likely, a tentative resolution comes when they have sex. Possibly, despite things seeming a little strange and on edge, they make love later. She never had any reason *not* to, and she's now better rested. Nothing prevents her from wanting to feel the pleasure and closeness with him that sex represents to her. So they have sex after all.

Very quickly, Groom's fears are relieved, and his confusion settled. All's right with the world again. She still loves and wants him. Emotionally, he is home.

Happy ending, right? Wrong.

Okay, maybe. The first few times of this, nothing usually gets broken unless one of them has a nasty reaction. They chalk up their confusion to strange flukes. Eventually, though, she might notice a pattern.

Even with Bride's relative innocence, she's probably been influenced by the sex lie. To one degree or another, she sees her sexuality as a steak that can draw dogs. Rightly or wrongly, Bride always wonders, "Is he interested in me or my body?" Even in her inexperience, Bride has still asked herself dozens of times when a man showed interest in her, "Is this about me or sex?"

Whether it's the first or fifth occurrence of some version of his mood swing, she notices the change. He was cranky and cold; now, he is content and close. How does she explain that phenomenon? Remember, she probably does not integrate sex into her identity, dividing "sex" from "self."

Given that lens, she'll probably interpret his change like this:

"He had *me* and was cranky; he had *sex* and is content."

That's the first way it's "resolved"—not good, and not really resolved. It is a wound that will likely become infected instead.

The second way I hear about this being "resolved" comes from her "research." Imagine she calls her mother or an older married friend. There's a good chance they will have faced a version of this moment in their marriage dozens of times. Their interpretation will likely fall into the same kind of self/sex divide. In other words, whoever she calls will probably be jaded.

So Bride talks about his bad mood, and the well-meaning but cynical woman responds, "Well, you didn't have sex with him. That's why he's acting like a three-year-old." Where does this conversation go from there?

Or maybe Bride reads a blog or grabs a popular Christian book on marriage that makes the (misled) claim that a man's number one need is "sex." Not love, not affection, not relationship, not approval, *sex*.

Bride is devastated. Groom was different; he was supposed to not want her just for sex! This "revelation" crushes her. It turns out her suspicions all along were right about him, too. He's just as objectifying as the rest.

There are good reasons why most women feel cynical about sex. Many fear they aren't enough, especially about their self-image. The world spends billions to convince them of this, and social media exacerbates the problem.[31] Now, the fear enters her bedroom with the one person she thought she could trust. So, of course, Bride feels mortified and let down.

And Groom has no idea.

If you hear me justifying men's childish behavior, please read again. I am not letting the guy off the hook. I am giving special honor to neither perspective at this point, merely pointing out the difference between their interpretation of the same experience.

Sadly, she only has her interpretation tools, and the evidence seems to fit. She thinks he just prioritized sex over her.

No sex equals irritable.

Sex equals lovable.

So what does she do the next time Groom goes out of town? That depends greatly on her life experiences. I have a funny feeling that I know what our Bride would do. In the Christian world, to "be a good wife," she will probably get more rose petals and new lingerie. But this time, when she seduces him, it will be less uninhibited, *less free*. Now, sex feels more like a job. This isn't intimate arousal. The fun, excited feelings diminish, and if the pattern continues, grow dormant. Bride now makes love with him to *avoid* the negative emotional consequences of *not* having sex with him. What else is she to do? She knows how important this is to him (note the word is "this," not "she").

Not only does Bride not want it this way, but Groom doesn't either. Remember, men consider the meaning behind sex the most important part! If he begins to sense a lack of meaning in sex with her, 97 percent of the reason for the experience is taken from him. He may continue to seek sex with her in an effort to rediscover the feelings or maybe just to accept the 3 percent, but if this cycle continues, they'll both know it.

Sex will become tainted for her, which means it becomes tainted for him. He senses she's forcing it, and she's merely acquiescing. She will often be having sex to "take one for the team" (an actual quote from a women's marriage conference), and he will perceive this in her lack of authentic, intimate freedom with him.

Now what she predicts and what happens when they have sex may not fit together. Once she gets into it, all the former feelings may flood back, but the anticipation is largely work rather than fun or play.

A common refrain from Christian wives with loving husbands like Groom is, "I am always glad when we have sex, and I usually really enjoy it, but I just am not very excited anticipating it." This is at least partially because she anticipates the feeling of division from him—*sex* but not *her*—(and also psychological fatigue, which we will look at in the next chapter), but in the act of lovemaking, she finds herself feeling bonded after all. She may even experience his affection and love that does not intuitively divide *sex* from *her*.

So how is it possible to develop an intimate, sincere, free, enriching sex life between men and women? It is clear that God intended sex to be the most powerful advantage and bond for the married couple, so why is it one of the most common dysfunctions? Why is sex among the most common sources of personal hurt, hopelessness, rejection, and resentment in every marriage, even good ones?

How does a couple like Bride and Groom, who sincerely, authentically, deeply love one another, have a free and fun sex life, and plan to only grow more intimate for decades, end up with sex being the pry bar that divides them?

How can this intended "advantage" end up feeling like cancer in some marriages, an afterthought in some, and merely "meh" in others?

Hopefully, I've put to bed (pun intended) several troubles that arise from confusion by covering the way men and women think differently. Merely understanding these differences can help tremendously.

Women, be at peace; I'm *not* about to pull a classic Christian speaker move and end by saying, "Well, sex is more important to men, so you should just give him sex whenever he feels like it." Nope, trust me, I have a much better, more biblical, and more empowering idea. Looking to God's design will provide the path forward.

If you are a newlywed (Well done! Reading marriage books before the crisis. You are elite indeed), you want to know, "How do we avoid this?"

The question for the rest of us is: "How do we restore what we lost?"

First, let's consider upshots so far.

Husbands, you have a lot of new information. Your wife may instinctively interpret your pursuit of her sexually as the *pursuit of sex instead of her*. Now that you know all the times you may have hurt her unintentionally, you have a great chance to be a place of growth and understanding for her. If you are sympathetic to her instinct to think of her sexuality as distinct from herself, you get to be the intentional, safe person who gets to help her see herself as you see her—an integrated whole! Thoughts, feelings, personality, beauty, sexuality, experiences, opinions, body—you get to wrap all these together when you think of her. Imagine if you could be a part of helping her rediscover the freedom to be pursued by you and bolster her self-image.

Women, when you freely engage in sex with your husband, you create the spark of those feelings of "home" and "welcoming." Like a roaring fire tucked in a fireplace in a cabin, beaten by a frigid blizzard, it provides warmth in a cold world. That's a pretty cool superpower! You, and you alone, have the pure power to light that fire in a holy and God-honoring way. Remember what sexual desire means to him when it comes from you: accepted, wanted, encouraged, desired, strong, and right. Those are wonderful things to be able to give to another person. He feels at home with you, entirely affirmed, unstoppable, and on top of the world! *You* can instill that in *him*. When you instill it in him, it can reciprocally create feelings like that in you.

When uncovering new, fundamental understandings, it can help to go over them again in different words. I hate to backtrack, but let's reiterate Groom's and Bride's different understandings of sex through the "start with me" principle before we move on. (Actually, I like to backtrack. It is too easy to miss something important in only one pass.)

We'll clarify the ideas of this chapter by focusing on husbands and wives separately.

To Women: Men Integrate Sex into Their Identity

Everyone builds their lives around how they think of themselves. Some identity statements are clear (married/unmarried, man/woman, orphan/adopted). We can deny the black-and-white statements, ignore them, pretend like our feelings dictate them, or change our understanding of them. They are objective, or we can also prioritize them. For instance, many men act like they're not fathers, and that's a serious problem. I can pretend like I'm not a father, but that *denies reality, since I am.* We should seek to integrate true things into our identity.

When something is well-integrated into our identity, acting on it comes naturally. (Theology—identity—activity.) As a well-integrated mother, my wife, Ginger, *naturally* keeps track of our kids. Amid unearthly chaos, her mom radar keeps track of them even if she's doing something else. She has an internal clock that runs down when one is too long unaccounted for. That's motherhood well-integrated.

Unfortunately, when men's feelings get hurt, we can simplify our deep, complex emotions by responding angrily. Often, when we express anger, we in fact feel hurt, confused, or embarrassed rather than angry per se. Given the significance of our sexuality to our identity, it is no surprise that Feldhahn reports that men's most vulnerable moment is reaching out to their wives sexually.[32] He writes: "Men are powerfully driven by the emotional need to feel desired by our wives, and we filter everything through that grid. Do I feel desired or not desired by my wife? If we feel our wives truly want us sexually, we feel confident, powerful, alive, and loved. If we don't, we feel depressed, angry, and alone. And this goes way beyond the amount of sex we're having."[33]

Wherever you are most sensitive, that's a good indicator of what you integrate most into your identity. Some things can be good to be a part of your identity, and others not. Our identity peels back in layers like an onion; the difference is that *now we reveal* something at the center—a core foundation.

As humans, we are sexual beings in the same way we are thinking or feeling beings. It's a part of our nature. We have the built-in purpose of producing children; the desire for arousal, sex, and pleasure; and the appropriate biological equipment. Obviously, this aspect, like any other, can be broken in a fallen world. Also, you may have chosen to accept the gift of celibacy to serve others without the distraction of marriage. (Though, if you're reading this book, I'll assume you're probably *not* celibate.[34])

Notice, though, that even if you're not "sexually active" (how a doctor would say it), you're still a sexual, or a "sexed," person. It's a fact. Even if you are a virgin, sexuality is part of your identity.

Think of it this way: If someone removed a man's sexuality from him, he would be devastated. If a man has a reduction in sex drive, performance, or related factors, it can create powerful discouragement, insecurity, and questions about his identity. Marketers know this and, therefore, advertise relentlessly to men about sexual health, especially erectile dysfunction. Some of this insecurity affects how many middle-aged men respond to midlife crises.

Women, however, most of you probably do not intuitively understand your sexuality as part of your identity. If someone pursues you sexually, you don't necessarily feel as though they are pursuing you. The pursuit itself may trigger insecurities.

You might say, "He just wants sex. He doesn't really want me," when for the man, rarely that could be farther from the truth. When we, as men, pursue our wives sexually, we intuit that we are pursuing them, not merely sex. The approval and desire of a man at his core is seeking to connect with his wife at her core.

Of course, it is always okay for a wife to say she is not interested in engaging sexually. Just know what feelings that might evoke in him and learn to handle it graciously.

To beat a dead horse a bit more to death: Feldhahn cites one of the men she surveyed to express the overall finding: "When she says no, I feel that I am *rejected*. 'No' is not no to sex—as she might feel. It is no to me as I am."[35]

In the old rom-com *Pretty Woman*, Julia Roberts is a prostitute hired by a businessman (Richard Gere) so that he can have disinterested sex on an extended business trip. At first, this seems like a great option. It's easy and uncomplicated—just business. Soon, though, he is climbing a fire escape to propose to her. That's because it's incredibly difficult for men to engage in sex without assigning identity-level meaning to it. The connection is key, as we have seen.

I've had many men tear up or cry when I explain this. "I've gone my whole life without being able to explain to my wife how I feel about sex!" Or "Someone finally gets me, thank you!" Or "I feel so heard!" These men are often in their forties or fifties. That revelation and bringing words to deep wells of feelings is incredibly gratifying and encouraging.

Women, you need to practice thinking along these lines: He wants my body because he wants me—I'm not divided in his eyes. In sex, he feels safest with you. Sex is the most intimate way for him to experience you. He wants to love you when he wants to make love.

To Men: Women Generally *Do Not* Integrate Sex into Their Identity in the Same Ways You Do

Men. You need to practice empathizing with your wives.

Too often, when husbands understand this identity split and finally feel understood, they tune out when I talk about how their wives feel. The solution to marital sex problems is to consider what the *other* person needs and desires. It's easy for us, guys, when we hear this new idea to forget that our duty is to love our wives first and foremost. I'm glad I can help you explain your feelings to your wife—but that's only half the battle.

Here's a way to empathize. Imagine: You're worth hundreds of millions; you've got cars, mansions, a yacht, a watch worth more than my truck, and more. Now, imagine being this rich and trying to date.

Right off the bat, you might think, "That would be easy!" Not so fast, tiger. If you're trying to have one-night stands or flings, then sure, it's easy, but let's say you're trying to start a long-term relationship. The problem becomes obvious fairly quickly: There's always the nagging doubt of whether she wants you or your money.

Wealthy people may think: do they want me or my money?

Women wrestle with something analogous: does he want me or my body?

However, given the ubiquity of abuse and assault and generations of narcissistic male cultures, it's no wonder women have learned to divide their sexuality from their identity. I'm always drawn back to the scene in *Robin Hood: Prince of Thieves*, when the Sheriff of Nottingham tries to rape Maid Marian in an effort to sire a child of royal blood (this is entertainment?). What struck me was the way the scriptwriter put these words in Marian's traumatic, heart-wrenching pleas: "You can take this body, but it will not be me." She repeats it over and over.

If you permit me to speculate, I think women learned to separate sex and identity because they "learned" over generations to protect themselves from the trauma they may experience from the abuse. If not abuse, at least ignorance and crass handling of her feelings.

For instance, according to one estimate, predators will sexually assault about one in six women in America.[36] That massive number will affect each one of the victims deeply. If your wife has experienced that, it would be good to cover it in counseling. Experiencing that can put up yet another barrier to healthy sex. As a psychologist, I could go on and on about how sexual assault will cause agonizing psychological damage. It's a truly vicious act that can destroy people at the identity level, though, again, you probably didn't need a master's degree to know that.[37]

This defense mechanism affects the healthiest marriages, as wives intuit this even if they have never experienced significant abuse. This separation of sex and identity is reinforced at multiple layers of culture. In advertising, women are told to show off their bodies to attract men. Women in the church are told that men will lust after them if they wear skimpy clothes, regardless of whether they like them or not. While I'm not saying women should wear immodest clothes, I am saying lust is on men. It is easily misunderstood that many men are primarily visual (which is often true; see FAQ 3), and men only want sex (which is not true).

So is it any wonder that it is intuitive for women to divide their sexuality from their identity? Men also face these issues but at much lower percentages. When men do struggle with splitting themselves up into sexuality and self, they often wrestle with similar intuitions that most women do.

Legalistic versions of the purity movement create this as well. If you are a "victim" of the purity culture movement and think sex is dirty and bad, you may struggle with married sex. I don't prize virginity because I believe sex is wrong but because it's *sacred* (cf. Chapter 6). If you've thought of sex as dirty and something to avoid at all costs, which the purity movement can unwittingly communicate, you may instinctively apply those attitudes to married sex. And, of course, sex is the farthest thing from dirty in marriage.

As individual men seeking to love their wives better and better, we can patiently nurture our wives back to Eden—naked and unashamed. Now that's a worthy ministry. We just have to figure out how to communicate our love for her whole being, consistently and gently, in ways she can experience from her head to her toes and from her heart to her brain.

The Self/Sex Divide: Who's "Right"?

The man's intuition is right, or at least it's ideal. I cannot imagine that God wanted anyone's identity to be divided from their sexuality. In the Garden, if Adam and Eve were naked and unashamed, they had complete vulnerability and openness with one another. In both of their minds, there was no fear of rejection or hurt from the other. Adam would never feel rejected by his wife, and Eve would never feel threatened by Adam or any other man. Anything that God created them to be, they would *be* that, and it would perfectly integrate into their holistic lives.

So, in my opinion, everything about them that God created them to be would be rightly ordered in their identity. Nothing would get in the way of the other thing. As we are now, we constantly need to prioritize things differently as our lives shift and we reflect on our sins.

I theorize that when Adam and Eve distrusted each other and lost vulnerability, when Eve no longer felt safe with Adam and Adam no longer felt certain of his wife's affirmation, their perfect vulnerability and innocence collapsed. When vulnerability collapsed, men began "seeing and taking" women for themselves (e.g., Gen. 38). This human sin led to debauchery, incest, polygamy, and abuse.

Fast forward to millennia later, and I believe women continue to protect themselves from emotional and psychological destruction by separating their identity from sex as a defense mechanism. To husbands, now that you know how this separation of self from sex came about, can you empathize with her a bit more? How will you change your attitude and behavior toward her? You might ask at this juncture, "How can I help my wife see herself as beautiful and the one I want? How can I open her up to sexual intimacy like before?"

That's the right attitude—starting with yourself.

I've taken this pivotal chapter to highlight the differences between male and female thinking about sex. Merely understanding this difference, though, is not enough. We need to deepen our understanding before we can apply it properly in Part III.

The first place to start is psychological energy.

---

1. Dr. Julianna Slattery, "Understanding His Sexuality," Focus on the Family Australia, April 5, 2018, https://families.org.au/article/

2. Historically, this kind of practice does crop up, e.g., in the practice of concubinage or the Latin machismo culture of having a mistress for sex and a wife for children. I'm convinced that even here, we find a greater longing for something beyond such a setup. The broken images of sex point to a deeper longing that the real thing truly satisfies. I'll talk more in-depth about this in Chapter 4 in the section titled, "What About the Sex Industry?"

3. Many know that a few thousand Greeks, led by the three hundred Spartans, faced this massive army for almost a week before being overwhelmed. Eventually, the Greeks were able to maintain their independence from the Persian Empire and Xerxes—one of the only cultures to do so. This man did not hesitate to sacrifice the lives of hundreds of thousands of men to achieve his ends. In fact, the invasion of Greece was primarily due to what he perceived as an insult to his father. Possibly more than half a million men died in that short-lived war.

4. Shaunti Feldhahn, *For Women Only, Revised and Updated Edition: What You Need to Know About the Inner Lives of Men* (Colorado Springs: Multnomah, 2008), 112.

5. Feldhahn, *For Women Only*, 116.

6. Stephen Snyder, *Love Worth Making: How to Have Ridiculously Great Sex in a Long-Lasting Relationship* (New York: St. Martin's Press, 2019), 13.

7. Feldhahn, *For Women Only*, 67.

8. Feldhahn, *For Women Only*, 115.

9. Laurie J. Watson, "Six Truths About Men and Sex," *Psychology Today*, August 12, 2017, https://www.psychologytoday.com/

10. Gottman et al., *The Man's Guide to Women*, 41.

11. Cathy Primer Krafve, *Marriage Conversations: From Co-Existing to Cherished* (Kansas City: CrossRiver Media Group, 2021), 71.

12. Feldhahn, *For Women Only*, 112.

13. Feldhahn, *For Women Only*, 113.

14. Janis Wright, "A Survey of Personality Disorders," AAFP, October 15, 2004, https://www.aafp.org/pubs/afp/issues/2004/1015/

15. Feldhahn, *For Women Only*, 93.

16. Shaunti Feldhahn and Jeff Feldhahn, *For Men Only, Revised and Updated Edition: A Straightforward Guide to the Inner Lives of Women* (Colorado Springs: Multnomah, 2013), 119–220.

17. Feldhahn and Feldhahn, *For Men Only*, 127.

18. Russell D. Clark and Elaine Hatfield, "Gender Differences in Receptivity to Sexual Offers," *Journal of Psychology & Human Sexuality* 2, no. 1 (August 7, 1989): 39–55, https://doi.org/10.1300/

19. I obviously think this expression of one-night stands and this perspective of cheap sex is hugely damaging and leads to terrible issues in marriage. I think sex outside of marriage is wrong. So I'm not condoning these guys' adolescent attitudes, just explaining them.

20. Malone and Harris, *Battles of the Sexes*, 120.

21. Chris Legg, "Talking to Kids about Sex Part I . . . Re-Released," November 12, 2019, https://chrismlegg.com/2015/05/30/

22. C. S. Lewis, book two, section two in *Mere Christianity* (New York: Harper Collins, 2012).

23. Julie Bindel, "Why Men Use Prostitutes," *The Guardian*, January 14, 2010, http://www.theguardian.com/society/2010/jan/15/

24. Nikolas Westerhoff, "Why Do Men Buy Sex?" *Scientific American Reports* 21, no. 2 (October 23, 2012): 60–65, https://doi.org/10.1038/scientificamericanbrain0512-60.

25. Farah Aqel, "The Psychology of a Rapist," DW.com, September 7, 2020, https://www.dw.com/en/the-psychology-of-a-rapist/a-

26. Ana J. Bridges et al., "Aggression and Sexual Behavior in Best-Selling Pornography Videos: A Content Analysis Update," *Violence Against Women* 16, no. 10 (October 2010): 1065–1085, https://doi.org/10.1177/1077801210382866.

27. Olga Stavrova, Tila Pronk, and Jaap J. A. Denissen, "Estranged and Unhappy? Examining the Dynamics of Personal and Relationship Well-Being Surrounding Infidelity," *Psychological Science* 34, no. 2 (November 2, 2022): 143–169, https://doi.org/10.1177/09567976221116892; Dylan Selterman, Justin R. Garcia, and Irene Tsapelas, "What Do People Do, Say, and Feel When They Have Affairs? Associations between Extradyadic Infidelity Motives with Behavioral, Emotional, and Sexual Outcomes," *Journal of Sex & Marital Therapy* 47, no. 3 (December 30, 2020): 238–252,

28. HuffPost, "Cheating Survey Finds That People Cheat with People Less Attractive than Their Spouses," October 6, 2013,

29. Feldhahn, *For Women Only*, 113.

30. National Sexual Violence Resource Center, "Statistics," accessed December 19, 2023, https://www.nsvrc.org/statistics.

31. Barbara Jiotsa et al., "Social Media Use and Body Image Disorders: Association between Frequency of Comparing One's Own Physical Appearance to That of People Being Followed on Social Media and Body Dissatisfaction and Drive for Thinness," *International Journal of Environmental Research and Public Health* 18, no. 6 (March 11, 2021): 2880,

32. Kathi Lipp, "Episode 205: Shaunti Feldhahn and the Ultimate Resource Guide for (Trying to Be) Awesome Wives," June 20, 2016, https://www.kathilipp.com/2016/06/

33. Feldhahn and Feldhahn, *For Men Only*, 132.

34. God calls some to serve Him through singleness, and that calling is a high one. If that's the case, then God has bestowed a different identity on you and called you to another purpose. Check out 1 Corinthians 7.

35. Feldhahn, *For Women Only*, 119.

36. Patricia Tjaden and Nancy Thoennes, "Extent, Nature, and Consequences of Rape Victimization: Findings from the National Violence Against Women Survey," Data set, PsycEXTRA Dataset, January 1, 2006, reproduced by the CDC, NIJ special report,

37. If you have been a victim, you can heal. It will take time, but healing from therapy, and more importantly from Jesus, is accessible to you. Platitudes like this won't help, I know, but I would be amiss to not say there is hope for a brighter future.

Five

PSYCHOLOGICAL ENERGY

A t some point during my sex talks, I offer a trade:

"Anyone who can give me $20,000 in *cash, right this second*, I will give you $40,000 in cash. No strings attached. Who's in? Anyone interested in making a trade?"

Invariably, someone shoots their hand up.

"You're in? Great. Okay, show me the cash."

They either pretend to have money or nod their head at me eagerly.

"Wait," I ask. "Do you have $20,000 in cash, dollar bills, on you right now?"

Then they sheepishly tuck their hands away.

I'll press them: "C'mon, it's a great deal, right? Two to one?"

Anyone would take that deal *if they could*. No matter how good of a deal, they do not have $20,000. So I raise the reward: $50,000? $100,000? $1 million?

No? Why not? It's the deal of a lifetime—$20,000 cash for $1 million!

But. They. Don't. Have. It. Raising the cash-out doesn't help the problem.

Now, if I said, "I will give $40,000 to anyone who brings up an initial investment of zero dollars," who do you think would be in? Well, of course, everyone would.

But if the initial investment is more than I can afford, the payoff doesn't matter. Hiking up the value only makes the person who can't take advantage of the deal feel worse and worse.

Bedside Chats

In therapy over the years, I've heard a similar story repeated. The wife is in bed, and the husband comes in and sits on the bed (or, in a couple of cases, I kid you not, brings in a chair), and he wants to talk. He does something like this every few weeks to every few years. Wives tell me about these with weariness etched in every line of their faces.

He then spends however long, with whatever tone (depending on the husband), trying desperately to help her understand just how important sex with her is to him. Wives, I hope that those of you flashing back to these moments right now are *also* suddenly realizing, based on the book thus far, what he was *trying* to say all along. He probably lacked the words or understanding to communicate his deep feelings. If that's true, go find him, give him a kiss, and thank him for trying, though failing, to explain his heart to you.

He probably tried analogies, bribes, math problems, movie references, childhood stories, and quotes from the sex chapters in marriage books to try to help you understand how much he desires/hopes for/needs/expects/is entitled to/demands sex with you. No matter his efforts, he makes no sense to you. You are feeling one thing—tired. You were probably tired before he came in, and now you are weary from this broken-record-sounding conversation. You probably even think, "I should've just had sex with him; at least I could have avoided this again." Oops—do you spot Bride's disunity spiral thinking there? She's having sex to *avoid* something bad, not because she wants to show and receive love.

Now, I must admit that I feel serious sympathy for the husband in these moments because I've been there. Ginger and I had many of these late-night talks for several years. I, in essence, used the investment terminology: "But this is worth $40,000 to me. It's worth $50,000, $100,000—no, $1 million to me!" But, of course, she lacked the energy for the initial investment.

One man surveyed said, "I think that my wife, after twenty-some years of marriage, knows how important my need for sex is, but I wish she knew how important it is to me that she needs me sexually. She probably does not need sex so much, but I need her to want and need sex with me."[1]

Surely, if she understood how important lovemaking is, she would join me in loving and desiring me the way that I love and desire her. How can she not understand that I want her to choose me like I want to choose her? After all, it isn't like it costs her anything to engage sexually with me, and she tells me that she loves sex with me. So why isn't she initiating? Why isn't she seducing me? Why does she refuse sex or seem "too tired"?

I cringe to think of how many men have heard my talks and later said, "But I've never come home to rose petals like Groom did in your story," as if *that* is the insight they were supposed to walk away with. Again, I understand. I've been there too. I felt confused and rejected, pouring my heart out, seeing nothing but weariness on her face and hearing it in her words but still feeling compelled to try to explain like some stupid kid.

I hope that maybe in this section, I can defang and maybe even translate those talks in a way that helps both husbands and wives.

Many years ago, after one of those times when I sought to make love with my beautiful wife, and she responded that she was too tired, I made an effort to explain how important sex with her was to me.

Of course, we generally had a great sex life, but our differences in thresholds and interpretations of sex meant that sometimes we weren't on the same page about engaging sexually. And, to the very point of this chapter, homeschooling five children, managing a home, shepherding friends and families, and tending to her easily distracted husband left her many nights with zero points of psychological energy.

During a talk like these described, I (apparently) asked her if she wanted to be the woman of my dreams and to make my dreams come true as much as I wanted to be that for her. I honestly thought at the time that this was a poetic way of communicating with her.

Here's what I was thinking: I want to be the man of her dreams, and I'm convinced that if I knew of something as important to her heart as sex is to my heart, I would make sure it became a reality. If she told me I needed to lose twenty pounds to be her dream come true, I would have done it. Make a million dollars? I'll figure it out. Take her to Paris? Keep a close eye on the fridge for those tickets! So if sex was that equivalent for me, why couldn't she make that happen?

In my head, I wanted to be the man of her dreams. So when she tells me her dreams, I want to make them happen. I knew that my sweet wife, of course, did want to be my dream come true, just like I wanted to be hers. Who wouldn't want to be naked and warm and close with the woman of their dreams? Why doesn't she want that with me? Doesn't the woman of my dreams want to experience the dream come true with me?

She doesn't want to have sex with me—therefore, she doesn't want my dreams to be true (so my thinking went).

Years later, I found a journal entry of hers. Ginger is, like me, not a consistent journal or diary keeper. We have journals with the first two or three pages written in them and the rest blank scattered in drawers all over our house. We are both wired like this (it explains why it has taken so long to get this book done). In this journal, there was one entry. Only one. Here it is:

> I realized that sex with me speaks to Chris's soul because he said, "You don't want to be my dream come true." I realized that most nights he needs *no* debriefing time from the day—just wants to get right into it. I feel like it is a thing because it does become one more thing when it doesn't feel like a relationship. When there is no transition between teaching the kids, wiping bottoms, correcting, playing, etc. . . . then continues the cycle of Chris wanting "me" but it doesn't feel like he wants me. I feel like I am never enough—I am truly disappointing to him. Obviously not his dream come true.[2]

Wow. It's still painful for me to read back. I had taken my feelings of rejection and, instead of seeking understanding before seeking to be understood, I had dumped those feelings onto her. In my ignorance and insensitivity, I had communicated the exact opposite of what I had hoped to. You can see that she is trying to make it something special ("sex with me speaks to Chris's soul"), but that isn't what she was thinking. She was seeing how "Chris wanting me" didn't feel like it was about her but about sex. After all, if I wanted to make love before debriefing the day's events, it meant I wanted sex more than her (her interpretation).

So did you catch *my* error in thinking about psychological energy?

There were several, but the main one was this: "After all, it isn't like it costs her anything to engage sexually with me . . ."

Since my identity is wrapped up in sex, it takes me $0 to invest and get a $40,000 return. So I thought that from a psychological energy perspective, she was choosing *not* to take the $40,000 even though it cost an initial investment of $0 (not true of most women). Therefore, I assumed there was another reason why she didn't do it (my interpretation). Since I knew she loved me, I assumed she must not do it with me because she had forgotten how important it was to me.

I assumed that sex was integrated into her identity like it was mine. I had no reason to question the idea that sex didn't "come naturally" to her like it did me. What if engaging sexually with me, even if she wanted to, would cost her more psychological points than she had to invest at that moment? What if pouring out my heart about how special and important sex with her was to me ($50,000, $100,000, even $1 million) wasn't solving the problem—but making it worse?

What if her feelings were "I would love to make love, but I just can't tonight because I don't have the psychological energy points?"

After all, *that is what she said.*

As in the example I started with, trading $20,000 in cash for $40,000 doesn't work if I don't have the $20,000 for the initial investment. It doesn't matter if I increase the return value to $1 million. You can't take the deal if you don't have the $20,000. All it succeeds in is making you feel worse that you can't take me up on it.

In *The Married Guy's Guide to Great Sex*, C. L. and J. J. Penner write, "Many women have no energy left for sex by the end of the day; it's been burned up by working at a job, keeping up the house, preparing meals, mothering children, and more. Even if you help, she'll feel burdened if she alone 'owns' all these duties."[3]

I lacked the understanding of what that meant. That made no sense to me. I thought, "Sex together is free, fun, orgasmic (more on that in a bit), doesn't take all that long, and it even burns calories." There is almost nothing her life lacks that wouldn't get better with more sex.[4]

However, she claimed that she "just didn't have it in her."

What I heard was that she "didn't love me enough" or "didn't understand how important it is to me . . ." It couldn't be a lack of love; ergo, she must not understand me. This leads back to yet another chat about sex, trying to make her understand, and her weariness grows. Now you see why I call this a disunity spiral—both people leave the conversations feeling hurt, misunderstood, unappreciated, and alone.

The damage caused by these misunderstandings is a big part of the motivation for the research that led to this book. When it comes to sex, this illustration represents the failing strategy of men everywhere. Men spend all of their energy trying to explain how important sex is to them. So when women don't have sex because they don't have it in them to meet their husband's desires, they feel worse and worse.

It's bad enough that men do this, but historically, Christian counselors and authors have taken this same strategy and created whole ministries. Before you know it, these authors say it's not only a need but the only way to prevent him from having an affair (see FAQ 5 about the word "need"). If she wants to affair-proof her marriage, she better figure this out.

Though some marriages are strong enough to translate this rubbish "affair-proofing your marriage" message into something valuable, most suffer under it. Many, like Bride, suffer in silence. Her arousal and desire and free choice of him, which is what he actually craves, is hurting in silence. She grits her teeth and bears it, thinking that if so many Christian authors teach it, she must be the problem.

There has to be a better way. To find it, we need to unpack this idea of *psychological energy*. Before you think we are diving into some academic psychologist nerd talk, I suspect that for many readers, this will offer the biggest percentage of explanation for what has gone wrong in your sex life. If you have ever heard yourself think, "Sure, I would love to mess around, but I just don't know where I will find the energy," or if you have ever been bewildered when someone who loves you said something like that, read on.

Psychological Energy

Each of us wakes up with some energy to face the day—physical energy, spiritual energy, emotional energy, and other kinds. I won't break these down individually. Instead, I'll lump them all into one heading: "psychological energy."

Psychological energy refers to the holistic expenditure options that we have in life. If there were some way to measure this energy, we wouldn't start with the same amount each morning. Temperament, health, attitude, and many more elements are all factors. And, of course, every day, we wake up with different levels in our tanks. If I get crappy sleep the night before, it'll affect the amount of energy I wake up with. Loads of financial debt could affect your energy by weighing you down. If you're depressed, that will *undoubtedly* affect your energy levels.

We spend psychological energy when we choose an activity (mental or physical) to do something, experience something, or even feel something. Typically it is an automatic expenditure.

When something "comes naturally" to us, that's usually a way of saying that it costs us little or no psychological energy. When we enjoy something, it may be a way of saying it adds to our tank. On the flip side, when we interact with things or people who are annoying, it takes something out of us. It's not a bad thing to spend energy. We all do it all day, every day, spending and gaining varying amounts of this energy. Jobs, chores, or social events can drain you, but fun interactions, coffee, petting a dog, introverted time, physical affection, and other things can return it.

Some activities simultaneously cost and add energy. These are investments. Exercise is a great example. It costs me psychological energy to work out, run, or almost anything else boring and physical. Man, if I can avoid it, I do. I have to *decide* to spend the points. But an interesting effect often emerges. It may cost me ten points of my overall energy to get on that elliptical, and I step off an hour later physically tired and sweaty but with twenty points more energy than I started with.

If I was down to twenty points before my evening workout, I would get done and now have thirty points. But getting the payoff takes an up-front investment.

Of course, there are so many factors here that it would be impossible to quantify psychological energy. However, once you understand these principles, the conversations they create between an intimate couple are super helpful!

What taxes your psychological energy?

What little things I do or say are energy drains?

What little things I do or say add energy?

What things come naturally to you?

What things are great for giving you psychological energy but cost an initial investment?

We tolerate differences that cause friction between us and our spouses by spending psychological energy. When we experience discord over temperament differences, different plans, or need to pick up each other's slack, we draw on our energy reserves. Of course, we spend points at work, in our friendships, at church, and in all kinds of relationships too, but being and doing what our spouse prefers over what we prefer costs energy.

You may remember me saying my wife loves babies. I do, too, but she is at another level. Anything about babies comes naturally to her. Nurturing is wired into her identity. An expression of this is that she loves things made for babies, tiny and cute things. As a pastor, I often get to go to the hospital to help greet a church member's newborn baby. I love making her jealous by sending her a picture of me holding the infant with proud parents.

For years, I would find a small baby outfit in a grocery bag from her shopping trip. Maybe a onesie, a little infant hat, or tiny socks. I would then gently point out that we didn't have any babies. She would respond that the outfit was just too cute to pass up! Surely someone has a baby that we could give it to.

When something is integrated into your identity, you need a reason *not* to do it; you do not need a reason *to* do it. Apparently, for my wife, not having a baby is not a sufficient reason *not* to buy baby clothes. Shopping for baby stuff is like a psychological energy drink for her. I like babies, but I hate retail stores. I have about a fifteen-minute headache countdown that starts when those automatic doors slide open. It costs me around twenty psychological energy points to be there longer than fifteen minutes.

So if at the end of an exhausting day I come home, and my wife, who has also had an exhausting day, says, "Hey, the church is hosting a baby shower tomorrow. Want to run with me to the store and buy some baby stuff for the shower?"

We are both near zero. I love my wife and know that spending time with her will be life-giving. Even just a few minutes will improve my attitude and probably even increase my overall psychological energy (seriously, she is that fun and that easy to be around; ask anyone).

However, she wants to go to a *store* to shop for baby stuff. If she is at zero points, this still sounds good to her. Buying baby clothes costs her zero points and is worth forty in return.

If I have twenty points left, I have a decision to make. Do I invest them in the store, or do I save them for something else? It's a fair question, and I might decide either way.

However, *if I'm at zero*, I will likely say (you guessed it): "I would love to, but I just *don't think I can tonight*." Hopefully, she understands. She can either wait for me tomorrow and hope I have more to invest, or she can go by herself to get the baby clothes. Hopefully you see the parallels to the way many wives feel about sex.

There is another concept that will help us understand psychological energy: thresholds.

Thresholds

I'm going to illustrate the threshold principle with a slightly silly example. I'll call this couple Greg and Sarah.

Greg and Sarah both love spaghetti. They have slightly different tastes on how to prepare it, but they both crave good pasta. In fact, Greg wants spaghetti three times a week (almost qualifying him for a *My Strange Addiction* episode on TLC). If he doesn't have spaghetti *at least twice a week*, he'll get grumpy and seem to experience withdrawals.

Sarah also really, really loves spaghetti. If she doesn't get it, she'll feel upset, but she only really craves it *once a month or so* before she feels bummed.

Then, these two get married. So here's the question: how often does the wife's threshold get reached? How often does Sarah get pasta withdrawals?

The answer is *never*.

You may have been tempted to say once a month; after all, that's her threshold. But because Sarah married Greg, he always reaches the threshold faster. How likely is it that Greg is going to wait a month before the family eats spaghetti? Not very likely. To Greg, it may seem like Sarah doesn't have the same cravings that he does.

She does, but not on the same timetable.

Do they both love spaghetti? Yes.

Will Greg be disappointed? Probably sometimes. Making spaghetti for dinner two to three times a week is a lot of work and might get old. His threshold gets hit so quickly that he probably won't always get the pasta on his timetable.

Tying this in with psychological energy, Greg has to spend some points *not* eating spaghetti at least three times a week.

Will Sarah be disappointed? Only in that she may become frustrated that Greg doesn't sufficiently appreciate them having spaghetti *once or even twice* a week. She may feel like the availability of pasta is never enough for him. Eating spaghetti is always fun for her, too, and Greg is a master at cooking it, but because of the difference in timetables, she will often eat pasta when she would otherwise choose not to.

She will have to spend some psychological energy to make and have spaghetti sometimes, *even though she enjoys it.*

Now, you may already be jumping ahead and thinking that "spaghetti" is a euphemism for "sex"—not necessarily. This concept applies to almost any normal area of life. If Sarah begins to feel stressed when the sink is full of dishes for three days, but Greg feels it every two hours, how often will Sarah feel stressed about the dishes? Almost never! Greg is not likely to tolerate the stress of a dirty sink for seventy-two hours, but he might feel frustrated that she "never does them." In fact, she would do them, but only within twenty-four to forty-eight hours. It never gets to that point before Greg feels bothered enough to clean them.

If I start feeling intense worry when my kids are five feet from the road, and my wife feels it when they are twenty feet from the road, how often will I feel stressed? Never, if she is around. And she and I are potentially going to face conflict over this difference, aren't we? "I am not worried enough" and "she doesn't trust me" sounds like how that would play out.

Financial spending, risk issues, time with friends, and bed-making are all examples. There are a million tiny instances of how thresholds can affect two people seeking to live their lives together.

Of course, it costs us very little psychological energy to operate within our own thresholds—they come naturally. It costs some psychological energy to seek to sacrifice my thresholds to serve my spouse by taking their thresholds into account. We can take their thresholds into account in two ways: Doing the thing sooner for our spouse with the lower thresholds or waiting for our spouse with the higher threshold.

Sacrificing for one another's thresholds is another expression of the OJ and chocolate milk thinking from Chapter 2. In other words, living with another person requires paying attention to and figuring out their natural thresholds.

Now, of course, this entire conversation, in principle, applies to sex. Maybe the spaghetti analogy was just a *little* slanted in this direction, I admit. Obviously, different people have different thresholds when it comes to sexy feelings. Some people's sexual feelings are more aggressive, some more adventurous, some more warm and tender, and some just less intense in general. But understand that our thresholds are complex, just like our personalities. One spouse might have a very low threshold for adventurous sexual activities but a very high threshold for warm and cuddly sexual activities, for example. Once again, the main lesson is in knowing and loving your spouse in the ways they appreciate the most.

Not surprisingly, conflict in marriage often occurs in the areas of the largest gaps in thresholds.

Men who feel hurt by their wife's lack of sexual desire, take a deep breath. The good news is your wife almost probably does enjoy sex with you. Statistically, her threshold is probably just at a different place than yours. That means she may not *seem* to enjoy sex as much because she never reaches her threshold for craving it in the same way that you crave it with her. Her higher threshold doesn't mean she doesn't love sex or you. That's some information to work with.

So, thresholds, learned or intrinsic, can explain part of how psychological energy gets spent differently and experienced differently by two people. However, there is some more vital insight that I think we can gain from some patterns in marriage satisfaction scores.

Wives, hopefully you understand why those bedside chats were happening (sorry).

Husbands, hopefully now you understand what she is saying when she says, "But I don't think I can tonight."

Wait, many of you just had a thought: "But, Chris, it wasn't always like this—so I'm still confused. When we were first married, she loved having sex with me. She was always ready, willing, and eager! She would seduce *me*. She rarely or never said, 'I don't think I can tonight' in those first years together, especially on the honeymoon. Just a few years later, that began to change. Can you explain that?'"

Yes.

Marital Satisfaction Scores

First, the disunity spiral hadn't started yet in most young marriages. You were totally ignorant, but somehow, things seemed to work anyway . . . right up until they didn't.

Debra Smith notes the spiral that happens when husbands and wives become too focused on what they primarily desire at the expense of what the other one primarily desires. We hope that the spiral works upward through selflessness, but Smith notes how it can be a death spiral as well: "Then after a woman stops meeting her husband's sexual [desires], a man is certainly not inclined to meet his wife's emotional [desire] for romance. And the cycle continues in a downward spiral until the marital relationship is nonexistent on all levels . . ."[5]

Once the disunity spiral has started, sex begins to look like a piece of exercise machine with tons of baggage hanging all over it. Now it has lost so much of its best value that it isn't what it used to be all about.

The second reason can be explained by a graph found in a work on the psychology of happiness:[6]

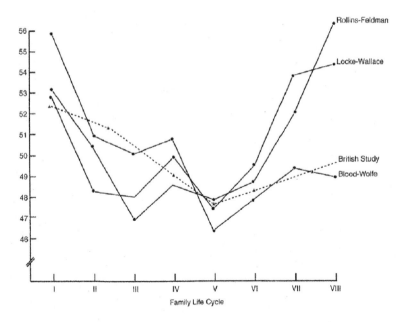

This graph comes from a meta-analysis of four studies of marital satisfaction over time (don't be scared by "meta-analysis," it just means a study generalizing the results from other studies to give the big picture). Notice the heading "Family Life Cycle" in place of a timeline, showing how a family's progress over time can lead to an increase or decrease in marital satisfaction.

I'll unveil what the "Family Life Cycle" stands for and simplify the data.

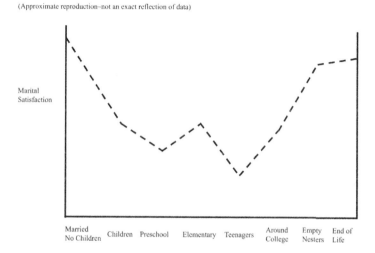

(Approximate reproduction–not an exact reflection of data)

Marital
Satisfaction

| Married No Children | Children | Preschool | Elementary | Teenagers | Around College | Empty Nesters | End of Life |

Let's unpack it.

Around the time of divorce, you can expect the couple's sex life to be in shambles. Okay, that's obvious, but why are they nearing divorce? In my counseling experience, there are two times that couples tend to separate, and there's evidence to back me up here too.

When you look at the meta-analysis graph of marital satisfaction, a few things probably stand out. Most marriages start out pretty satisfied. Certainly, some drop suddenly after the honeymoon; you hear about people who describe their first year(s) of marriage as pretty horrible. Likely in these cases, at least one person was not prepared or mature enough for marriage. However, for the most part, the data point for the first years of marriage for most couples is pretty high.

Then, somewhere in the three-to-five-year zone, the data point drops precipitously and typically seems to bottom out at around seven-ish years. What is this? What causes this sudden drop in marriage satisfaction? Children.[7] Keep in mind during all that I am about to say I love kids, and I especially love and enjoy *my* kids. My coauthor in this book is one of them, right? So I love kids, and we have five of them. Kids are great.

I also call them "emotional vampires." They suck psychological energy points like nobody's business. The little leeches are never satisfied.

The authors of the study "Attachment, Marital Satisfaction and Divorce During the First Fifteen Years of Parenthood" put it clinically but clearly:

> The birth of a first child presents a significant challenge for married couples, as their relationship undergoes a transition from a dyadic unit to a family of three or more. This transition may affect the family system in many different ways, both positive and negative. On the positive side, parents often experience a sense of gratification and joy over having a new baby. On the negative side, they may also experience exhaustion, lack of time for themselves, and more disagreement over issues pertaining to care of the baby and the division of family labor. [. . .] These strains and difficulties may affect the quality of their relationship as a couple adversely.

They continue:

> Indeed, a recent meta-analysis reveals that although child-less couples experience a decline in marital satisfaction over time, parents are significantly less satisfied than non-parents are, and number of children is reliably related to marital dissatisfaction. [. . .] Research has consistently shown that the transition to parenthood poses a serious challenge if not a crisis for marriage.[8]

Those snippets kind of say it all.

When couples have children who are especially early on in their infancy and again when they're in their teens, statistically, marital satisfaction plummets. Think about it: have you ever known a divorced couple who didn't have kids? They're rare. Why is that?

Well, the answer may be obvious: the stress-inducing and time-sucking children mean the spouses lack the psychological energy that they have been spending on each other! Peeling back another layer reveals it also becomes harder and harder to find time for sex, a result and cause of an unhealthy marriage. In a hard time, when sex is meant to smooth out the bumps, it can become a hassle to the wife because it takes energy she doesn't have.

As one woman said, "For guys, it seems, sex provides relief or escape from exhaustion. For women, we have to pull ourselves out of exhaustion in order to want to have sex."[9]

Remember, it takes a certain number of psychological points for the wife to engage in sex (it costs twenty even though it is worth forty). Children tend to drain those points. Men desperately want to engage sexually with their lover to help regain that energy and connection (it costs zero but is worth forty), but women lack the energy to start it! Voila, a recipe for a train wreck.

At the end of a long day of carpooling, soccer practices, lunch prep, diapers, and the harrowing cries of babies, all your wife wants to do is sleep. She also wants you, but possibly not sexually (or in any other way that costs psychological energy). She needs the points regained before she has enough energy to make love to you. This is crucial, though. If you do something like this for your wife, it cannot be a "one and done." It takes consistent work and sacrifice.

This brings us neatly to another vital principle within the heading of psychological energy—margin.

Margin

In 2004, Richard Swenson wrote the groundbreaking book, *Margin: Restoring Emotional, Physical, Financial and Time Reserves to Our Overloaded Lives.*[10] Simply put, "margin" is "the space between our load and our limits and is related to our reserves and resilience. It is a buffer, a leeway, a gap; the place we go to heal, to relate, to reflect, to recharge our batteries, to focus on the things that matter most."[11]

When it comes to resources, the "margin" represents the leftover resources we have fun with. What do we have fun with? The money left over after the bills. When do we have fun? With the time that is left over after everything that must get done is done.

A great danger exists in marginless living. When our schedule is totally packed, what happens when one event runs long? A domino effect takes over. Now we are late to everything else. "Marginless is being thirty minutes late to the doctor's office because you were twenty minutes late getting out of the bank, because you were ten minutes late dropping the kids off, and you were a block away from the gas station when you ran out of gas, and you forgot your wallet."[12] In case you needed more convincing, God hardwired margin into the Ten Commandments in the form of *rest*.

If a surprise medical bill comes up when we live paycheck to paycheck, marginless, it cascades into overwhelming debt. Well, the same idea applies to psychological energy. What psychological energy do you have fun with? Whatever is left over after all the energy you must exert is exerted—the margin.

Now, ladies, imagine getting home and your husband wants to make love. You are completely out of psychological energy because you didn't create margin in your day; anxiety, fluster, and frustration are not friends to romance or arousal. As marriage goes on, both spouses typically have less margin—especially with kids. Let's say that engaging in sex requires your wife to spend twenty psychological energy points. Remember, this isn't a bad thing.

When you were first married, what used up her energy most days? Probably very little. Even in her job, she probably didn't have much responsibility since she was young (like you). If you were like us, you owned almost nothing and lived in a small apartment, so there wasn't much to stress about at home. (It doesn't take long to tidy up six hundred square feet.)

Also, and I will talk more about this in the arousal section, she probably felt pretty good about herself, and you were probably looking pretty good, too. Add to this, you had tons of psychological energy you could easily invest into her. You had the margin to pay attention to her in romantic, fun ways.

So, early on, she started each day with whatever 100 percent was and probably ended each day with as much as 60 percent left in the tank. Maybe she didn't intentionally think about sex all day, but when you show interest, she intuitively looks at the bank of energy and feels the points available to spend. She might even intuitively realize sex will be an investment that returns her more points than she started with.

But then child number one appears. Seven in ten parents lose three hours of sleep per night each night of their child's first year of life. That's around one thousand hours of sleep lost the first year, which equates to 133 nights of sleep.[13] It takes parents an average of six years to get their sleep back on track.[14]

What happens to the psychological energy you have fun with? The little vampires suck up anything you give them. Unless you intentionally *impose* margin, it will not exist.

The psychological energy he used to spend on romancing her, focusing all of his energy and attention on her? Limited. The margin she spent thinking or planning for sex or just engaging in arousal? Reduced. Add to that diminished energy to spend on exercising, spending time with friends, and other psychological energy increases, and you can see the problem forming.

In hard times, God intended sex to smooth out difficulties in a marriage. So the lack of sexual intimacy's power to bond the couple is lost. It's like a survivalist who cannot find enough food, so they run out of energy to look for food. It becomes a cycle of defeat.

Now add in a few of those "bedside chats." Add in a grumpy and confused Groom to go along with his fatigue. Add in Bride's complete exhaustion (at times), a sense of failure, body changes, hormone changes, and viola: the disunity spiral.

As I write this, I'm surprised any marriage makes it through this stage. Of course, I know why they do. We may not have as much free energy or sex, but when we look over at the baby breathing gently in the crib, we are more in love with our spouse than ever. The "one flesh" ideal of marriage conquers again. But can we thrive rather than just survive? Yes, and wherever you are in the disunity spiral (if you're in one at all), you can reverse the ill effects to thrive not just with sex but with your marriage.

Look at the graph again. Pretty quickly after bottoming out, the satisfaction begins to rise. As your child gains some independence, it will feel like a pay raise in the psychological energy department.

With great fondness, I remember when my children could feed themselves for the first time. I was in charge of early mornings, which meant breakfast was my responsibility for years. At first, the ritual of getting a baby to eat a spoonful of squished something was painfully tedious. Of course, it can be adorable, but at 6:00 a.m., trying to get them to open their mouths to eat was not fun. Apparently I'm completely unable to feed a child without opening *my* mouth for every bite, which feels a bit silly. I was highly motivated to help them learn to use a spoon for themselves. It was an immediate energy bonus once I could just watch and ensure nothing catastrophic happened. And don't get me started on the joys of sending a child to "go get breakfast" while staying in bed—one of my life's highlights.

And potty training. It's amazing when a child can take themselves to the bathroom without help, and you don't have to change their diaper.

More psychological margin added to the tanks.

You should celebrate the increase in margin, but often by that point the damage is done from all the misunderstandings. You may also see a noticeable decline in satisfaction about eighteen years into marriages that bottom out again around twenty years before rising. Want to guess what that dip represents? If you guessed teenagers, you're correct.

For many couples, the disunity feels unfixable, then add in the mix the second most emotionally challenging era of marriage—the teen years. Teenagers are amazing, by the way. It's a unique age of opportunity and just about my personal favorite era so far, but once again, they can be needy, demanding, and exhausting. Plus, instead of feeding them with a spoon, you need to take them to sports, school, and other activities. "I told you so" is no longer an as-proper-technique for communication or instructions. The adolescent brain needs practice using logic, persuasion, and even disagreement in this stage of development, which is as exhausting as it is necessary. At the teen stage, kids start becoming independent—which means they might drift away from what you think is best for them, which creates more stress. Oh, and God forbid (that was a prayer, by the way) that you allow a teenager to get between the two of you, splitting your marriage. Teens do this as they seek allies in life, and it spells doom for marital intimacy.

Remember, you *actively tend the garden*, or it wilts. Actively tend to your marriage, or it will wilt. Kids can represent something of a drought to persevere through.

This sheds light on why some men and women commit adultery. Remember, the person outside of your marriage usually has a lot more psychological margin than your spouse; after all, they're not raising your children or putting up with you. A single man or a woman already disconnected from their spouse is at a major advantage when it comes to psychological energy to spend on you. If you marry the person you cheat with, and especially if you have children with them, you will find yourself back where you started. I'm convinced that's part of why second marriages fail more often than first ones, and third even more than second.[15] The problem is most likely *your* ability to love someone with limited resources, not your spouse.

If you, husband, can invest in your wife's energy bank during the day, she might have more left over for you sexually, which will fill both of your tanks.

If you, wife, can remember what sex means to him and communicate your desires, you might make margin for the energy to engage in the freer, joy-filled sex of your youth in the evening. This will create a life-giving cycle. Especially in the difficult seasons, the investment and these vital practices will not happen naturally. They must be chosen, scheduled, protected, and practiced.

How do you both do this? Glad you asked. That's what the rest of the book is about.

In order to change the cycle, you will have to invest in making sure that you and, to the degree it is up to you, your spouse, make margin. In the section "Whole Life Seduction," we will move into top-tier levels of strategizing how to make this a reality.

Sadly, otherwise, the disunity spiral gets deeper and deeper, tighter and tighter. When you start reversing gravity, you usually can't take short-cuts. You have to spiral *up*, which takes the foundation of Part I, the understanding of Part II, and the application of Part III.

Once life gets demanding, it is necessary to intentionally save energy to invest in our spouses, or our lives, jobs, kids, and other priorities will devour it all.

With a new wind in our sails, more encouraged to invest in sexuality, we can unpack what God meant sex to look like before sin broke it.

This raises a question: Is it possible to spend points that you don't really have?

To answer, allow me to digress and talk about submarine movies. My favorites, by far, are *Crimson Tide* and *The Hunt for Red October*. I love the tension, the alien feel of the environment, the constant risk and danger, and the bravery required to live in such a blind and perilous oceanic world. However, I'm always confused about a recurring plot point. During a crisis or battle, the captain will always ask engineering if they can go to more than 100 percent on the reactor (something you might also hear in space movies). In *The Hunt for Red October*, some version of this happens three or four times.

The engineer always responds, "One hundred and ten percent on the reactor is possible but not recommended, sir."

The captain always replies, "Then go to 110 percent."

Despite what my coaches said about giving 110 percent in a game, I know just enough math to know 110 percent of a whole doesn't exist.

So I asked an engineer friend about this dubious plot point. He explained that engineers create equipment specs with a recommended number for the output. So the reactor comes with a series of instructions from the builders with its maximum. Really, the captain is asking the engineers whether the reactor will survive going above that number or will melt down and imminently kill everyone. In movies, engineering says that while you can go above those specs for a short time, you better not push it, or the whole thing will come apart.

The captain should never go above the recommended specs for long, and he should only do so in rare situations. Otherwise, over time, the reactor will melt down and lead to irreparable damage or worse.

That is my answer to the question: Is it possible to spend more psychological energy points than you have? You can, but you are defying what the great Creator designed us for. Over time, consequences will compound. When one spouse spends too long overdrawn, the entire system, marriage, and families will fray at the seams. It's best to protect the system with grace and patience.

Reinterpreting Bride and Groom

Now we can replay Bride and Groom with a healthier understanding. They understand that their marriage is a living parable of God's love for His people; they understand how each other interpret and intuit sexual engagement; they understand they must "stock the fridge" with what their spouse desires with grace and good gifts.

For Men: How to Start Reinterpreting

Imagine you're Groom, back from your business trip. You anticipate a sexy encounter with your beautiful wife but instead discover her 99 percent asleep in her pajamas. What is your reaction?

"Okay. I can interpret this differently after reading that *brilliant* book by Chris Legg that helped me understand this moment. She is probably out of psychological points, or she simply forgot about the option of sex. I can work on seducing her tomorrow. For now, I can pray for her, brush her hair for a bit, or go straight to sleep because I'm quite tired." This new interpretation allows you to avoid stewing in insecurity.

The next day you can still share about how you would love nothing more than to enjoy her in sex when you get back from a trip. But be clear to also tell her she doesn't need to feel pressure if she forgets or is too tired.

Instead, say, "If you do think about it, it means a lot to me." Or maybe, "Okay, I gotta confess, I really loved that welcome home last time with the rose petals, but I am still happy to be home with you. Is everything good between us?" or avoid the mention at all, since you have your elite understanding. Instead, find out about her time while you were apart.

Or, if you're stinging from the rejection, despite your understanding, say with vulnerability and gentleness, "I know it's irrational, but not having sex hurt my feelings last night." I guarantee she would prefer that over you being grumpy and uncommunicative. It's a clear win-win. She will feel a much higher sexual draw to you if you communicate like this, trust me. Our inner boyish hurt feelings aren't attractive in the slightest.

Mutual love and mutual sacrifice include the byproduct of wonderful sex. Men, you must realize that your wife won't always remember or want to have sex. When she doesn't, it needn't wound you. Of course, you are allowed to feel disappointed, and you're even allowed to gently communicate those feelings to her. Her rejection of sex is not a rejection of you.

Remember (and this is key), why do we find so much meaning in sex? Her desire for us. So suppose we manipulate her, intentionally or unintentionally, to get our way and get sex. In that case, she's not doing it because she desires us, which defeats the whole point, leaving you and her disappointed! This should remind you of the gift principle. I'll break it down in case you forgot.

1. You could allow her to engage sexually with you (which feels the best since she's actively affirming and pursuing) on her own time—inspired and encouraged by you, creating the right atmosphere for sexual intimacy.

2. You could ask her or initiate it (which is totally appropriate and still amazing), and then, if communicated well, she gets to feel desirable, and so do you when she welcomes you in. This is a perfectly good and necessary option in marriage.

3. You could manipulate or demand it, which is entirely inappropriate and doesn't fulfill your greatest desire in sex, which is for her to freely give it. Emotional blackmail is a formula men often use (creating a major emotional price for saying no). It's kind of a dastardly combination of number three and number four.

4. You could purchase it (through a prostitute or treating your wife like one, which is not only sinful, it doesn't even deeply satisfy your desire).

Even if you feel you're getting closer to her through sex, she may not feel the same. Which means what? Do you need to be second-guessing her feelings all the time? Not at all. You simply need to learn attentiveness. Pay attention to her, the details, what she likes, what she wants, how she's feeling, if she's tired, if she's in a bad mood, if she doesn't like what you're doing. In her heart, if she loves you, women want to want you.

Feldhahn's findings back this up. In response to the question "If you could magically change your sex drive and/or some of the reasons you don't want sex as much as your husband does, would you?", *82 percent* of women said yes, they would magically increase their sex drive.[16] And, for happily married women, *100 percent* said they wanted to magically increase their libido.

Why? Presumably because they desire their husbands. They want to want to engage sexually, even when their psychological energy or hormonal drive just isn't all there.

Here's another insight from Feldhahn: Men, your physical body probably does not physically turn her on sexually (no matter how much you work out). Of course, she may appreciate the strong, masculine physique, but the linkage between the eyes and arousal seems not as strong (as reported by women in Feldhahn's research).

"For her, sex *starts* in the heart."[17] For men, it seems more holistic—starting and ending in the heart, mind, and body, all intertwined! How to start working on her heart, then? Since we've laid the groundwork for marriage, you should know your next steps. Find out what she loves. Apply the sleuthing principle. When you get time alone, make sure you're prioritizing her preferences and what she loves. Show her that you desire her and want to know her, including her emotions.

A healthy, intimate sex life is integrated and intimate, *not* transactional. I am *not* encouraging you to "take care of her emotional needs, and she will take care of your sexual needs." That's how so many damaging marriage books have tried to deal with this issue.

Rather, I'm hoping you'll be able to have a complete understanding of how to bless and encourage your wife in such a way that she will be more able to naturally integrate her sexuality into her identity and then, as she shares that identity with you (intimacy), your sex life becomes healthier too.

I will expand on this later, but I also want you to recognize that you'll have a responsibility to satisfy her sexually just as much as she does to you. She may not enjoy sex with you because you're not attempting to gratify her. She should be pleasured by sex too, by the way!

Let's cut out the immaturity and the adolescent manipulation and pursue our wives like men.

For Women: How to Start Reinterpreting

So, wives. Now that you know your husbands probably integrate sex into their identity, you can start tearing down the unhealthy self-image dichotomy that's been on repeat in your head for years. Even if you are one of those women who integrate sex into your identity intuitively, you probably still have had the message that all men cared about is sex, which either still depersonalized the act for you or made you feel even more like the freak since your husband hasn't seemed to care as much as he is "supposed" to.

When you have sex with your husband, you are affirming him and who he is. For you, the primary ways you receive love or experience intimacy at the identity level might be through his verbal affirmations or appreciation or any number of things, and all of these are probably important for him as well, but for most men, he experiences those same feelings at a core level when you make love with him.[18]

Imagine you're getting dressed up to go out to a wedding, so you bought a new dress just for this occasion. You've done your makeup for a laborious twenty minutes and come out to the living room asking, "How do I look?" You accompany this question with a graceful twirl in your new outfit.

At that moment, you probably want affirmation from your husband, not a critical review of your color palette or style. It is technically okay if his response is lukewarm, but it would probably feel hurtful or like rejection.

At this, your husband may think you look great, but he may also think, "She knows I think she's beautiful . . . So why does she want me to say it all the time?" However, if he loves you well, he will tell you he thinks you look great every time and will not "grow weary of doing good" in his encouragement (Gal. 6:9). And it can't be just any man who tells you that you look good. It means more from your husband!

All individuals have unique ways they like to receive love. So pause for a second and have in your mind the most affirming thing your husband does (or you wish he would do).

Got one? Hold on to that feeling for a second.

That feeling you get from that is *probably* how your husband feels about you choosing to experience sexual pleasure with him. Consider all of the implications of that analogy. In most cases, the more enthusiastic you are about sex, the more intentional and strategic, the more you give forethought and consideration to sharing yourself fully with him, the more powerfully he will feel your affirmation."

You might respond to your husband's irrational thoughts ("She didn't have sex with me, so maybe she doesn't love me!") with "That's ridiculous. We had sex last week. He knows that I love him. Why do I keep needing to show him?"

But remember how you keep asking him to compliment your outfit, focus attention on you, go on a date, pay a bill, do the dishes (or whatever example you came up with)—it's the same concept. He needs to be reminded just like you do, time and time again.

He's no more lecherous for wanting sex with *you* (because he loves you) than you are haughty for wanting his compliment (because you love him).

Let me run another scenario by you. You come out in your dress and pop the question out, but he doesn't even look and says in a grumble, "Fine." That's the equivalent of you refusing to engage sexually with him. If you insult or disparage him for sex or make him feel crushed for wanting sex with you, you'll wound him as if he had unironically said, "Your outfit stinks!"

The problem is that women often fail to understand the gravity of sex's effect on men's feelings at the identity level just like men often fail to understand the gravity of what affects your feelings. Debra White Smith noted, "One day I realized that I was expecting him to be a full-blown Romeo while I was being only half a Juliet."[19]

All of us must be diligent to understand our spouse and reflect on ourselves, too.

If communicated gently, you can always provide corrections to his sex technique, just like he can provide gentle corrections to your outfit. But for the most part, rejecting sex with him or frustrating that desire in him can feel like a rejection of him as a man. At this stage, let me reiterate what I've already reiterated: It is okay for you to say no to sex. I'm not locking you into some kind of behavioral legalism. Rather, I hope this understanding will help you handle him more gently and graciously.

Here's an obvious difference: all the wives reading this book are yelling at me right now: "Complimenting my outfit is the most minimal effort possible. It literally takes two seconds. Sure, I enjoy sex too, but sex can be hard work!"

I one-hundred-percent agree. Sex is kind of in its own category, so all analogies fall apart in practice. So maybe him mowing the lawn is a better comparison . . . but somehow, comparing mowing the lawn and sex just feels wrong. (Though they seem to take similar amounts of physical energy. Sex burns about four calories per minute, and mowing burns about five, according to a quick Google search.)

I hope to show that your husband has just as much responsibility for gratifying your sexual desires as you do his. I merely want you to understand your man's heart behind desiring sex with you. I actually have a whole chapter for your husband to help you both get to the point where you want to have sex with him by giving you the energy to spend on sex later, so hang tight.

For now, I want you to start using this chapter's *interpretation*. When your husband talks about sex at strange times, or it seems to move him more deeply than makes sense to you, just know that it's a part of his nature. It doesn't excuse his selfishness or lack of empathy, but it can help you understand what is going on inside his head and heart—and that is the very definition of intimacy. Practice thinking: "He wants sex with me; that *means* he wants *me*!"

Let's go back to the Bride and Groom story. When Groom comes home from the trip, if you have the energy to spare, try to remember that a good way to invest the energy may be to welcome him with sexual intimacy. If not, then you might send him a text so he's less disappointed, explaining how rough your day was. Even better is to add something sexy to the text and say you can't wait to make love with him tomorrow. If you communicate something along those lines, I suspect that he won't get his feelings hurt in the slightest. When he realizes that you probably intuitively separate them, he is on his way to pursuing you and will hopefully do his own reinterpreting.

Interestingly, and we will delve more into this later, these truths mean that he wants you to pursue him, especially sexually. This is an interesting paradox. Men naturally pursue women sexually in an active way. That natural ordering is not a bad thing inherently. But if you take an active role in initiating, it will mean the world to him! Men love active partners in sex, even though women's drive is often a "responsive" or "passive" sexual drive.

Do you want to love and bolster your man's confidence at a whole new level? Initiate sex! Bring passion and attention to your husband in the bedroom, even just every once in a while, and this will make him feel like Superman. Just like if he reached out to pay compliments, encourage, help, or whatever ways best uplift you without you asking, being intentional about sex can increase both your arousal and his.

The reason why I set up the basics about marriage and love in the beginning and spent so much time on it was to prepare you and your husband to love each other sacrificially. This may entail sacrifice for you, and even if it does, continue to make what means the world to him your top priority.

In all that, women, remember he will not love you perfectly. He won't understand every inmost part of your emotions. If you're being honest, do you even understand the innermost parts of your emotions?

While he should pursue you and grow, you can avoid a standard of perfection. Especially if he is starting this for the first time or relearning how to pursue you like when you were dating, he's going to start out shakily.

Please, please affirm his attempts and encourage him.

Remember the "start with me" principle.

Since you're not worried about his performance, and you ought to focus on him in your relationship, making love to him and showing your affection will motivate him to work harder and serve you throughout the day better, just like when he loves you in the ways most deeply connected to your identity.

I know that many of you have had decades of bad experiences. Many of you could use healing from broken and abusive sexual experiences. This is some of the hardest work a person can invest in—but the freedom that can come from doing trauma-healing work is profound. Many more have emotional pain from abuse or harassment, even from people who should've been trustworthy. I am so sorry for the dreadful things you've experienced. I'm inspired by the men and women who I have seen find freedom within this grief. I'm also honored to help couples through it in so many cases.

I've also been impressed by the husbands who are eager and patient while their wives heal from the abuses of their past (or from wounds he created) if she asks it of him clearly and graciously. Most men are willing and able to work on their issues if they believe true appreciation and mutual love are the results for them and their wives.

---

1. Feldhahn, *For Women Only*, 114.

2. Yes, I got her permission to include this entry here.

3. Clifford L. Penner and Joyce J. Penner, *The Married Guy's Guide to Great Sex* (Colorado Springs: NavPress, 2017), 23.

4. Just check out the lists of benefits in these articles! Center for Women's Health, "The Benefits of a Healthy Sex Life," accessed October 31, 2023, https://www.ohsu.edu/womens-health/benefits-healthy-sex-life; Pamela Rogers, "The Health Benefits of Sex," *Healthline*, April 12, 2023, https://www.healthline.com/health/healthy-sex-health-benefits#health-benefits.

5. Debra White Smith, *Romancing Your Husband: Enjoying a Passionate Life Together* (Eugene, OR: Harvest House Publishers, 2013), 13.

6. Norbert Schwarz, "Global and Episodic Reports of Hedonic Experience," in *Calendar and Time Diary Methods in Life Course Research* (Thousand Oaks, CA: SAGE Publications Inc., 2009), 156–74, https://doi.org/10.4135/9781412990295.d15;
Daniel Gilbert, *Stumbling on Happiness* (Toronto: Vintage Canada, 2009), 221.

7. Jean M. Twenge, W. Keith Campbell, and Craig A. Foster, "Parenthood and Marital Satisfaction: A Meta-Analytic Review," *Journal of Marriage and Family* 65, no. 3 (August 2003): 574–83, https://doi.org/10.1111/j.1741-3737.2003.00574.x.

8. Gilad Hirschberger et al., "Attachment, Marital Satisfaction, and Divorce during the First Fifteen Years of Parenthood," *Personal Relationships* 16, no. 3 (September 2009): 401–20, https://doi.org/10.1111/j.1475-6811.2009.01230.x.

9. Feldhahn and Feldhahn, *For Men Only*, 146.

10. Richard Swenson, *Margin: Restoring Emotional, Physical, Financial, and Time Reserves to Overloaded Lives* (Carol Stream, IL: Tyndale House, 2004).

11. Richard Swenson, "Margin," November 3, 2023, accessed December 19, 2023, http://www.richardswenson.com/margin. This quote from his website about the book summarizes the point quite well.

12. Richard Swenson, *Margin*, 1.

13. Snüz, "The Truth About Sleep: Snuz Sleep Survey Results," accessed January 5, 2024, https://www.snuz.co.uk/sleep-centre/news/the-truth-about-sleep-snuz-sleep-survey-results/.

14. David Richter et al., "Long-Term Effects of Pregnancy and Childbirth on Sleep Satisfaction and Duration of First-Time and Experienced Mothers and Fathers," *SLEEP* 42, no. 4 (January 14, 2019), https://doi.org/10.1093/sleep/zsz015.

15. Todd M. Jensen et al., "Differences in Relationship Stability between Individuals in First and Second Marriages," *Journal of Family Issues* 38, no. 3 (July 10, 2016): 406–32, https://doi.org/10.1177/0192513x15604344.

16. Feldhahn and Feldhahn, *For Men Only*, 134–135.

17. Feldhahn and Feldhahn, *For Men Only*, 142.

18. Joshua M. Ackerman, Vladas Griskevicius, and Norman P. Li, "Let's Get Serious: Communicating Commitment in Romantic Relationships," *Journal of Personality and Social Psychology* 100, no. 6 (January 2011): 1079–94. In one study, it was shown that men are more likely to say "I love you" to their partners six weeks earlier. Men were also happier if they hadn't yet had sex with their partner and their partner said "I love you," whereas women were happier if she heard it from a man after sex. Why? They theorize because men think it will mean they will have a meaningful and engaging sexual encounter, whereas for women it means he's devoted to her even after sex.

19. Smith, *Romancing Your Husband*, 17.

Six

BECOMING ONE: AN ANCIENT VISION FOR SEX

I lead trips to Israel, one of my life's highlights and regular joys. Perhaps the greatest challenge in putting together the tour is choosing which sites to visit. I lean toward places where I can teach from my passions (shocking, right?). I don't usually prioritize the traditional sites, places where biblical figures "supposedly" did XYZ based on little evidence. For example, we typically don't go to the church supposedly built on the house with the upper room or the precise spot where Jesus allegedly died. While I see the value in the pilgrimage mindset to visit sites of traditional interest, my co-teachers and I choose based on the historical significance and, even more so, teaching locations that recreate the experience of the people living thousands of years ago.

At one spot, we hike up a dusty, dry, hot, rocky hill to a surprise destination. As we walk, greenery starts to appear around a trickling stream. Eventually, we arrive at the source of the brook, an area called Engedi. The waterfall is called David Falls because David hid from Saul there in 1 Samuel 23:29. Some believe David wrote Psalm 63 while camped near this spring: "A psalm of David. When he was in the Desert of Judah. You, God, are my God, earnestly I seek you; I thirst for you, my whole being longs for you, in a dry and parched land where there is no water" (v. 1).

David's words to the Lord feel palpable when we arrive at the freshwater pool after we've hiked in the heat. Wasteland surrounds the spring for miles on all sides. What a relief David and his devoted men must have felt when they arrived, haggard and desperate, at this freshwater spring.

So what do I teach about at this phenomenal, awe-inspiring site? Marriage. Why? Because my wife is like a spring of freshwater in the desert. When life beats me down like the dry Middle Eastern sun, she refreshes my soul, and I, hers. Psalm 63 is about David's love for God, but since marriage is a parable of the love between God and His people, it seems like an apt place to unpack the beautiful truths of matrimony.

Still not convinced? Let's read from David's son, Solomon, who writes about his betrothed: "My beloved is to me a cluster of henna blossoms in the vineyards of Engedi" (Song of Sol. 1:14). The Engedi image strikes me deeply. I use it as a teaching example frequently, and I have pictures of it everywhere. When my eldest son and his wife married, I gave them a ceramic pot filled with water from Engedi.

Not only does the spring of Engedi represent marriage, but it also represents the refreshing, secure, life-giving nature of sex with our loving spouse.

Sex is Sacred

We began this book by covering the fundamentals of marriage. We also examined some common misunderstandings about sex. We started to gain some clarity with a discussion about psychological energy. Up to this point, I've provided a fresh look at a well-established view of marriage that stretches back thousands of years to the Bible. The Christian ideal of marriage does not change, even if what it looks like on the surface shifts from culture to culture. (For example, nowadays, people get to choose who they marry instead of their parents picking for them—that's pretty neat.)

However, if you paid close attention to the marriage chapters, you might notice my definition excluded sex.

If marriage is as I've defined it way back in Chapter 1 (based on God's word), then it could do with an extra spice—a secret sauce. Wouldn't it be nice if some unique form of sacrifice could be experienced together as a sacred form of enjoyment? It would be fantastic if the two lifelong, committed individuals could engage in something special for only the two of them. It would be a private and intimate act that was their special, secret bond, helping their marriage run more smoothly, giving them an advantage over all other potential competitive relationships, and symbolizing the joy we experience in God's presence.

If only there were a physical way to join two people together to make the difficult process of becoming one that much easier.

Hmm. Oh, right, *that* is sex.

And it is sacred. It is a holy expression of the purity and power that God created marriage to exhibit in its living parable. As we whet our appetite on this feast of goodness prepared for us, however, I want to be realistic.

We are about to set the table for the concept of intimacy. Intimacy is essentially not possible to build without trust. If you are in a marriage without trust, where you don't feel safe, or one of you lies, cheats, or is unreliable or unwilling to mature, the next chapters are not for you. I'm not talking about the normal ways that our spouses are imperfect and flawed. I'm talking about deep breaches of trust and especially an unwillingness to change or get help. This special barrier might include adultery, habitual lying, an unwillingness to talk about issues, substance addiction, or other vices that make trust impossible.

If this is you, you need to stop here and rebuild trust. You cannot *earn* trust. It must be given freely. However, you can be *trustworthy*, which *inspires* trust over time. You may need help with addictions, dishonesty, or drawing healthy boundaries. I consistently see untrustworthy spouses who are frustrated with a lack of intimacy, but let me repeat: intimacy is not really possible without trust. Read and apply the materials in *Healing Your Marriage When Trust is Broken* by Beall, *Emotional Blackmail* by Forward and Frazier, or *Tender Warrior* by Weber, for examples of how to become a more trustworthy person.[1] No books can replace the therapeutic relationship. If you are not a trustworthy person, I encourage you to get help from a professional counselor who can help guide you through the character change called for.

If the trust is still strong enough to support intimacy, read on.

So what do I mean when I claim that sex is sacred? Sex plays a special God-ordained role in our lives in this institution He created. We have referenced these concepts before, but remember, in Genesis 1 and 2, God designed, created, and ordained marriage and the sexes. Jesus confirmed this by combining these passages in Matthew 19:4–6:

> He answered, "Have you not read that he who created them from the beginning made them male and female, and said, 'Therefore a man shall leave his father and his mother and hold fast to his wife, and the two shall become

one flesh'? So they are no longer two but one flesh. What
therefore God has joined together, let not man separate."

God created sex to bind and connect people with explosive power to
further the "two shall become one flesh" idea.

Becoming One

Let's unpack Genesis 1:24, the passage Jesus quotes.

I believe God created males and females to complement one another in
such a way as to mutually represent God's image. In other words, men
need women and vice versa to paint the fullest picture of God's image.

I mentioned earlier that roles in life are often analogies of God. For
instance, the definition of *father* (an identity) is to reflect God's paternal
traits. This is why Paul can be a spiritual father to Timothy (1 Tim. 1:2).
On the other hand, mothers reflect the maternal traits of God. Each of
these need to exist to reflect God fully. Men and women together reflect
God.

In the creation account, God takes man's side and forms woman. The
phrase "a helper suitable for him" is intriguing. However, the word
"suitable" is probably best understood as "corresponding to him" rather
than any other meaning of the English word.[2] This makes more sense
of the way God created Eve. "Helper" certainly does not refer to sub-
servience since the same word refers to God in sixteen of twenty-one
occurrences in the Old Testament.[3]

Then man in Genesis 2:23 spontaneously speaks a poem (women often
have this effect on men, remember the hidden Shakespeare):

> This at last is bone of my bones / and flesh of my flesh; / she shall be called Woman, / because she was taken out of Man.

You can hear the palpable relief in his voice—*finally!* A companion! He names her woman since she was a part of him. In some sense, corporately, men and women make a whole. The narrator of Genesis is then inspired to comment:

> Therefore a man shall leave his father and his mother and hold fast to his wife, and they shall become one flesh. And the man and his wife were both naked and were not ashamed (Gen. 2:24–25).

Let's unpack that first sentence. As we've mentioned, marriage means prioritizing your spouse above all others. In the Jewish world, leaving your father and mother didn't usually mean leaving geographically. Most families would live in compounds, building their house connected to the house of their in-laws or parents. It more likely refers to leaving as "forsaking for the sake of" his wife. Then the next phrase, "and they shall become one flesh," provides a deep well of truth.

Pinch the flab under your arm. Slap your thigh. All of that is "flesh." Your physical, meaty bodies "become one," but *in a spiritual sense*. Here, we run into an issue. As modern Westerners, we think of the physical and spiritual as fundamentally separate. The writer of Genesis did not. Nor did any of the authors of the Bible. The spiritual and physical intertwine. Just from this passage, I wouldn't say "become one flesh" necessarily refers to sex. I would say, however, that sex is part of what becoming one flesh means.

In sexual intercourse, "becoming one" has a physical expression of what's already spiritually happened when you married your spouse. Becoming one flesh is part of your identity as a married couple, and an integral part of that is sex. Remember, theology → identity → action.

Notice how Paul quotes Genesis and uses it in an argument against people engaging in prostitution. He writes in 1 Corinthians:

> Or do you not know that he who is joined to a prostitute becomes one body with her? For, as it is written, "The two will become one flesh." But he who is joined to the Lord becomes one spirit with him. Flee from sexual immorality. Every other sin a person commits is outside the body, but the sexually immoral person sins against his own body. Or do you not know that your body is a temple of the Holy Spirit within you, whom you have from God? You are not your own, for you were bought with a price. So glorify God in your body (1 Cor. 6:16–20).

Here's the main point: When one commits sexual sin, they sin against their own body. If a man has sex with a prostitute, he becomes one flesh with her. The purpose, or meaning, of sex, is *to make two into one*. Thus, he says your body is not yours to give away. God has bought your body because he bought *you* with the price of Jesus's blood.

We can imagine the Corinthians saying, "Well, it doesn't matter what I do with my body as long as my spirit is okay." Paul contradicts this sentiment. He calls our body a *temple*—a profound image of where the spiritual and the physical meet.

Women, this can help dissolve self-image problems: God has bought you, body included, because it, as an aspect of you, is holy, like a temple. God cherishes you and pays a high price for you because He loves you.

And the "you" *includes* your body.

Never allow your body to become one flesh with another person unless through marriage. Paul's argument ties together "becoming one flesh" and sexual intercourse inextricably.

Our whole being becomes wrapped up in our spouse when we love them and consecrate that love and identity through making love. That unification is a beautiful aspect of creation that existed in the Garden.

So the purpose of sex is to unite two into one. This phrase is the very definition of the English word "intimacy." Some have created a memorable definition for intimacy—"into you, me." That's not bad. Intimacy means guiding someone through the different aspects of your life. Depending on their relationship with you, there are aspects of your identity they can access and others they cannot. (These are called "boundaries.")

When you first get to know someone, they will walk you around the most open aspects of their identity, like their work and hobbies. Then, you get to know their more intimate thoughts and emotions. Later, they may open up secrets, shame, traumas, victories, and proud moments. We can call this mental and emotional intimacy. Their views on purpose, life, value, meaning, and other deeply important aspects will come to light as intimacy develops. Scripturally speaking, once within the safety of the marriage covenant, you begin the process of being guided around their *bodies* in sexual intimacy.

Dr. Welch notes, "The intimacy everyone seems to crave so much these days is not just about sex, although that is a part of it; it is not just about communication, although that too is a part of it. Intimacy is, at its core, about letting your spouse past your defenses and protective walls to a place where they truly see who you are."[4]

The moment that sex disunifies a husband and wife and becomes a barrier in all of these areas of intimacy, its point is defeated.

Years ago, I would go with my father to the American Wilderness Leadership School outside of Jackson Hole, Wyoming (not exactly suffering, I admit). He taught there each summer for several years, and I loved going. I am convinced there must be a reconstruction of it on the New Earth someday. Several pairs of high-powered binoculars were mounted on stands in the main room, which always intrigued visitors. We locals would climb several peaks each year, some quite challenging. The binoculars allowed us to view the whole path and our destination before we set off. With them, others could also keep an eye on us as we hiked.

This chapter, "An Ancient Vision for Sex," is meant to act like those binoculars. We're scoping out the path laid down by God to the top of the mountain. We must hold fast to the boundaries we are convinced are God's path (biblically) for our marriage. As such, we should never seek to please our spouse at the expense of God's design. Within His vision, we sacrifice and serve. In order to live more fully in that vision, we submit and devote.

I know that for so many, you have reached this point in the book and, Lord willing, for the first time are aware of the disunity and how it came into existence. You felt lost on the mountain of marriage somewhere, and for some, a lethal storm was blowing in. Your marriage could not last much longer and even if it did, it sure wouldn't be much fun. Now, you can see the top and where you went wrong. With a bit more mapping out, you can continue the hike.

So let's unpack a vision for sex that can become the peak we are aiming at. For at the top of the mountain is a Garden summarized in the phrase "naked and unashamed."

There are three main ways sex joins two people into one, which gives us an outline of the path ahead.

Procreation

Sex allows us to pass on our genes to our offspring. This command from the Lord to become co-creators with Christ and fill the earth extends back to Adam and Eve. God blesses the act of procreation and bringing forward abundant life (being "fruitful"). God looked at them and said, "Gotta fill this whole earth up with humans, so get to it!"

In procreation, we have the opportunity to unite ourselves and become one at a physical level by bringing our genes together and producing a new person. This miraculous version of two becoming one isn't subtle at all. Indeed, a whole new person, a spiritual human, is *created* in this process by God through the act of conception.

Having, loving, raising, and discipling children unites parents together over a common purpose. It can pose significant hurdles, especially to your sex life, as we discussed. I can attest, however, as a father of five children, that having kids is well worth it.

Millennials and Gen Z have fewer children and later in their lives.[5] There's certainly no moral issue I see with that, necessarily. God calls people to celibacy and singleness and knows every child who will be born. Having (conceiving, fostering, and adopting) children is good. Remaining single for ministry is also good, but having children far outweighs the inevitable challenges. Ginger and I got pregnant while I was studying for my master's and in a low-paying part-time ministry job. We were poor, certainly, but having our firstborn (after two miscarriages) continued to prove God's blessing in a way that finances never could.

There's a great deal you have to figure out along the way, but it's all worth it.[6] Ginger and I love parenting—I'm sure we could write a whole book together. While procreation is a massively important part of sex, especially theologically, I can't make it a focus of *Sex and Marriage*. Other Christian books cover the topic splendidly.

Partnership

The cultivation of absolute openness and freedom recaptures the Garden of Eden in beautiful ways. In Eden, Adam and Eve shared perfect, unadulterated, and open intimacy. Let's recapture what it must have been like and cultivate *that* for our marriages.

When we fully love and desire to grow the other person selflessly, each partner knows they can be open about their inner thoughts, feelings, and desires.

Two people who open up with the certainty that the other will secure and treasure who they are reflect the kind of love with which God loves His people. We would want for nothing if we possessed a perfect form of this security. Nothing in life would overwhelm us. No challenge would overcome us. You could always return to your spouse in any situation: doubt, fear, or heartache. Of course, our spouse can never provide the security that only God can, but we can be a rock to each other as images of God. Even in small moments of joy, like drinking a cup of coffee, reading a good book, watching a show, or completing a project at work, you can share that with your best friend, from whom you withhold nothing. Imagine being able to provide that for someone else.

This profound feeling of security is one of the greatest gifts you could ever give. Sex intertwines with this. Adam and Eve were naked and unashamed. In marriage, shaming one another has no place. Should we encourage each other? Yes. Help each other reach our goals, bringing one another closer to truth and growth? Even exhortation? Absolutely. But shame? Absolutely not.

We ought never to fear our spouse's harsh critique or harboring of shame toward us when we're naked. We want to submit our bodies to each other in sex. And in sex, we become most vulnerable. We should only become most vulnerable with whom we most trust. Adam and Eve didn't even notice how they were naked; they were so trusting and free of danger. What a wonderful ideal!

This trust and freedom is for men and women to enjoy. Consider Paul's revolutionary statement to the Corinthians about sex in marriage. Paul's world was incredibly different from ours, and the equality this statement brings would shock readers in those days.

> The husband should give to his wife her conjugal rights, and likewise the wife to her husband. For the wife does not have authority over her own body, but the husband does. Likewise the husband does not have authority over his own body, but the wife does. Do not deprive one another, except perhaps by agreement for a limited time, that you may devote yourselves to prayer; but then come together again, so that Satan may not tempt you because of your lack of self-control (1 Cor. 7:3–5).

Way too often, people will use 1 Corinthians 7 like a hammer to drive home a point about the frequency of sex and condemnation of saying "not today." Many will use it to say, "Every wife has to give her husband sex all the time, any way he likes it." When it comes to application, I feel the need to call BS on anything that treats this passage as envisioning something that ignores Paul's other teachings, especially in the same letter (cf. 1 Cor. 13)!

First, sex ("conjugal rights")[7] is clearly a critical part of marriage that Paul isn't at all squeamish about. He is saying to have sex, have it often, and give it as a gift to one another without withholding. There are many times when it feels difficult to get sex started, but both of you should affirm your spouse despite it being a sacrifice.

Second, when it comes to this picture of partnership, husbands must especially be sensitive to your wives. You don't get a free pass to do whatever you want sexually because of this passage. Sex should be filled with *love*, and it should be *unifying*, not just for your pleasure, especially not just the pleasure of men—and luckily, Paul defines love for us in chapter 13. Husbands and wives, as you give sex freely, remember to do it in love as defined in these ways:

> Love is patient and kind; love does not envy or boast; it is not arrogant or rude. It does not insist on its own way; it is not irritable or resentful; it does not rejoice at wrong-doing, but rejoices with the truth. Love bears all things, believes all things, hopes all things, endures all things (1 Cor. 13:4–7).

Husbands, if you are insisting on your way, irritable, envious, or rude, then you're not approaching your wife rightly.

Paul doesn't permit our demanding sex. Impatience, lack of empathy, unkindness, or anything else unloving is not permitted all of a sudden in sex because each of us gives up the authority over our bodies. Love and sacrifice should permeate sex just like everything else in our marriage.

Finally, Paul's last comment in 1 Corinthians 7 about self-control hits me a little sideways (the Bible does that sometimes). The phrase "so that Satan may not tempt you because of your lack of self-control" feels off. Do we have sex because we can't control ourselves otherwise? What's Paul, a single man, getting at with this comment?

I think the third point must be something like this: some people wield sex like a weapon or carrot. They intentionally withhold it or, God forbid, threaten with it. I would caution against even joking to this effect. We've all heard: "Bob's going in the doghouse tonight!" or the husband joking, "I better watch my mouth or it might be the couch for me!" In this context, withholding sex becomes punishment. Conflict is necessary and healthy in marriage, but punishment escalates and solidifies disunity rather than helping reach a resolution.

So, here, Paul is at least partially cautioning against weaponizing sex. He's saying, "Give your covenant partner what they desire sexually; give and receive sex freely in love, and never actively withhold it for any reason other than prayer." The temptation to seek affirmation is very real. The temptation comes from so much more than merely the physical, hormonal "uh-oh, my husband's feeling hot tonight, and I'm exhausted, but I don't want him to go to pornography or another woman—I'd better give it to him." That is *not* what Paul is saying. When significantly withholding sex causes your husband or wife to feel unappreciated, unloved, or unaffirmed, *that* is where unwarranted temptation enters the picture. The disconnect is the danger, not the lack of sex per se. The failure to connect can create a temptation to connect somewhere else—in any of many ways (emotional, physical, etc.); God has given sex to confirm and strengthen connections of those kinds.

Some people seem to think that the "sex" concept in the Bible fails to transcend the mere act of penetrative intercourse. Is it really that common to think of sex that way? What if asking about sex was a way of asking whether you and your spouse chose, aroused, experienced, and pleasured one another as a part of the living parable of God's love for His people? Surely this is what God intended for His word to indicate—naked and unashamed, right?

Men, when was the last time you considered that your wife enjoys sex and could enjoy it more if you did what pleased *her*? Are you having sex with her, assuming that she won't enjoy it, and essentially using her for sexual release? This command to give each other conjugal rights includes you, pal. If you can focus on giving her pleasure, watch how that increased enjoyment leads to better sex for you both! I'll discuss the application more in Part III.

The first step to intimacy and vulnerability is *trust* because what that person does with the information is scary: Will they judge me? Shrug me off and ignore me? Get angry with me? Leave me? Laugh at me? Gossip about what I share with them? Emotionally blackmail me? Women are often just as guilty of these abuses as men.

Chances are, if you're married to a human, *they will eventually break your trust.* That's where forgiveness, confession, apologies, and communication come in.

Timothy Clinton addresses this concept in *Attachments: Why You Love, Feel, and Act the Way You Do*: "Are you there for me? Can I count on you? Do you really care about me? Am I worthy of your love and protection? What do I have to do to get your attention, your affection, your heart? These are questions of attachment. When they cannot be answered positively, your psychological, relational, and even spiritual foundations can be shaken."[8]

Doesn't it make sense, then, that our intimacy affects our sexual experience? It defines it!

Pleasure (Illicit, Erotic, and Intimate)

This section is not yet about the mechanics of intimacy within sexual engagement; I'll cover that later. Here, I'm helping explain how intimacy is key to true sexual power within the marriage. *The true power of sex is intimacy, even in reference to pleasure.*

I categorize sexual pleasure into three kinds of experiences:

- Illicit. This kind of sex refers to sinful, secretive sex. This is entirely off the table for Christians. Think of this kind of sex like a house fire—hot but destructive, or like methamphetamine—powerful but lethal. Think of this as "experiencing a secret."

- Erotic. This sex includes physical arousal and erotic satisfaction, which serve an important role in married life. Erotic sex diminishes over time and depends on circumstances, so it's not absolutely necessary. Think of this experience of sex like a bonfire, hot without destruction but also without much investment, or like dessert, yummy but you will die of malnutrition if that is all you have. Think of this as "experiencing sex."

- Intimate. Sex like this is about fully "having" your spouse. It means knowing and being known by them in a vulnerable, open way. Think of this as the hearth fire, the stove fire, the kiln—one of the fires that can also get hot but has real investment quality, like a five-course meal. Dessert can be a nice aspect, but only as a part of a greater whole. Think of this as "experiencing your spouse."

Erotic and intimate sex often overlap. This makes sense; we get to have intimate experiences while enjoying erotic arousal. But, if we lack the erotic, we can still experience sexual *intimacy*.

We should aim for intimacy and erotic sex, but in marriage's essence, we *need* the intimate. The erotic comes and goes, though efforts can heighten it. To further the erotic, we need to understand our spouses deeply, i.e., through intimacy. So it turns out that intimate sex is the way to both. Of course, if sex is the only way you seem to connect intimately, this indicates a serious problem and makes intimate sex impossible. Conversely, if sex is not intimate, it's less likely to be erotic—especially for women.

This is critical. Since sex is intuitively more central to men's identity, it feels intimate *more easily*, whether their relationship is intimate in other ways or not, which can pose a danger. Sex can give the *false impression* of intimacy in other areas where none exists.

For women, sex is incredibly intimate, but usually only if the context and connection are intimate *prior* to sex. If a woman feels emotionally connected, then sex will become more intimate for her and probably more erotic as well.

Men can go straight to sex from nothing particularly romantic because, to most men, sex *is* romantic. When the woman wants him, she chooses him in his favorite way.

As women start engaging sexually, they have the rest of the day in their minds. If you were rude about how she forgot something at the grocery earlier, she'd remember it in bed that evening. And, thankfully, if you went to the grocery for her as a gift, she'd remember that in bed, too. This makes sense. Most women want to understand that sex is about her, not about sex, and romance, which we'll discuss in-depth later, communicates her preciousness to you.

Men: you need to realize that true intimacy not only arises from sex but must be cultivated in other places, too, and true intimacy nurtures sex. You can't live in an illusion.

Women: understand that men want to romance you, but to them, sex is an obvious and amazing way to connect with you intimately, so why wouldn't they take this route every time?

This is why sex during the honeymoon comes so easily to most. You're enjoying dinner at romantic, fancy restaurants every night, constantly lounging on the beach together, exploring the area, chilling out and talking, and experiencing every conceivable romance together *and* having sex. Were the surroundings romantic? Check. Were you having each other sexually? Check. Were you enjoying spectacular dates? Check. You had a lot of leftover psychological energy and you were investing a ton in one another.

However, as the schedule fills up, romance becomes less frequent, dates can become less and less creative, and the status quo is underwhelming. You'll still search for intimacy. Most husbands understand marriage requires intimacy outside the erotic, but their difference in perspective can lead to conflict when busyness forces you to prioritize. For most men, sex is high-reward intimacy with a low initial energy commitment. For him, lengthy, sumptuous dinners are great, and he probably loves those (if you're on good terms), but sex demands less investment and similar or superior levels of romance.

Healthy marriages require regular intimate sex, but even this should not become an *expectation*—the bane of all relationships. You need to prioritize time with one another outside of sex, obviously. Dates and time together are essential in all times of life, but so is intimate sex, to the degree both of you feel content. A lack of erotic sex may or may not reflect poorly on a marriage, but a lack of intimate sex always reflects poorly.

You want your spouse to be your best friend, but even your best friends outside of your marriage you don't have sex with. So sex becomes a privileged, sacred kind of intimacy between you and your spouse.

Erotic might mean buying the lingerie you want to see her in. Okay, that isn't bad, but it isn't enough to build a marriage on. Intimate sexuality is when you can buy the lingerie that she wants to be seen in by you. Those are *not* the same.

In *The Man's Guide to Women*, the authors survey discontented women. They find that "the first complaint is: 'He is never there for me.' The second complaint is: 'We are lacking in enough intimacy and connection.'"[9]

One of the greatest predictors of satisfied women in a relationship was men who could regulate their anger and emotions, making women feel "safe and heard."[10] On the flip side, what do men report? In a "general way, a man wants to be desired and to feel like the woman in his life wants him, adores him, and approves of him just the way he is."[11] If you've been reading up until now, neither of these sentiments should come as a surprise since we've talked about how men and women interpret sexual desire.

At our cores, humans desire affirmation, love, and to be understood. With this key, we can unlock our spouse's heart by affirming, loving, and understanding. Opening yourself up to this requires trust, which loops back to where we started this discussion. Practical considerations, not just the big life things, require trust.

Do you remember the first time you gave tips on kissing to your partner? How did they react? Apply the "start with me" principle: how did *you* react when your spouse gave romantic advice or tips? Were you defensive? Angry? Or did you humbly listen?

If we felt safe sharing ways for our spouse to pleasure us better and we in turn listened to them, think of the sexual freedom and eroticism it would reward us! The better you know someone, the better you can plan a party for them. Are they an introvert who likes to talk about deep things? Plan a dinner party with a few close friends. Do you know their favorite food or desserts? Do you know the kind of vibes they like?

The better you connect with your spouse, the "better" sex you can give them. Here, we return to the sleuthing principle. I believe the truest pleasure and fullest intimacy occur when we make love to one person and take joy in the fact that we are giving pleasure.

One of the purposes of marriage is to place boundaries around one of the most powerful forces that humans can experience. Sex is powerful. A commonly used illustration, and I use it all the time, is that sex is like fire. Fires require boundaries (fireplaces, firepits, candlewicks, etc.). In the cold wilderness of our everyday lives, the warm glow of sex provides life. A fire outside a fireplace can cause a wildfire that burns down everything it touches.

Intimate sexual experiences often naturally involve erotic sex, too, but it isn't necessary. What makes them the best? They have a compound interest. Their value grows as we invest in the same person year after year. We get better at experiencing *them*! This gives a healthy dose of reality and hope to those with diminished erotic drive or power (every year, my invitation to be on the cover of a fitness or style magazine seems less likely). How can I compete when I cannot compete on the erotic (or illicit) playing field? Don't ask our culture, because it doesn't know.

However, ask those who have been married, each trying to do it God's way for a long time, spending decades honing their skills at knowing and loving each other. Ask them what "naked and unashamed" means after they don't look as hot naked as they once did. The very concept of intimate sex should bring hope and new life to all of us as we lose some of our vigor.

I mentioned my grandparents earlier. They were married for sixty-two years and were sweet, warm, flirty, and even a little seductive the entire time I knew them. I suspect after six decades, they knew each other so intimately that they could create more sexual energy in a glance across the room than most newlyweds could in a week!

The fire in the fireplace can heat up just fine.

Don't Defile the Marriage Bed—Otherwise, No Holds Barred!

Once sex is in the fireplace, any fuel, starter, or lighter goes.

I have searched all through Scripture, and except for instances of ritual impurity, I cannot find a single restriction placed on the sexual behavior of a married couple. Obviously, everything we do should be kind and loving, but when it comes to specific sexual behaviors, the things condemned are always about something outside of the marriage covenant, and in those cases, *all* sexual behavior seems forbidden.

Of course, many sex acts that men and women can engage in are not specifically mentioned, but therein, they are not forbidden either. Keep in mind that this is not because the Bible is somehow squeamish about sex. Incest is specifically forbidden (Lev. 18:6–18). Is there anything more taboo than incest? Actually, maybe bestiality (sex between humans and animals), which is specifically mentioned and forbidden as well (Lev. 18:23). Clearly, the authors of the Bible, under the inspiration of the Spirit, are not afraid to forbid sexual acts between humans because it's gross to talk about.

Of course, sex acts should be agreed upon and mutually enjoyed when possible. We ought to be selfless, but if something is extremely uncomfortable for your spouse, work together toward mutual pleasure. And some acts are, for medical reasons, ill-advised, like reckless anal sex.

However, the Bible never says, explicitly or implicitly, "In sex, a husband and wife should not . . ."

In Hebrews, we find the closest thing to such a prohibition: "Let marriage be held in honor among all, and let the marriage bed be undefiled, for God will judge the sexually immoral and adulterous" (Heb. 13:4). How would one defile a marriage bed? Sexual immorality. I am confident that "sexual immorality" in this context refers to that very list from Leviticus 18, which talks about adultery, incest, bestiality, among others. Adultery can be understood to mean "sex with anyone other than your spouse."

In other words, unless the married couple brings someone else into their marriage bed or involves someone else in their sex life (pornography, polyamory, etc.), their marriage bed remains undefiled. The Bible is only anti-sex outside of marriage. *It is very pro-sex within marriage.* Before the covenant, we express purity by keeping our hands off (so to speak). Within the covenant of marriage, we celebrate the exact same purity with no holds barred (so to speak).

Christian ethics allows everything agreed upon, done in love, in sex by a married couple.

I stake a great deal of my thought on the idea that God means for us to integrate our lives with the spiritual. The spiritual truth about what sex represents and the spiritual engagement of marriage does not take away from the physical aspects. Marriage is holy *and* practical. Indeed, marriage is practical when it is holy. Humans are one-hundred-percent spiritual and one-hundred-percent physical. We're spiritual and physical "amphibians," as C. S. Lewis once remarked.[12] We discuss the integration of the biological and spiritual more in Chapter 9.

I'm a romantic and love the tales of knights and medieval stories of chivalry. I appreciate the holiness and reverence that medieval knights and kings seemed to grant sex. However, they and many other early Christian fathers fell prey to the trap that separated the spiritual and the physical, made the physical dirty, and followed piety at the expense of following Jesus in an embodied way.

When God created Adam, He formed him from the dirt. After He breathed life into him, he "became a living being." Previously, the King James Version translated the Hebrew word *nephesh* as *soul*, as though the real person is in the soul and the body is merely a shelter. God created a whole person when He created humankind.[13]

Dreaming About the Garden

Adam and Eve experienced completely integrated identities. The pursuit of and acceptance of intimacy with God is the foundation for recreating the Garden. Anyone can experience some degree of Garden perfection on Earth. Someday, we will have a city even better than merely the

Garden (I believe the Garden is within the eternal city described in Revelation 21 and 22). There, we will understand once again what it is to be truly human as God intended.

In the meantime, we can get more glimpses and tend to other relationships in an effort to reconnect with Eden. Obviously, marriage is intended to be the main human relationship for recreating the Garden experience. We learn to be vulnerable and safe and naked and unashamed with one other human, as fully intimate as possible, in coordination with our intimacy with our Creator.

How do we recreate this in the context of sex?

It is especially meaningful for wives when their husband takes the lead in exploring intimacy with God as a couple. Though I love to see when a husband leads his family in spiritual activities like prayer and Bible Study, neither spouse should neglect the spiritual in the other. (As a good guide, I'd recommend *Husband in Pursuit: 31 Daily Challenges for Loving Your Wife Well* and *Wife in Pursuit: 31 Daily Challenges for Loving Your Husband Well*.)[14]

Any excuse for ignorance, in the general sense, should be over by this point. I've intended for these understandings to be the core value of this work. It should have given you enough to begin to apply already. If there were nothing else in this book, I pray this would have radically changed your marriage life, especially in regard to sexual intimacy. Now that I've hopefully put to rest some key excuses for cluelessness, repentance will open up.

Repent

The Hebrew prophet, Hosea, once called on Israel to "return, O Israel, to the LORD your God, for you have stumbled because of your iniquity" (Hos. 14:1).

The Hebrew word used for "return" here is transliterated as *"shub."*[15] It is a primitive root that can mean or be attached to any concept of returning, literally or figuratively. It is strongly connected to the idea of "repenting." In the Hebrew and New Testament Scriptures, "repent" is usually understood as turning away from one thing and toward another. When we stumble away, intentionally or not, from the truth, we need to return to it as soon as possible. When we, like sheep, have gone astray, we need to return to the Shepherd and the love He calls us to.

Whether historically accurate or just a good way of comprehending the word, I was raised with the idea that "repent" was a military term (or like one).[16] It was a word that was an instruction to "do an about-face and keep marching." Imagine a soldier marching at normal speed due north; the sergeant gives the order "repent." In response, the soldier should now pivot 180 degrees and begin to march at the same speed due south.

After we gain new insight, we must repent. We must assimilate the new insight into our lives and allow it to transform our opinions, understandings, emotions, and behaviors.

Repenting is often the most challenging step when gaining new information. For thirty years, people have been coming to me in counseling settings, telling me that they "just need some tools." Rarely is this accurate. Usually, they have plenty of tools for success, but lack the willingness to change their thinking or behavior.

Not convinced? When I start counseling couples, I sometimes ask them to make two lists (separately from one another). In the first column, I instruct them to write small things they could do to bless their spouse. In the second column, they write some small things their spouse could do for them. Even if their marriage is in dire straits, it's astounding how often their predictions of what would bless their spouse are *correct*.

In other words, most couples know how to bless their spouse—they have the right tools. They just don't use them. How much more vital is it to repent when we gain new understanding and new tools?

Given Feldhahn's essential insight to this book, she charges us to apply our understanding: "Once you realize that your man is actually saying, 'This is essential to my feeling of being loved and desired by you, and is critical to counteract my stress, my fears, and my loneliness,' well . . . that suddenly puts it in a different category. So how might you respond?"[17]

From now on, I'll focus on applications for introducing and upkeeping your marital sex and romance. Up to this point, the lessons should hopefully have changed attitudes and behavior. If not, before you try to put into practice any more tools or applications, it may be necessary t o *repent*, in prayer to God and probably face to face with your spouse. Ever since I found Ginger's journal entry, as I mentioned in Chapter 5's "Bedside Chats," I've periodically repented of those bad habits and wrong mindsets to my wife. Reinterpreting past conflicts may make you realize your insensitivity, ignorance, or tendency to hurt your spouse, even (or especially) unintentionally.

An essential, but not sufficient, part of repentance is apologizing. Even if you never intended to hurt your spouse all those years, you should apologize if you suspect you wounded their feelings. Apologizing does not necessarily admit wrongdoing. It's an acknowledgment of having hurt them, right or wrong; apologizing is a real and practical tool for experiencing a powerful marriage and sex life.

My version of the "bedside chats" with my wife hurt because they piled shame on her for not making love with me more often (without me realizing it) even when she lacked the psychological energy to be aroused. I should apologize for that, and I did. And, in the future, I'll surely need to apologize again.

What should you repent of? What should you apologize for? What needs to be discussed between you and your spouse?

Refreshed with the insights from Parts I and II, and hopefully, with a repentant heart, we add and implement what we've learned.

Recap

Women, learn to trust your husband as he proves himself trustworthy, and open up to his efforts to love you. He won't be perfect, but neither will you. Realize that you can start thinking about sex as affirming who you are; he is affirming you as a person in his heart when he pursues you sexually.

Men, do you realize how precious your wife's heart is? How vulnerable and soft? When she trusts you, and you put her down, you're crushing her and making her close up. Treasure her well in the little things. Empathize with her always, especially in sex. It might take years to break down her barriers, but the process will prove wildly worth it.

You might express the sentiment of this chapter differently than I did. That's fine, but *communicate that*. If these chapters do nothing but make you think and talk deeply about these issues, I consider it a success.

Maybe your marriage is entirely flipped—maybe both of you are part of the percentage that is unlike the typical. Perhaps the husband separates sex from his identity, and the wife doesn't. That's fine—discuss it! (And in that particular case, read FAQs 1 and 2.)

In Part I, we looked at the nature of marriage—a redemptive, grace-filled powerhouse capable of providing healing, pleasure, and joy, but only when lived out according to God's design. In Part II, to apply the sacrificial principles, we turned to examine the differences between our preferences, perspectives, intuitions, and interpretations about sex. We ought to be motivated to understand and empathize so that we can serve one another (so that we can please God, if for no other reason). The need to serve, understand, and empathize applies to essentially every area of married life, but over the years, I have seen this pattern of misunderstanding about sex devastate what was meant to be a great strength of marriage.

Finally, we can focus on applying the principles from Part I and Part II into Part III. The application involves intentionality and anticipating the practical barriers. Let's dive in.

1. Cindy Beall, *Healing Your Marriage When Trust Is Broken: Finding Forgiveness and Restoration* (Eugene, OR: Harvest House Publishers, 2021); Susan Forward and Donna Frazier, *Emotional Blackmail: When the People in Your Life Use Fear, Obligation, and Guilt to Manipulate You* (New York: HarperCollins, 2019); Stu Weber, *Tender Warrior: God's Intention for a Man* (Colorado Springs, CO: Multnomah, 1999).

2. Allen P. Ross, "Genesis,'" in *Bible Knowledge Commentary: Old Testament*, eds. John F. Walvoord and Roy B. Zuck, (Colorado Springs: David C Cook, 1985), 31.

3. "H5828—'ēzer—Strong's Hebrew Lexicon," Blue Letter Bible, accessed October 31, 2023, https://www.blueletterbible.org/lexicon/h5828/kjv/wlc/0-1/.

4. Welch, *10 Choices*.

5. Amanda Barroso, Kim Parker, and Jesse Bennett, "How Millennials Approach Family Life," Pew Research, May 22, 2023, https://www.pewresearch.org/social-trends/2020/05/27/as-mille nnials-near-40-theyre-approaching-family-life-differently-than-pr evious-generations; Hanna Seariac, "Research: Why Is the Age of Marriage Increasing? Is Marriage Worth It?" *Deseret News*, June 5, 2023, https://www.deseret.com/2023/6/5/23749905/why-is-age-of-marriage-increasing.

6. Interestingly, I understand it that some ancient church fathers thought that sex was *exclusively* for procreation. They also believed that sex was a less spiritual activity that would distract from the Holy Spirit's influence. Some taught and still teach that the pleasure from sex, even within marriage, was somehow a necessary evil. Addressing them directly would take us too far afield. In my view, and I believe the Bible's view, sex is meant for more than that.

7. Though the Greek word here (*opheilen*) is a more general term about "obligations," "responsibilities," or "duties," I do think that in the sexual context of 1 Cor. 7, this specific usage being about sex makes a lot of sense. However, I also like the idea of the more general "husbands give to your wives what you ought and wives give to your husbands what you ought" because it reminds me of the "render to God what is God's" from Jesus in Matt. 12. Jesus clearly is telling us to give our whole self to God, since we bear His image. I like the idea that husbands should not withhold anything about a great marriage from their wives, nor should wives withhold anything about a great marriage from their husbands.

8. Clinton, *Attachments*, 12.

9. Gottman et al., *The Man's Guide to Women*, 13.

10. Gottman et al., *The Man's Guide to Women*, 10.

11. Gottman et al., *The Man's Guide to Women*, 12.

12. Lewis, chap. 7 in *The Screwtape Letters*.

13. Eugene F. Roop, *Genesis: Believers Church Bible Commentary* (Independence, MO: Herald Press, 1987), 39.

14. Ryan Frederick, *Husband in Pursuit: 31 Daily Challenges for Loving Your Wife Well* (Tacoma, WA: Lion Press, 2017); Selena Frederick, *Wife in Pursuit: 31 Daily Challenges for Loving Your Husband Well* (Tacoma, WA: Lion Press, 2017). While I haven't read the book for wives, I'm sure it's great too.

15. "H7725—Šûḇ—Strong's Hebrew Lexicon," Blue Letter Bible, accessed October 31, 2023, https://www.blueletterbible.org/lexicon/h7725/rsv/wlc/0-1/.

16. A bit of research led me in a circle. Some people seem to think it originates in military language, others don't. The linguistic concept is a bit tricky, so even the best scholars disagree about its nature.

17. Feldhahn, *For Women Only*, 121.

PART III

APPLYING SEX IN MARRIAGE

S ex and intimacy are intrinsically linked. If sex was intended to be well-integrated into our identities, then seduction should be a well-integrated part of the whole of our marriage!

Here, I will define seduction as creating the right conditions to draw and inspire our spouse into a state of enjoyment and arousal with us. It is a form, or application, of the intimacy in our marriage. Our whole lives are wrapped up in levels of intimacy—especially our marriages. So we cannot separate our "everyday" lives from sex, nor can we separate sex from our everyday lives. To create wonderful sex with our spouses, we must engage in *whole-life seduction*. The sex life of the intimate marriage is not in competition with the rest of the marriage. In a way, sex is like a metaphor for the rest of marriage since physical intimacy reflects intimacy more generally.

So, how, on any particular day, do we get from routine to the act of sex? Seduction. Seduction is nothing more than the effort to create feelings of *romance* (feeling wonderfully special to someone) and *arousal* (readiness to engage sexually) in your spouse.

Whole-Life Seduction

Whole-life seduction is about creating and tending the garden of your marriage so that it bears the fruit of sex through romance and arousal. Whole-life seduction is experienced in holistic *investment* in your spouse so they feel wonderfully special and freely desired. Through communication, you can help them do the same for you.

For this reason, each application section is about investment into romance, arousal, and pleasure. These applications will help you spend the time, effort, money, and energy that God has given you to steward where it will do the most good. Back to the garden analogy, this final part will show you how to water the plants, till the soil, and dispose of weeds. As always, the key is in caring and knowing about your spouse. Instead of selfishness, Part III hopefully inspires you toward personal growth.

I've taught the mindset of whole-life seduction for a few years, so imagine my satisfaction to find the concept in Feldhahn's work in her new 2023 book! Just before publishing *Sex and Marriage*, we read Feldhahn's *Secrets of Sex and Marriage*, coauthored with sex therapist Dr. Michael Sytsma. Imagine the satisfaction of discovering even more of the principles I had developed over the years encouraged or confirmed by their further work. For example, in their Chapter 8, they talk about holistic seduction: "Living seductively means bringing your best self to the party."[1] Read it after you finish *Sex and Marriage* if you want to go even deeper. We were overjoyed to discover so much consistency between their research and our findings! We barely got it in time to integrate some of their new findings into this book.

The application of the principles in this book leans toward the husband because most wives care more about the setting and romance surrounding sex, as sex isn't as intricately integrated into their identity. But as I've reiterated, sex and seduction is for every married person. If these tendencies are switched or just different enough in your marriage, read Part III through that lens. Plus, there's plenty for wives in Part III too, regardless of the generalities. And, good news, guys, once we learn to spot it, most of our wives are giving us insights all day on how to seduce them with more precision and prowess. Seduction in a covenant marriage is really just about loving your spouse better into a garden of experiencing all of God's best.

Whole-life seduction is about creating a marriage in which all forms of intimacy are intentionally sought out for your spouse and for your marriage in an effort to create the best *living parable of God's love*. For a whole-life seduction, we need to be in contact with our whole spouse—body, soul, spirit, and strength.

Whole-life seduction relies on the principles of agape sacrifice, "sleuthing," and "starting with me." How do I sacrifice in an effort to create a garden of intimacy in which sexual encounters are a fruit that grows naturally? These principles are not transactional (boooooo!) but align with what we all really want in our sex life: freedom, fun, grace, pleasure, joy, and glory to God.

What follows are investment strategies for *romance, arousal*, and *pleasure*.

1. Shaunti Feldhahn and Michael Sytsma, *Secrets of Sex and Marriage: Eight Surprises That Make All the Difference* (Ada, MI: Baker Books, 2023), 176.

Seven

INVEST IN ROMANCE

S adly, the Bible doesn't speak directly to every subject or answer every question we want answered. This is especially true about topics that weren't as culturally relevant thousands of years ago or aren't morally or spiritually purposeful. However, blessedly, this is not the case when it comes to romance. Though ancient cultures did not prioritize romance since marriages were usually arranged, praise God, we have the little book entitled "Ruth."

These wonderful four chapters introduce us to a Moabite woman (Ruth) and her Jewish mother-in-law (Naomi). They are in dire straits. To summarize, these two widows have few prospects for stability or safety. What they have going for them is Ruth's character and poise, and the fact that God has not forgotten them.

At the lowest point in the story, we are introduced to a man of similar character and caliber to Ruth—Boaz. During the two central chapters, we watch them fall in love. Even though they seem clueless about the building romance, the all-knowing older Jewish mother Naomi sees it. She watches them serve, protect, and sacrifice for one another. She also notices the generous gifts Boaz always manages to send Ruth home with. The reader hears Boaz and Ruth's awkward and touching conversation on the threshing room floor, where they confess their feelings for each other. Both are stunned that the other chooses them. I wish I could delve more in-depth into this story—seriously, go read it.

This touching romance in the foreign, ancient culture of Israel nevertheless feels familiar to us modern readers because the core features of romance transcend culture. Romance means a willingness to be sacrificial, generous, gentle, and look silly for someone else. It means wanting to create whatever your special someone desires, so they feel like your special someone. Romance is inspiring and magnificent, but more than anything else, it's a choice. Choosing to treat someone as a treasure is one of the most wonderful gifts of grace you can give another person.

Where Your Treasure Is . . .

The importance of romance can be found in Jesus's words from the Sermon on the Mount: "For where your treasure is, there your heart will be also" (Matt. 6:21).

It is not a very nice thing for Jesus to say. It even sounds mercenary, but it's true. As humans, our hearts tend to follow our treasure. If we gamble money on a football game, our hearts *follow* the game. If we spend exorbitantly on a dog that needs to be groomed every month, our hearts are invested in that dog. More than just money, treasure can refer to time and energy as well. So Jesus encourages us to invest in the eternal kingdom of God so that our hearts will follow.

I coach couples who have "fallen out of love" to set aside a weekend or two on their calendar. I make each of them secretly create the weekend of a lifetime for their spouse. In the counseling sessions, we strategize to determine their spouse's favorite activities, foods, and interests. We make lists, research options, budget, and get excited. You know what happens?

As one of them schemes to create a special weekend for their spouse, they often "fall back in love." They invest their treasure—time, thought, intentionality, money, etc.—and their heart begins to follow, just as Jesus predicted.

I'm almost always working on long-term, large-scale projects for my wife. I wrote a poem that took several years; I created a twenty-year photo album; I've planned dozens of trips and surprises. This is not me boasting. I'm telling you about a discipline in my life based on the teachings of the great rabbi Jesus. Of course, Jesus was talking about investing in the kingdom of heaven, but loving our spouses is surely one way to increase the kingdom. I think investing in my wife is one of the best stock options for investing in the kingdom. She gets to enjoy feeling loved by me, but I get to enjoy dozens of hours of my heart drawn near to her as I invest my treasure.

A few years ago, I taught through the sex and marriage material at Pine Cove, which, in addition to youth camps, hosts summer camps for families (which I highly recommend). After one of the breaks, Ginger whispered something she'd overheard from some of the ladies. They were saying how lucky Ginger was to be married to someone who was "naturally romantic." She thought maybe I should clarify some things.

I *am* an extrovert and naturally interested in getting people's approval. I'm also quite adaptable. Maybe those traits give me some kind of advantage when it comes to romance, but otherwise, I can assure you that I am *not* "naturally romantic."

In fact, I am not sure it's possible to be naturally romantic. By my definition, "romance" is a discipline. It takes expenditure (time, money, sleep, psychological energy) for something that isn't always very special to me but *is* special to my lover. Ideally, it's special to us both, but typically, what makes something romantic is the way it serves the other person. It's not particularly romantic for me to buy my wife a gas grill for Valentine's Day. If I buy her flowers, especially the kind of flowers that only I know she likes best, which I think are fine but which she adores, *that* is romantic.

A "romantic" definition of romance might be "anything that communicates a mysterious, deeply held desire for another person to make them feel special." Here's a thoroughly "unromantic," pragmatic definition: "Romance is the expenditure of resources to bless *your special person* in a way they will appreciate even if you don't."

Regardless of how you define it, you will not be very good at romance unless you're disciplined and intentional. So let's strategize together.

Romance Projects

I like to have a long-term project, a medium project, then little habits in the everyday to pursue my wife. A long-term project might be writing a bit of poetry every few weeks to be compiled into something a few years from now. A medium-term project might be planning a weekend getaway. An "everyday" romancing would be making the bed every morning. I also like to go out on dates with my wife every few weeks.

My wife does a wonderful job of loving me in countless little, medium, and big ways. That said, I mentioned before the anecdotal evidence from my counseling practice that if a man pursues his wife, the marriage essentially *never* fails. I think there's something special about a man's pursuit of his wife, but I digress. It's critical for both to actively romance one another.

Romance requires planning, habit, and discipline, which are all a part of *agape* love. Out of these roots, our marriage will bear fruit of fun, sex, joy, excitement, adventure, and support. Do you like reading together? Do that. Do you like playing video games together? Do that—without the children. Take your spouse to a nice restaurant, or a picnic, or a movie, whatever they like and you can afford.

What works and makes sense in your marriage will change over time, and all three categories don't need to be full steam ahead every day. Instead, think like this: "When was the last time I did something big for her? Well, it's been a few months. Probably start time to planning something." Or "Did I do anything to actively love my husband today? I guess not. Time to do something small!" And "When was the last time we had an evening just to ourselves? It's been a couple of weeks, so it's time to block a Friday off in the calendar!"

Even if you don't like planning or logistics, you'll need a bit of it. At the very least, you'll need to make a habit of carving time out on the calendar. If you're both spontaneous people, just use the guidelines to reflect on when the last time you did something big "spontaneously" was. Then, hurry up the spontaneity (as silly as it sounds). I'll strongly caution against the idea that "the romance isn't genuine if it isn't spontaneous." In fact, I'll outright reject it as a Hollywood cock-and-bull story. It's the easiest and most crippling excuse *not* to romance. Ninety-nine percent of the time, this attitude leads to less romance, not more. All things being equal, we drift away from romance unless we are intentional. Basing romance purely on spontaneity will mean basing romance on feelings, on *eros* love. We want to cultivate eros through romance, not base romance on eros—a classic cart before the horse situation.

If you use the everyday, medium-term, and long-term categories, your treasure will be put in your spouse, and your heart will follow. If you're doing none of these, start somewhere! Some men and women struggle with the creative aspect of this, so to jump-start you, I've included a quick list here.

- Tell your story of how you met and fell in love. Write it down or record it for them. You can purchase a book online with prompts to help. Fill it out with them in mind.

- Create a photo album of your life together. Gather photos, create a timeline, and get it made and shipped. This project took me three years, but it's among her favorite gifts.

- Plan a special trip of a lifetime (even if you do this several times in your life). Figure out their favorites and surprise them over and over with how well you know them.

- Write a word that describes them on their mirror (dry erase), a new one each week.

- Hide surprises for them around the house, like notes, gifts, or treats. This is especially good for when you're gone on a trip for a while.

- Have something special crafted for them. Find a blacksmith, jeweler, potter, musician, or painter to create something you designed especially for them.

Romance is the expenditure of resources in an effort to let someone else know that you want them to feel wonderfully special. The "wonderfully special" is pure poetry. The "expenditure of resources" is strategy and discipline. The more intimately we know someone, the better we should be at choosing the things that make them feel wonderfully special, even with limited resources.

To explore this subject and get more ideas, check out *Romancing Your Husband: Enjoying a Passionate Life Together* and *Romancing Your Wife: A Little Effort Can Spice Up Your Marriage* by Debra Smith.[1] In these books, Smith gives insightful ways to improve the romance of your marriage. My favorite aspect is her description of her and her husband's experiences navigating new attempts to romance each other. If it's new or fresh to your marriage, it may start clunky and awkward—that's okay! It's all a part of the process.

Limited Resources Romance

In times of limited resources, you must be more creative in investing your resources. If you are short on money (as many newlywed couples are), psychological energy (as many young parents are), or short on time margin (as parents of teens are), then your awareness must increase all the more.

Mark (my coauthor and editor), for the first-year anniversary with his wife, set up an elaborate spa evening, but he made it in-house. He turned their 700-square-foot apartment into a parlor, rearranging their plants, buying cheap candles from Target, cutting a sign out of cardboard, getting massage oil, spending a couple of hours on YouTube learning massage techniques, purchasing face masks, and ordering a couple dozen yards of tulle. The total cost came out to around fifty dollars and a few hours of preparation. You might be fifty years old with millions at your disposal, but a pillow fort is what your marriage needs, not another five-star resort holiday where you work the whole weekend. Lots of money is not essential to romance.

Indeed, be careful of finances. Women, if you *expect* five-star resort experiences, you're putting unwarranted pressure on your husband. I know most of you don't anticipate this kind of treatment; you just want to be known, loved, and cared for. Watch out, though. Depending on your lifestyle growing up, the treatment you expect may take a financial toll you're unaware of. Of course, plenty of wives take care of finances in a relationship, but the feeling of responsibility can sit heavily on a guy's shoulders. Husbands often feel stuck when their wives say, "I want you to spend more time with me!" while they simultaneously spend more and more money.

Those not in the corporate world can't easily understand how much work it takes to move up the competitive ladder. I've known many men who, after decades of slaving away over the corporate game, look back and realize they should have spent more time with their wives and kids. This sentiment is so common it's a trope. Maybe if they knew their spouse appreciated their *efforts* so much and not the *size* of their portfolio, they would feel a little less panicked about chasing higher salaries.

Another practical tip when you're low on energy instead of low on cash is *get a babysitter*. If one of you doesn't want to hire one, please reconsider. If your parents live close by, use them. In the first century AD, families mostly lived in houses close together, sometimes stacked on top of each other. This extended family communal home would probably make for some intense conflict with in-laws, but the upshot was the whole family raised the children, not just a couple and certainly not single parents. The truth is, *we're not built to raise our kids on our own*. If you're far from your family, babysitters or spiritual parents in your church are essential in the early years. You'd be surprised how often an empty nester in your church would love to take your babies for an evening—*for free.*

In the earlier part of my marriage, I would come home from work (probably exhausted myself), throw the kids in the bathtub for about an hour, and let Ginger have her time to do whatever she wanted. This was an act of love in and of itself; I didn't "expect" to have sex because I did that every night. But she did have more psychological points for lovemaking later if she wanted to; and much of the time, we did end up wanting sex together.

Wives, romancing him may mean something obvious, like buying yourself lingerie and creatively seducing him. Husbands, romancing her may mean something obvious, like planning a summer vacation.

Or your husband might want a spa day with cucumbers for his eyes—to relax in the hot tub with a glass of wine. Maybe your wife wants you to buy something kinky. Maybe she hates flowers, but she would kill for a gas grill!

That's the trouble with writing this whole chapter; I can only give you generalities and guidelines. Keep the principle in mind here: What will make your spouse feel special feelings, and what lets them know they create those special feelings *in you*?

Romance and Personality

In addition to romancing with limited resources, we need to learn to romance our spouse by understanding their quirks, desires, and ways of thinking. Gary Chapman's immensely popular book, *The Five Love*

Languages, is a good starting point.[2] The system isn't foolproof (make sure not to let it create expectations). I also think it was a mistake to put sexual engagement under the heading of "physical touch," since I think sex should represent an expression of any and all of the languages, but it's still a great conversation starter if you feel stuck. Chapman divides the "love languages" into five categories: physical touch, quality time, gift giving, acts of service, and words of encouragement. All of us love any and all of these, but some feel more natural and uplifting. I'm amazed at how often people discover Chapman's material, and it's the first time they realize people like to be loved in different ways. It's a little disconcerting, but it explains a lot.

You could also look into personality tests. All personality guides are rough approximations. Some are better than others. The best one is Myers–Briggs. (I think the Enneagram is the worst, although it has spawned an entire Christian literary movement.) As an example from the Myers–Briggs, say your husband is a strong "J," which is a "judger." This probably means they'd rather plan things ahead of time with an itinerary. This will give him a sense of security and calmness. On the flip side, say your wife is a strong "P," which is a "perceiver." This means they'd likely rather adapt on the fly to feel a sense of adventure and excitement. These tests can serve as another great catalyst for discussion.

Appreciation and Romance

How about something that costs no time and no money? Appreciation.

Appreciation is possibly the most romantic expression. Why is it tough to communicate appreciation when our wife does something for us? Why does it feel strange to express gratitude for our spouses' everyday responsibilities? Why is it tough for a wife to thank her husband for facing the stressors he takes on for their family? Pride is a possibility, but perhaps it's more defensive than that. Maybe we think if we give our spouse a "well done," they won't feel motivated anymore. Of course, we all know deep down we're *more* motivated by appreciation, not less, but maybe that's our irrational concern anyway. Or perhaps it's because we feel a sense of competition with our spouse and want them to appreciate what *we* do?

Honestly, I don't know what we each may feel that appreciation costs us, but we don't do it enough! So here's a homework assignment: Tell your spouse three things you appreciate about them. Let it cascade into more things if you can think of them. The more genuine appreciation you can jam-pack into your day, the more romantic and brighter they'll become.

Appreciation is a treasure that we can invest in them that protects them *and us* from bitterness and resentment. In the process, we encourage our favorite things about them, which encourages more of the same! A basic rule in counseling is to reward what we want more of. Appreciation is a powerful reward. Seriously, think of something right now that you appreciate about your spouse, maybe something no one else knows about, and tell them. Watch their face brighten, their smile appear, and their shoulders relax a little. Keep sleuthing the appreciation that means the most to your spouse.

Romance is a discipline; world-class romance means disciplining yourself to communicate appreciation for the things no one else even notices.

Romance and Sex

How does romance intertwine with sex? If both husband and wife can romance and arouse each other, we get seduction, and seduction leads to sex. Even if it takes each person sacrificing for the other, the end result is beautiful. Typically, women feel more inspired to make love to their husbands when he romances her outside the bedroom. He's not romancing her to get sex. He's romancing her the way she wants to be romanced, creating special feelings in her. The husband desires sexual intercourse because it creates romantic, special feelings in him in and of itself. So she's arousing him to create feelings of romance in him. All of this arouses her, which means both are romanced and aroused—sex follows.

This may be surprising to some of you ladies, but your husbands will often appreciate your assertiveness in seduction. You may have grown up thinking men were the only ones who were "supposed to" lead or initiate, especially sexually. Actually, most husbands want you to lead out in sex and show your desire for them. Dr. Kevin Leman puts this point well: "Some of you have been taught while growing up that, to be attractive to a male, you have to be sweet, soft, and follow a man's lead. But do you know what that husband of yours secretly wants you to be? Sexually assertive! [. . .] There's not a man out there who doesn't want to feel prized, loved, and sexually desirable."[3]

Remember, when you show your desire for sex with him, you're affirming *him*. It's easy to see how, given what sex means, sex and special feelings (and thus romance) are intertwined for men. His wife sexually pursuing him becomes a powerful romantic experience. Remember, sex makes many men feel at home, welcomed, known, and loved, and these strike romance.

However, there is a trap that gets set in these conversations. Speakers often treat sex in marriages as transactional—"You give me this in exchange for that." It's an egregious error. This mindset can undo a lot of our work so far, so it'll be one of our focuses in Chapter 8.

We've seen five ways to go about romancing each other. This includes dates and poetry, video games and reading, getting babysitters and time alone, romancing with tight resources, and ways to be intimate with your spouse. Ultimately, it's up to you to figure out what works best for your best friend and lover.

---

1. Debra White Smith, *Romancing Your Husband: Enjoying a Passionate Life Together* (Eugene, OR: Harvest House Publishers, 2013); Debra White Smith and Daniel W. Smith, *Romancing Your Wife* (Eugene, OR: Harvest House Publishers, 2005).

2. Gary Chapman, *The Five Love Languages: How to Express Heartfelt Commitment to Your Mate* (Chicago, IL: Moody Publishers, 2009).

3. Kevin Leman, *The Intimate Connection: Secrets to a Lifelong Romance* (Ada, MI: Revell, 2019), 102.

Eight

BARRIERS TO ROMANCE

A s often as there are voids—failures to be romantic—there are, of course, barriers to romantic feelings. In other words, things we do or say or even steal from our spouse give that feeling of being wonderfully special. Sadly, one of the most insidious and cancerous of these is encouraged by some of the most famous Christian teachers, pastors, and marriage books—*transactional thinking*.

My wife and I were at an event for couples and families a few years ago, and the event began with a common activity in which the couples share their highs and lows from the year before. It became clear that several of the couples were barely making it. In some cases, the husbands referenced their wives finally following through with "the week." It did not take us long to discover that the year before, a well-meaning speaker and pastor had taught about sex. He used outdated and dangerous material that says men's top "need" in marriage is sex. (Which we have shown to be false. It is not *sex* but what sex *means* that is special to most men. Even what sex means is not a "need" per se). Using this assumption, the pastor then challenged the women to initiate sex every day for one week and to choose different lingerie for each of those nights. The materials and the teacher taught created an incredibly strong sense of "transaction" when it comes to sex. They treated sex as a commodity that wives have and owe their husbands, especially in return for gifts and favors.

The men didn't know how to correct this thinking since it's tough for most men to intuit any distinction between engaging sexually and feeling desired, and the women, striving to be good Christian wives, tried to accept and even apply this homework assignment (shudder). They even tried to laugh as the pastor called for high fives from the husbands in the audience for trying to help them.

I know this pastor. He is a good and godly man. He is a sound teacher of Scripture. Christian publishing from the last thirty to fifty years had misled him to the detriment of dozens of marriages. He is not alone—these books have probably misled millions.

Transactional Sex, "Sex Starts in the Kitchen"

Often, Christian and secular marriage authors just say stuff (I can be guilty of it too). They seem unaware of the way that their own personal experiences inform what they then may project as absolute truth. I recently encountered one of these authors who casually mentioned, "At least 60 percent of marriages will experience infidelity." But this is just patently false. It's more like 10 to 25 percent (up to 45 percent if you include nonsexual affairs).[1] Of course, it makes sense that a therapist is going to overestimate infidelity since so many clients come in with infidelity as a presenting issue, but this kind of misstep can create lasting damage. A person hearing this statistic may feel more paranoid about their faithful spouse, or, on the other hand, they might feel like it's not so bad to cheat after all.

One of these patterns has to do with presenting marriage as essentially "transactional." I do not remember who or where, but years ago, I heard someone theorize that cavemen wanted access to sex and cavewomen wanted protection for their offspring, and viola—marriage! Fine, theorize away, but as mentioned before, I believe marriage was not an unfortunate but necessary exchange of resources but rather designed to serve a theological purpose!

However, so many Christian marriage books over the last few decades have presented marriage as essentially the same thing: a negotiated exchange of resources. He trades providing her "needs" in an effort to get his "needs" from her. This exchange is not the vision presented in God's word and as you will see, it can be toxic.

Here's an excerpt from a Christian bestseller that does an excellent (terrible?) job of expressing the nature of a transactional marriage. I have no doubt this concept was communicated in an effort to help, and I am sure it has helped many (sold over two million copies), but I think these concepts can be easily misunderstood and misapplied, and I want to help us avoid that error.

> He (the husband) makes a commitment because he trusts her to be available to him whenever he has a need for sex, just as she trusts him to meet her emotional needs. Unfortunately, in many marriages, the man finds that putting his trust in this woman has turned into one of the biggest mistakes of his life.[2]

Do you see how this is not about the integration of two into one, but the exchange of what one "needs" for what the other one "needs"? Neither sex nor emotional desires are "needs" (see FAQ 5). This is not grace or love; this is a negotiation for what I'm willing to give in order to get what I want. I believe that this is flat wrong, and I've written *Sex and Marriage* largely as a response to this transactional way of thinking.

Thousands of pastors and teachers have used books tainted with *the sex lie* and *transactional thinking* for decades. Some of these teachers have been talented and sound enough to make something valuable of the compromised books, but I know that for many, disunity was sown into marriages, and the power and dignity of true intimacy was stolen from people who assumed that someone who could get a book published and become a bestseller was a true expert.

I am sorry so many of you were misled. As a pastor and therapist now, I refer only to books by theologians that speak to the theology of marriage (like Chan's *You and Me Forever*), books based on research (like Feldhahn's), or good efforts at meta-analysis, which is sort of how I see my efforts in this book.

I don't want to cite more negative examples. This decision is not motivated by cowardice, but, especially as an inexperienced writer, I never want to become a weapon against another believer. I hate calling into question the integrity of anyone who claims to be seeking God's best for people when I don't have any good reason to doubt their intentions.

For this reason, rather than rake several of these books and speakers over the coals in the limited time I have here, I decided to include Amazon reviews from several of the best-selling Christian marriage books to show what I'm talking about. I want us to see how easy it is to interpret anything that seems to endorse a transactional mindset in a damaging way. These are actual comments from Amazon from various Christian marriage books that are the most famous and the most transactional. We're not endorsing these comments (many of these bestselling books have high average reviews), but they sound exactly like the remarks I've heard in my counseling office.

"We got through four chapters over a few weeks and then tossed it in the recycle bin. It reads like it was written in the 1950s. Granted there are some good discussion questions that led to some great conversations between my new husband and me, but it was just nearly intolerable to read. I peeked at later chapters and was outright offended by some things. **(As a woman that I know nothing of my own sexuality and that I need to count calories and wear the makeup that my husband prefers. WOW.)"**

"The other one-star reviews sum up my issues with this book—**it's sexist, overly simplistic, and very dated.** The author doesn't back up any of his claims, just cites questionnaires he's given to his patients over the years."

"What do I need to do to keep my husband from having an affair? **Give him sex whenever he wants and stay skinny throughout our marriage.** What does he have to do to keep me from having an affair? Make sure he has a well-paying job. Horrible advice for the modern couple. If I could give it zero stars, I would."

"Basically this whole book is built around the idea that all problems in a marriage are because a woman won't have enough sex with her husband. **If a woman would just have more sex with her husband, all problems will magically be fixed.** It's also completely based around religion and tries to come up with biblical rationale for his reasoning."

"It also carries the thought pattern of the wife fulfilling her husband's needs and suggests it is her fault if he strays because of a lack of sex at home. **Sex is taught as something that is only for men.**"

"**One of my problems with this book is that no matter the problem it always fell on the wife to fix it.** A husband cheats then his wife needs to give him more sex so he isn't tempted to look elsewhere. Husband wants to divorce; his wife didn't do a good job of showing him appreciation and satisfying him sexually. I could go on and on with these different examples that didn't sit well with me or my husband [. . .]."

"**The expectations and misunderstandings that this book seeded took us years (literally *years*) to overcome.** I wish I had never tried to educate myself with this drivel and had just approached sex with the same love, patience, and selflessness that makes every other part of our relationship satisfying. If you are considering this book because you think it speaks for women and will clue you into how your wife thinks and feels, read some of the other reviews from women, it won't."

"This book also teaches that a woman needs love, not sex. This book basically teaches **that a man is entitled to sex** and without it doesn't feel respected, who cares what the woman wants out of sex. I need to make her feel loved, whatever that means. If you have this book I urge you to throw it away."

I cringe to read them. While many reviewers suggested this kind of thinking was acceptable in the past, I disagree. It may have been common, but it was never the best. The value of sex is the empowerment of intimacy (exactly as biblical theology would predict) and not transactional interactions like two addicts who depend on an addictive substance.

As I mentioned earlier, I once had a client say, after reading one of these books, "So men want a prostitute who cleans their house." You can imagine that this concept didn't make her feel more united to her husband. Her husband responded, "Well, all women want is an emotionally brilliant therapist of a husband with a steady paycheck."

Pitting two people against one another—the opposite of intimacy.

Dr. Steven Snyder relates the worst possible scenario:

> Some women who've lost desire will keep having sex with their partner out of a sense of responsibility—or just to keep the peace [. . .]. All your sexual self knows is that it's being forced to do something it doesn't want to do. It doesn't like that one bit, of course. So what happens next is no surprise: You lose desire. Sex begins to feel like an obligation. Now you really lose desire. Most low-desire women eventually realize that obligation sex isn't the answer. But then there's still the problem of what to do with a partner who's still interested. Under the circumstances, many women start avoiding anything that might turn their partner on.[3]

Consider this last quote, especially if you sense that your spouse has become less affectionate. Could it be your spouse is under the impression that if they are affectionate, you may immediately move to sex—which they are afraid to trigger?

The wrong kind of obligation can rob marriages of joyful sex. Expectation and rigidity will rob it of freedom, but, of course, marriage entails sexual intimacy!

Too often, the phrase in this chapter title, "sex starts in the kitchen," comes across as "bargaining for sex" or, even more darkly, a kind of purchasing sex with good behavior. I put the heading "sex starts in the kitchen" in quotes because there is *something* true in the sentiment (which we have already unpacked in Chapters 5 and 7). That is, sex is often more intrinsically romantic for men than for women. In addition, sex usually requires more psychological energy from women to start, but when only part of the story is told, it sounds transactional. Here's an example from Dr. Kevin Leman, writing to men to serve their wives as a part of "when sex actually begins":

> It begins when you remember to take the garbage out and pick up your dirty socks and put them in the laundry where they belong. It continues when you rub your wife's back and give her a sweet kiss as you make her coffee in the morning before you both go out the door. It continues when you text her, "I'm thinking about you" over lunch. It ramps up when you add, "Don't worry about picking up that dessert for the party tonight. I know what you like. I'll pick it up and meet you at home."[4]

The call to serve is admirable. I've found some great nuggets from his book, *Sheet Music: Uncovering the Secrets of Sexual Intimacy in Marriage*, where he delves into the intimacy of sex.[5] Since you have the interpretation tools from this book, you can probably see a potentially beautiful application of this exact teaching (which I think Dr. Leman intends, by the way). See how this fits in with all these puzzle pieces? His point is helpful for guys to hear, and at some level, it's true *if the mindset of both the man and the woman are good.*

Nevertheless, I still feel unsatisfied with Dr. Leman's explanation. After men read this, they may still be confused when she doesn't just want to jump into sex. After all, he did these "romantic" things. If we're not careful, we're going to end up helping our wives with chores *for* sex, or we'll end up expecting sex as a reward or an entitlement. "Sex starts in the kitchen" implies that if I start in the kitchen, it will end in sex!

If he invests in protecting some of her psychological energy by helping with chores, like working in the kitchen, then *if* she gets in the mood later or is willing to be seduced later, she will have the energy points she requires to engage! In other words, it is a *part* of the whole-life seduction mindset, which is not about transaction but about knowing and serving.

If we think through the lens of energy, it helps clear up why women care about the context surrounding sex. If your wife is worried about the state of the house, she will feel drained. If she's spending all day overwhelmed with kids and projects around the home, her tank will be depleted by the end of the day. And remember, it takes most women energy to get started. Remember to sleuth your spouse's preferences to help her feel loved with limited resources. The accuracy of the idea that "sex starts in the kitchen" is that she needs her mind clear, responsibilities taken care of, and most importantly, the energy to get sex started.

One of the amazing things about sex, wives, is that sex encourages your husband; it affirms him as he loves you. Though he shouldn't feel entitled or serve you so that you'll make love to him, having sex does affirm him just like his service affirms you. And remember, making love probably even replenishes *your* energy if you have it to invest at the start.

Remember the picture your marriage should be: Freely giving and giving up our preferences for the other. Both of you should work toward the same goals: freedom, life, and abundance. However, both sexes need to avoid the impression that sex is a commodity that the woman has and trades for other advantages for herself. Either spouse should not view making love as a bargaining chip for chores, work, or kindness in an effort to get sex in payment. This mindset only encourages disintegration, leading to women thinking of their bodies as meat and men feeling entitled to sex as long as he does chores.

Imagine the consequences of the transactional mindset. A husband is half-heartedly doing the dishes, checking off a to-do list. At the end of the day, when he says he wants to have sex, his wife says, "What about the lawn?" He slaps his forehead—he forgot that one chore. So sex or no sex? What if he wines and dines her, but she suddenly comes down with period cramps? Does she owe him a debt? During the whole date, will she think, "He's just doing this to get sex!" Or maybe, "I bet he expects sex in exchange for this date, but I have a furious headache. What should I do?"

Of course, the reverse is quite tragic, too. Imagine, after a wonderful date, the wife shuns her husband's advances because she remembers that it's only the first date in six months—and he needs to do better than that to "get some!" She wants to hold the carrot on the stick in front of him a bit longer. Not very romantic at all.

Transactional thinking creates a tall barrier to romance and sex indeed.

Expectations

You've probably noticed by now I don't like expectations. In every chapter, I probably mention the danger of expectations at some point, so it's past time to talk about it. Part of the reason why we feel so lost is we compare ourselves or others to impossible standards (think of the touched-up Instagram model). It is one of the many reasons why pornography is so incredibly damaging. Before I go too far down that path of talking about pornography, let me explain the concept of expectations psychologically.

Expectations are natural. Our brains are hardwired to group experiences under headings to make predictions so we can amply prepare. This ability is one-hundred-percent necessary to function in day-to-day life, especially to survive psychologically. Some basic expectations: I will wake up tomorrow. I will go to work tomorrow. My car will get me to work. Politicians will lie. These expectations are *predictions*.

If you don't have to go to work tomorrow because there's a holiday you forgot about, you feel good. It's a positive breaking of your expectations. (Woohoo!) Positive, broken expectations are surprises.

If your car doesn't turn over the next day because your kid left the overhead light on, how do you feel? That broken expectation feels a bit different, and you might have colorful language to describe it. Expectations can be broken in positive or negative ways, but the result is usually negative.

If you have an emotionally dysfunctional family, going to Christmas will have hurt feelings associated with it. So you need to be mentally prepared for those fights; you have an emotional war ahead of you. You're expecting (*predicting*) how Christmas will turn out based on your past experiences, which allows you to set your mood accordingly.

So you expect to have verbal fights and for Christmas to go terribly. Naturally, then, every Christmas, you'll be on edge. These expectations may exist without you even knowing it.

If you marry into a wonderful family, and your in-laws have awesome holidays, Christmas means presents, warm cocoa, holiday spirit, and jolly times. Even so, you'll have your expectations leftover from your childhood. That means you'll be ready to fight and on edge, expecting a trap at any moment.

You may even think to yourself, sitting at your in-laws' house, everyone else having a great time: "Why am I in such a rotten mood?"

It makes sense because you *expect* the holidays to lead to all kinds of trouble.

Your mood may lead to conflict with your spouse and alienate your in-laws. In this case, you have to *unlearn* your expectations so you can enjoy Christmas with your in-laws. You have to shift your predictions.

As a marriage counselor, I can say right now that these buried and unknown expectations, which I call "life rules," will probably be the greatest source of tension in your marriage. Uncovering these with the aid of others would help every couple immensely because everyone has them.

Other expectations are like demands—they are *normative*. In other words, a boss expects that you show up on time to work. Otherwise, there will be consequences. The IRS (sadly) expects you to file taxes. Other humans expect you not to steal from them.

Often, however, predictive expectations can become normative expectations. Let me give an example of how this idea of expectation can affect your marriage.

Do you think the wife should do the dishes and you should get to watch TV after dinner because that's how your dad did it? Well, your wife may have grown up where her dad did the dishes and her mom read a book after dinner. So your life rules come into conflict. After dinner, what happens? Your wife reads a book, you watch TV, and the dishes don't get done, but you both expect (*predictive* and *normative*) them to be done . . . hmm. Do you smell that? It smells like dirty dishes and an argument brewing.

We each have hundreds of unknown, invisible expectations and life rules that we have to deal with in marriage.

And this point becomes clear: you have expectations about sex and romance. Both of you. And it built up for decades without you even realizing it. The James Bond movies, pornography (which statistically guys are exposed to when they're thirteen, though many, myself included, were introduced much earlier),[6] *The Bachelorette*, hundreds of skimpy magazines in the checkout lines, *Cinderella*, and hours of movies that include romance and sex all can contribute to these hidden expectations.

Perhaps most important, though, are your friends, family, and mom and dad. Maybe your mom and dad never showed physical affection in front of you, or *ever*, for all you know. These will affect your expectations. Your wife may wonder why you never show her affection in public or around others, and it might deeply hurt her feelings. You might not have thought about it—you're just subconsciously mimicking your parents.

Jessa Zimmerman puts it like this: "Sometimes these messages have been loud and explicit. Sometimes, sex has seemed almost invisible, and no one was talking about it. Either way, your brain puts together a picture of how sex works, what it means, and how you are supposed to feel about it. You build an image of what to expect. By the time you started to be aware of sex and were becoming a sexual being, what were you expecting? What specific ideas did you form about what sex should be?"[7]

We often equate the *predictive* expectation with the *normative* expectation. In other words, this is how sex *usually* seemed to work, so this is how it *should* be. I predicted I would get to watch TV after dinner, so that's how it *should* be. Some expectations are there because of pornography or unhealthy past sexual relationships.

I hate to break it to you, but you're simply *not* going to be having a candlelit dinner in Paris every date night. In the arena of romance, you may have some Disney fantasy expectations. I'm cautioning you against expecting those unattainable romantic feelings that you see in movies and chick flicks.

Let's return to Bride and Groom for a second and remember how Groom expected rose petals, seduction, and sex the night he got back from the trip.

If Groom hadn't expected (predicted) "welcome home sex," then when his wife was 99 percent asleep, he wouldn't have been so upset the next day or that night. Understanding how his wife thinks would help deal with his *false expectations*. His expectations didn't even come from bad sources; they came from a beautiful act of love from his wife from the last time he went on a business trip. But these expectations for rose petal seduction are misguided, regardless of how good the source is. It becomes a lose-lose scenario for him.

I want to be super clear about this. I'm not saying you need to lower expectations. I'm saying that you need to *get rid of them* wherever possible. I view them as, at best, a rarely necessary evil. March them up a mountain, place them on an altar, and set them on fire—let it be a pleasing aroma to God.

Again, we typically mean two things when we use the word "expectation," and they are better and clearer options. We mean *predict*, as in "I expect that it will rain later," or *boundary* or *requirement*, as in "I expect you to not sleep with anyone other than me in our marriage."

In the former case, I don't know that what word you use really matters since there is no real personal connection to it. In the case of the latter usage, it is better to make this a request, plea, or, if necessary, a boundary (for guidance on how to set boundaries well, I recommend *Boundaries* by Townsend and Cloud[8]). It seems like an important boundary, for example, to set with your spouse so that they do not sleep with anyone else. For things you desire, communicate this as a hope and prayer with and for them, and then communicate appreciation and celebrate them for their faithfulness!

Imagine your parents always expected you to get straight As. When you got As, did your parents celebrate your hard work and accomplishment? Probably not. But what would happen if you got *one* C? You probably got lectured or punished.

A better way is to have a minimum grade in mind, with consequences attached, and encourage rather than tear down. Then, when your kids get all As, it's a huge celebration. If they get mostly Bs, that's also great. But notice, if you have high expectations, the best success becomes *meeting* expectations, and then it becomes impossible to celebrate.

This harkens back to Chapter 1's "Coming Up with Marriage from Scratch," when we talked about how giving love freely is the heart of relationships, especially marriage.

What I mean is this: Enjoy the moment for itself when possible, and don't worry about what you *expect* will happen. Don't build anything on the expectation of sex or whether you'll steal a great potential joy from you and your spouse. Let me share a simple equation and rewind the Bride and Groom story again.

Groom *expects* to have amazing sex when he gets back from his business trip.

Expectation → Have awesome sex

Let's play out three scenarios and see what they lead to if Groom *expects* this kind of rose petal sex.

- Doesn't have sex → Serious disappointment

- Has sex but no unique and exciting seduction → Disappointment

- Has awesome sex → Meets expectations

Yikes. So it's pretty much a *lose-lose-okay* scenario. This doesn't seem ideal.

Let's play out the three scenarios again, but this time, Groom has no expectations, only desires and hopes:

- Doesn't have sex → Still disappointed (he can't help it) since he had desired to engage sexually, but he's okay. No one gets all of their desires met all of the time, after all.

- Has some sex but no crazy seduction → Fantastic—what a fun gift to experience this together!

- Has awesome sex → Wow! Amazing, what an awesome surprise!

With this mindset, it's pretty much an okay-win-win scenario.

This is an attitude shift and a reality check that will fundamentally change your marriage. As humans, this process is extremely difficult, I grant that. It can be hard to diminish predictions and normative expectations. Remember, husbands, you get to come to your wife and talk through your feelings if you do feel disappointment (new skill acquired!).

Your wife will not think you're weak for expressing disappointment. She will just be relieved that you've come to your senses. In the case of Groom and Bride, let's say that they didn't have sex, and Groom feels a bit of natural disappointment. Imagine if Groom asks her about her weekend the next day. She will probably spill all the craziness of yesterday that happened while you were gone that you knew nothing about. She had to go to her sister's house and help with a crisis, run a bunch of errands, and deal with a work emergency, so she was completely exhausted by the time you arrived at 11:00 p.m. When you hear her side of the story, you'll empathize with why she forgot about sex or why her tank of psychological energy was empty by that time.

At this point, you can express how you were looking forward to making love with her, but being with her is enough, and you're glad to be back with her. You can also talk about how you were looking forward to sex, but add how you entirely understand that her day was exhausting, and also ask, "How can I help with your sister?" or "Could I get a few chores done for you?"

Don't feel afraid to communicate to her, "I was looking forward to sex with you, so I'm a bit disappointed, but trust me, I totally get why it didn't happen last night." Maybe at that point, bring up how you guys could have a nice dinner that night and then have sex afterward.

Less expectation, less expectation, less expectation.

More communication, more communication, more communication.

Communication Breakdown

The general communication failure between the male and female sexes is the topic of thousands of books (and again, the differences are generalities, not universals).[9] My example is anecdotal, but it might offer some insight. Consider a man driving and a woman in the passenger seat. He's in the fast lane, maybe fifteen feet behind the granny car going seventy in a seventy-five mile per hour lane. She comments, "Babe, you're following that car in front of us too closely."

He might rudely retort, "Well, I can pull over if you wanna drive." Or maybe he'll look at her incredulously like she just insulted his family name. At this point, I want to ask: Why is defensiveness such a common response? And why is she caught so off guard by his tone?

Men appear to more commonly communicate *critically*, whereas women more commonly communicate *consultatively*. Critical communication is typically information I think you need to correct an error. Consultative communication is meant to give you information I believe you want so that you may make a change, even if only for my sake or our relationship's sake. The difference is subtle but can be a real barrier to romance.

Two women are riding together. The passenger suggests, "I think you're riding that car kinda close." The woman driver hears, "I think the car is so close, it's causing me anxiety, and I know you would never want me to feel unnecessary anxiety." See how the consultative communication gives a peek into her friend's emotions? She is not necessarily saying anything negative about the driver. She's implicitly saying: Here's how you can help my anxiety. Typically, a woman driver will respond, "Oh, I'm sorry," and then slow down a little. This is not an admission of guilt—merely a simple adjustment to the feelings of another woman. In essence, the driver is saying, "You're correct. I did want that information, and I want to make the easy change so that you feel cared for and less anxious." Again, all this happens implicitly.

It's a different story with two men in a car. He could be falling asleep at the wheel and barreling headlong into an eighteen-wheeler, *maybe* another man would say something—but probably not. "Hey, you're riding that car kinda close, buddy" immediately and definitively can be interpreted as "You moron. Didn't your dad ever teach you to drive? You're basically one major failure." Okay, maybe that's a bit of an exaggeration, but not much. So unless a man is trying to pick a fight, why would he communicate about it? Even if he is anxious, why bother the other guy? It's not his problem. They can both die in an explosive car crash, but at least neither one loses face.

When the man is driving and a woman is riding shotgun, trouble easily breaks out. She thinks he hears and understands the *consultation*, but actually, he hears *criticism*. He interprets her "bid" as disrespect or a lack of confidence. In insecurity, he defends himself rather than seeking to comfort her. Ironically, he doesn't realize she was only seeking comfort from the start.

When men know the whole picture, they usually respond differently. If she were to say, "Honey, I don't know why, but I am feeling some anxiety about how close you are behind that car. It would really help me feel more relaxed if you backed up a little. This isn't about your driving; it's about my emotions, whether irrational or rational. It would mean a lot if you would be willing to slow down a little." While most women might know those undercurrents, for whatever reason, a lot of men don't. "Overcommunicate until clarity" is a great rule of thumb. It will fill the cracks this book will inevitably leave. As you move forward, sweep aside assumptions and be as clear as possible. If one of you gets frustrated and you're confused about why, overcommunicate until you achieve clarity, even if it feels ridiculous. With charitable listening, overcommunicating will resolve the frustration ninety percent of the time.

This communication failure is extremely relevant to romance. Talk about the details of romantic experiences. Set time aside to talk about your feelings and what you appreciate. Even more importantly, you get to ask the other person what they appreciate. For example, do this for kissing. For instance, *The Married Guy's Guide to Great Sex* encourages couples to ask each other about the other person's kissing: "If either of you isn't happy with the other's kissing, take an evening to show and tell each other how you like to kiss. Take turns leading. Note that a good kisser is usually not too hard and not too tentative, not too wet and not too dry, lingers but not too long, and uses his tongue gently and playfully but not forcefully."[10]

Some people have some pent-up pride and hold on to what triggers them sexually or romantically. Let me help you out again: give that up. There's some part of you, especially ladies, who might think, "Well, he should *know* what turns me on after seven years of marriage! I'm not going to tell him. He hasn't earned that knowledge." Stop that. Immediately. You're constructing unnecessary barriers to romance.

This communication barrier applies to romance generally. It also can apply to sex. Men usually interpret tips as *consultation* in the bedroom, which is a good thing! I suspect because men wrap their identity up in sex so easily, they interpret correction positively. If a man is trying to give his wife an orgasm, and she says some version of "that feels good, but a little slower," he probably won't get defensive. He knows that she is the only one who knows what is going to give her the orgasm, so he better listen to her consultation. And, in his mind, he's just happy she's chosen him through sex! Nothing to complain about there.

Most wives tell their husbands a dozen times a day how to romance them. Sometimes it's subtle. Men, pay attention, and, women, make it more obvious. Bottom line: Don't let a lack of communication spoil your romance or sex lives.

Fighting without Resolution

Barriers to romance aren't always bad. Many are inevitable. In a healthy marriage, you will get into conflict, even fights. I lack the space to delve into how to argue and fight well here, but two basic principles include (1) listening intently and (2) doing everything possible to cool off rather than heat up the argument. So no swearing, try to keep a lower voice, and no threatening gestures.

The third and most important principle is resolution. You are not done until the relationship is restored. Feldhahn discovered that successful couples always make it clear to each other that they will restore and reconcile. Sometimes they may go to bed in disagreement but *not* in doubt over whether they'll be okay.[11] If, for any reason, you cannot conclude a conflict (it's just too late at night, someone has to go to work, the baby starts crying, etc.), it's important to assure each other that you *will* reach a good-faith resolution. "I love you, and even though we disagree, we *will* work through this" is all it takes. Then, physically affirm your words—a hug or kiss to seal the promise. Never threaten or blackmail with divorce or even hint that the argument might *not* work out.

What must come *first* is some kind of resolution, *then* physical affirmation. Physical affirmation does not replace the hard work of arguing, empathizing, leading, submitting, and trusting. I know couples who will sometimes have sex in an effort to resolve difficulty. I'm all about that connection, so long as you've reached a healthy pause point to the conflict. Unresolved conflict is like a cancer cell; the cell may start small, but until resolution, it can easily grow.

Mental Illness

As a mental health professional, I struggled with where to put these few paragraphs about the role mental illness can play in sex and marriage. As mental illness raises serious barriers to romance (in addition to marriage generally), this seemed the best place for it.

We all have to deal with depression, anxiety, and other uncomfortable emotions in our lives. For many of us, however, these take on much more significant life-altering roles that are chronic and cyclical beyond what matches reality. In other words, becoming depressed when there's nothing to be depressed about or anxious when nothing should cause us anxiety. This can act as shorthand for mental illnesses more broadly. Feeling anxiety because a bear is chasing me is not a mental illness. Feeling intense anxiety from meeting a small dachshund because a dog hurt us as a child is something to work through in therapy. Feeling anxious every day, so much that you can't go outside, is a mental disorder.

Mental illness serves as something of a "tax" on our psychological energy. When we are taxed beyond our means, it is that much more difficult to spend energy on another person, even if we want to do so; strangely enough, even if we feel like doing it! It's also more challenging to be romantic with someone who cannot easily communicate how much they appreciate us, even if they love us.

If your marriage involves mental illness, depression disorders, anxiety disorders, developmental disorders (like autism), addiction disorders, PTSD, and any of the others, it's vital that *both* of you become experts in the disorder and learn to communicate as a team about it. Most of us could use professional help at times in our lives and marriages, but in these cases, counseling is that much more important. So try to find a professional who is something of an expert in the issues you face. Read books about the disorder, follow blogs, and form a community with others. Above all, learn to communicate openly with each other about the illness.

Not long ago, I worked with a couple where one spouse was diagnosed with autism. As is common for such folks, he naturally placed people into clear-cut categories, into buckets, in his mind. Once he put them there, he struggled to see them as anything else. Due to some misunderstandings and misinterpretations, he began to see his wife as someone solidly in a bucket labeled: "trying to mess up my life." I'd worked with several marriages with this pattern of autism and learned to watch for this. After meeting with her, I became convinced she loved him dearly, but he couldn't see it.

So I challenged him to reexamine the evidence and see if the label "she loves me but doesn't always understand me" worked as a more effective category than "she is trying to mess up my life." Fortunately, he had placed me in the "expert" bucket, so he was willing to try.

Two weeks later, they came in and seemed like a newlywed couple, brimming with happiness and affection. He reported that "she loves me but doesn't always understand me" was, in fact, a superior bucket to put her in! They were both overjoyed with their new life together.

Mental illness does not need to spell doom for marriage; it presents unique challenges for sure, but also unique opportunities to love and serve each other beyond what we think we could normally give. A marriage like that becomes a unique picture of the gospel of grace.

Every couple will differ in their barriers and investments in romance. But if you avoid these pitfalls and invest in the places I've suggested, you'll put your marriage in the top ten percent (I made that up, but it feels right). While you should apply these chapters on romance to sex, there's more to say about sensual arousal. So I've set aside parallel chapters on arousal.

---

1. Tara Parker-Pope, "Love, Sex, and the Changing Landscape of Infidelity," *The New York Times*, October 28, 2008, https://www.nytimes.com/2008/10/28/health/28iht-28well.17304096.html; Nicholas H. Wolfinger, "America's Generation Gap in Extramarital Sex," Institute for Family Studies, July 5, 2017, accessed January 5, 2024, https://ifstudies.org/blog/americas-generation-gap-in-extramarital-sex.

2. Willard F. Harley Jr., *His Needs, Her Needs: Building an Affair-Proof Marriage* (Ada, MI: Revell, 2011), 50. I always want to give other Christian authors and speakers the benefit of the doubt. I assume Harley had the best intentions and I would prefer not to offer a citation here because I hate to throw stones. However, I do believe this mindset can be toxic and it is unethical to fail to cite a quote like this.

3. Snyder, *Love Worth Making*, 122.

4. Leman, *The Intimate Connection*, 99.

5. Kevin Leman, *Sheet Music: Uncovering the Secrets of Sexual Intimacy in Marriage* (Wheaton, IL: Tyndale House Publishers, 2010).

6. Alyssa Bischmann and Christina Richardson, "Age of First Exposure to Pornography Shapes Men's Attitudes Toward Women," *American Psychological Association*, August 3, 2017, accessed December 28, 2023, https://www.apa.org/news/press/releases/2017/08/pornography-exposure. According to this study by the APA, the average exposure is 13.37.

7. Jessa Zimmerman, *Sex Without Stress: A Couple's Guide to Overcoming Disappointment, Avoidance, and Pressure* (Winter Park, FL: LegacyONE Authors, 2018), 25.

8. Henry Cloud and John Townsend, *Boundaries: When to Say Yes, How to Say No* (Grand Rapids, MI: Zondervan, 2008), 25.

9. See Malone and Harris, *Battles of the Sexes*.

10. Clifford L. Penner and Joyce J. Penner, *The Married Guy's Guide to Great Sex* (Colorado Springs: NavPress, 2017), 17.

11. Shaunti Feldhahn, chap. 4 in *The Surprising Secrets of Highly Happy Marriages: The Little Things That Make a Big Difference* (Colorado Springs: Multnomah, 2013).

Nine

INVEST IN AROUSAL

I love doing premarital counseling. It's fun to watch the couple almost forget I'm in the room as they snuggle, sneak secretive touches they think I don't see (or they don't care), and talk as though they are going to win the lottery on the wedding day. They laugh spontaneously at even vaguely funny things. They instantly apologize for anything that might be taken as a slight. They're dialed in when we talk about sex and romance. I cease to exist the minute they walk out the door as they discuss intensely and intimately what they just learned.

They are aroused—and not merely in the sexual sense. Their internal radars are highly sensitive to each other's experience. We all know these feelings will not always be there; they are feelings, after all. However, like the ripest fruit and most vibrant flowers, feelings of arousal can grow if we tend our marriages in the right ways.

To understand sexual arousal, imagine a door. Picture the door closed but with a doorknob and several locks. This side of the door represents the everyday feelings of life: time pressures, stress, grief, hope, satisfaction, disgust, contentment, frustration, disappointment, confusion, and more. On the other side of the door is potentially free and satisfying sex. In order for sexual intercourse to be positive, enjoyable, and uniting, you have to be on the other side of that door. That door represents arousal. Now, the mere desire to engage sexually is not the same thing as arousal. A spouse can want to make love later but not feel any arousal from the thought alone. Looking forward to sex later will probably start unlocking the door, however, which is useful to remember.

Arousal makes us want to engage in sexual behavior, especially with a sense of urgency. The feeling is of being "turned on" or even more directly (and hopefully not crass to anyone) horny.

Just wanting someone else's feelings to change is not helpful (remember that $20,000 and the $40,000?) If it were, counseling would be easy. Bob Newhart's skit on counseling is hilarious and pertinent here. He yells, "Stop it!" when the client talks about their problems. One lady says she has a fear of elevators. His response? "That's ridiculous—stop it!" He assumes their problems are solved after he yells, "Stop it!" at them. This comically efficient therapist charges by the minute.[1] This isn't quite how it works.

However, without thinking about it, we do this in our marriage all the time: "Be less angry! Be less anxious! Be content! Be more aroused!" So we need to figure out how to create a space where these feelings are grown and inspired, not demanded or forced.

Hormones play a key role in arousal, but like all hormones, there are ways we can behave or think that will increase or decrease their pull. Sitting inside in the dark all day won't activate much serotonin. Getting out into the sunshine won't necessarily make us happy, but it might get us a boost.

Ways of acting and thinking will shut and even lock the door of arousal. At the same time, arousal is something of an autonomic response in the human body. For example, paralyzed people can still get aroused sexually.[2] Like so many autonomic responses in the body, some are aspects of arousal in our conscious control while others aren't. Most emotional states are affected by and affect hormones. So it might help us to compare it to an oppositely charged emotion: anxiety. Anxiety responses like increased heart rate, blood pressure, and shallow breathing are autonomic, but at the same time, anxiety can be influenced. For example, breathing exercises can diminish anxiety. More globally, our environment, the people around us, and our fears also affect our feelings.

I believe arousal is much the same. Instead of running away, like anxiety influences us to do, arousal makes us run *toward*. There are aspects of arousal outside of our control, but we can influence the arousal of our spouses. Part of being a good lover is working to inspire arousal in your spouse, especially whenever you are hoping to engage sexually. More on that later. For now, let's linger on hormones for a while since they play such a significant role.

Hormones and Arousal

After I brought up hormones, you may be thinking to yourself (*self. . .*), "Wait, isn't all of this just about hormones anyway?"

Well, yes and no.

There are generally two views to explain why men have sex so central to their identity and why women don't: biological and cultural. In other words, there are nature versus nurture camps. Those who take the biological view will generally do so with evolutionary terms. Thinkers in that camp will talk about hormones and the need for men to "spread their seed" to ensure the species' survival.

Authors, teachers, pastors, and psychologists will often divide biological motivations (drive, hormones, and reproduction) from spiritual motivations (sacrifice, bonding, oneness) and emotional motivations (acceptance, pleasure, satisfaction) from one another. My belief is that identity is the integration of these categories, not their division. We are material *and* immaterial; we are biochemical *and* spiritual. As I mentioned earlier, C. S. Lewis (or at least Screwtape) refers to humans as "amphibians—half spirit and half animal."[3] I prefer to think of us as one-hundred-percent spirit-animals. The aspects of who we are are integrated into a whole person and not able to be disentangled. In fact, even theologically, I do not think they can be truly disintegrated.

Given human nature as spirit-animals, does biology point to a difference in the sexes? *Battles of the Sexes* covers some groundbreaking science in the realm of sex and sex differences. It establishes that, yes, nature and biology play a significant factor in male and female differences. "One of the areas I could not ignore in my research was the distinctly unique biochemistries of the sexes. Just like the 1990s brain biochemistry research, sex differences research is based on 'hard' or natural science [. . .]. The pattern was clear: males and females are different on a biochemical basis throughout animal species. For humans, that pattern is especially true during young adulthood (ages eighteen to thirty-nine)."[4]

Some general differences that they found were statistically obvious: Men are far more likely to drown or be burned or injured; thirty-five times more likely to kill each other; ten times more likely to be put in prison; and more.[5] The authors point to the amygdala as one of the biological culprits. They write: "The amygdala, which is the brain's survival command and control center, is about twice as large in the male brain. Due to its survival-related nature, it is very difficult to turn off when it signals for action to be taken. In males, it is particularly reactive to all kinds of sexual stimuli."[6] Additionally, "Men's brain centers for sex (found in the hypothalamus) are twice as big as the sex centers in women, and indeed most men think about sex about six times more often than women do."[7]

Testosterone is the sex hormone that makes men, well . . . men. The hormone develops a human into a biological male. Females have testosterone too, just less of it. The hormone does many things, like make men grow facial hair, contribute to bone density and muscle growth, and more.[8] A 2022 review of the evidence confirms that there is a "strong relationship between [testosterone] and sexual desire."[9]

We can characterize men's desire as "assertive" sexual drive, and women's more often as "receptive" or "responsive" sexual desire. Women still desire sex, but they don't as often "bring it up," so to speak.[10] Snyder puts the distinction like this: "Like the screen-saver program on an old-fashioned desktop computer, a woman's system will often stay in "sleep mode" until someone moves the mouse."[11]

Husbands: Sometimes women will have the same strong, "instinctual" urge for sex, but most don't. However, your wife may generally show love by *receiving* sexual advances. Just because your wife doesn't bring up sex as frequently doesn't mean she doesn't desire you sexually. Remember, your wife likely struggles to sympathize with your zealous, primal, assertive desire. And, always, always remember you ought to rule those urges, not vice versa.

One of the authors of *Battles of the Sexes* is a certified nutritionist and taught dietary classes. She discussed different addictions with her classes over the years and frequently polled the students to see what things were most addictive to whom. Hierarchically, men often rated sex as one of the most addictive things, often around the levels of cocaine. Women, on the other hand, rated the addictive quality of sex about the same as food.[12] In addition from her research beyond this simple survey, women's amygdalae are apparently more aimed at food, whereas men's are aimed at sex. (I'll avoid making any comments on stereotypes!)

There are some real gems in these studies relevant to your marriages, but again, never forget my caution about generalities at the beginning of the book. Toss this information if it's not relevant to you.

This study and countless others show that sex is generally more important to men, and it appears that a large part of this includes biological influences.

Wives: many men naturally and biologically, on average, pursue sex with more vigor at the most fundamental brain/hormonal level. It's *not* a "need" like food or water, but its draw is biological and strong and in the same neurological realm as motivation for food and drink and survival, and those pulls are more often stronger in men. And remember, his testosterone connects to meaning and emotions. Feldhahn writes, in regards to sex, "Know that you're responding to a tender heart hiding behind all that testosterone."[13]

If hormones lead us one way, like men having a higher sex drive, that doesn't mean it's also not true that men experience a greater depth of meaning from sex. Both can be one-hundred-percent true at the same time. God created sex and for a purpose. *Of course* He biologically hardwired us a particular way to follow that purpose.

Biology and even evolution can "explain" these traits at one level (albeit imperfectly), but this view doesn't need to contradict the biblical, meaningful view on sex.[14] For instance, women generally integrate children into their identity more strongly than men. Most possess a nurturing, mothering instinct. Women more often worry and think about their children. So when women switch their identity from not-mother to mother, they then act on that identity by mother*ing*: nursing, loving, and caring, which biology supports. That doesn't mean the father doesn't reflect these things as well (well, except for the nursing part). Remember, I'm pointing to tendencies, majorities, and strengths, not absolutes.

This difference in identity (motherhood and fatherhood) is reflected in biology. One study showed that men and women have different neurological responses to infant cries, even if they're not parents.[15] Though this science is fairly new, some are studying the effects of oxytocin as a hormone playing different roles in men and women. It probably affects different tendencies in men's and women's natural responses to caretaking.[16] Does this "biological" or "neurological" science somehow take away from the meaning and value of motherhood? I'll posit no, it does not.

Of course, culture also plays a major role in shaping how we view sex and in what produces different hormone responses as well! The denotations of gender in any given culture provide markers for biological sex. Clothes are the primary example. Gender roles possess a great deal of biological pull but are largely cultural. Society may or may not reinforce that women should raise children and men should win the bread for the family. I'm not committed to the traditional, old-school American view that "men must have a career and women must stay home." That's not taught in the Bible. Even in Ephesians 5, when Paul talks about the household and headship, he does not restrict their husband-wife relationships to anything so narrow or cultural.

We can take key pointers from Jewish thought, which is deeply in tune with the biblical worldview. One author puts it this way:

> For the Jewish tradition, God created each one of us as an integrated whole, with no part of us capable of living apart from any other part of us. The body, the mind, the emotions, the will, and the spirit are all involved, at least to some degree, in everything we do in life, and they affect each other continuously and pervasively. This integrated view of the human being has an immediate implication for our sexual activities—namely, that on a level as conscious and deliberate as possible, our sexual acts ought to reflect our own values as individuals and as Jews.[17]

And, as with everything, sin twists and breaks that hardwiring. God created sex for a purpose, but we have twisted that purpose. That's part of our job as believers to look to God's Word to sort out the messed up, sinful aspects of the world, and our lives follow it.

In sum, *both* culture and biology shape the way men and women approach sex. For example, the current cultural zeitgeist pulls us into sexual promiscuity and argues that happiness can be found in *eros* rather than *agape* love. Even assuming there is no God, moral consequences, or wrongness to adultery or sex outside of marriage, the stats show that this lifestyle does not lead to lasting happiness.

So, though biology and culture will influence our beliefs, we can overturn them to a more accurate understanding. What I'm trying to do in this book is overturn misconceptions, no matter where they arise from. Culture and biology both tie into and influence our beliefs, but our beliefs take the cake. Our beliefs can rein in the potentially adverse effects of our instincts or culture. Being spirit-animals means we *can* rule over the animal.

Practical Tips for Unlocking the Door to Arousal

There are also several good books that offer ideas for helping your spouse keep the door unlocked and open to seduction and arousal. Particularly, this section is aimed at husbands, as wives usually have more locks on the door to arousal.

I feel the need to apologize for this book's title, *Get Her in the Mood: Seventeen Easy Steps to Seduce Your Wife Tonight*, as it sounds manipulative or transactional. While I found a few errors in this very short book, I was overall pleased with the heart and tone. The author authentically seems to want to make sure his wife feels loved by him. Notice that he also seems aware that it's common for women to see loving affection and intimacy as the pathway toward arousal.

I'll share a few of his tips here.

- "Make sure that you start the day with a long full-body hug in bed, and tell your wife how much you love her."

- "When you first see each other after work, give your wife a ten-second hug right away . . ."

- "If it feels right, give your wife an affectionate (but not sexual) kiss, after you hug."

- "When she answers you, make sure that you look her in the eyes. And *really* listen to what she is saying. Allow her to take the conversation in any direction that she chooses."

- "At dinner, remind her of a memory that you both share . . ."

- "Gently lift up her hair with your hands and kiss her lightly on the back of the neck one or two times."[18]

Another author offers this guide for seductive touch: "The area across her back right above the curve of her buttocks, which is called the sacral curve, is often a very sensitive pressure zone. By gently applying pressure with your entire hand, you may excite her in a way mysterious to you both. Stroking the whole of her back or lightly tracing the area with your fingers is another inventive move. As one lady said, 'This is why you have hot breath and why we women wear backless gowns.'"[19]

Notice that most of these are physical touches, but they aren't necessarily sexual, as she likely defines it. These touches do not have to and should not always lead to sex. That kind of physical touching can really encourage your wife that you love her for who she is and not merely for sex (which even if she *knows*, she needs to be *reminded* of).

A survey respondent to Feldhahn and Sytsma's research wrote the one thing she wished her husband knew was "how much nonsexual soft touch (hand holding, hugs, back rubs) is important to initiate sex for me, and how much I wish he would do that." And, cross-checking with her later answers, "Sure enough, in her other survey answers she indicated her spouse wasn't particularly curious [about how to please her]."[20]

Women usually need a reason *to* engage sexually. Wives, can you start considering what gives you a reason to think sexually? Most evenings rarely create any margin for affection, much less arousal. So work together to change this, adding *margin*. Even when the margin for engaging sexually exists, what if arousal doesn't?

Well, she could give her husband a "few seconds" to arouse her, for example, with slow kisses up and down her body or soft, slow manual stimulation of her clitoris, and see what happens. Or just wait until another time. But how much nicer would it be if she had taken a few moments out of the day to allow some feelings of arousal to drift through her soul, opening up the possibility of sex?

If the act of initiating sex is where the rubber meets the road for your conflict, and you want to go more in-depth than what I've included here, *Secrets of Sex and Marriage*'s Chapter 8 is entirely dedicated to growing in the skill of initiating sex, and I highly recommend it.

Start with these questions for each other: What traits do you find most attractive? What do you find most compelling? What draws you to me? You may be surprised at what they find arousing. There is a humorous video out right now that shows two women at a park "checking out" men.[21] The angle of the video makes it look like they are talking about buff guys working out. It turns out that they're really checking out men playing with an unruly child, changing diapers, and engaging in other nurturing behaviors with kids. It gets weird when they fantasize about a daddy duck who is leading his ducklings, but until then, it makes a good point. Don't assume or be disappointed if what arouses your wife is different than what arouses you or even what you want to be arousing about you.

If you work out every day of the week to become more attractive to your spouse, you might be (partially) wasting that time. If you put on red lipstick to seduce your husband, you might be wasting lipstick. You won't know until you ask. Wearing a certain cologne, a romantic date, perfume, a certain color of lipstick, dancing together, lingerie, kissing your spouse up and down, snuggling, showering together, back scratches, stripping slowly, or any thousand things will start to unlock the door of arousal. Communicate what those things are to the other person. Often, though, this communication can run across some touchy subjects.

Looks and Hygiene

I've heard more times than I'd care to count wives say that they wish their husbands would pay closer attention to their hygiene. Of course, there can be a place for sweaty post-workout lovemaking or sod-covered gardening sex, but cleanliness is most often wives' preference.

Husbands, if you're committed to serving your wives, work to help make the barriers for engaging in sex lower and lower for her. If you smell good, feel smooth, and brush your teeth, it will probably be easier for your wife to make love, meaning it will take less psychological energy to get started. That makes sense, right?

You are a team, working together to lower the thresholds of sex for each other, working together to arouse each other. This goes back to the idea of getting a PhD in your spouse. When you're Sherlock Holmes for what makes your spouse happy, you'll find sex easier and easier to jump into.

Looks and physical attractiveness are tricky matters. I've typically found that men would rather be chosen by someone less "physically attractive" than their ideal (everyone's standard for this is unique) if they knew their spouse would desire and choose them. Instead of beer goggles, it's like love goggles. You can't get much more beautiful than two people in intercourse, fully themselves, naked, unashamed, and passionately "choosing" each other. Some kind of arbitrary "objective" attractiveness scale is largely pointless and vapid. Men may joke, often crassly, about their preferences for women, but even then, to guys, it will feel empty rather than ringing true. All through this book, I challenge the stereotype that men only want sex at the expense of all else; of course, the evidence *does* point to the fact that men tend to put more emphasis on physical attractiveness than women do when choosing a partner.[22] Given this tendency, it's extra important for men to remind their wives daily that they're beautiful, makeup or no makeup, sweatpants or no sweatpants, pregnant or skinny. According to the apostle Paul, it's the husband's job to "nourish and cherish" his wife like Christ does the church. Cherish her beauty, nourish her confidence, no matter how a broken and fallen world would label her.

That said, your husband or wife will have preferences about your appearance. Within healthy limits, there's space to ask and discuss this question.

Take, for example, the issue of weight. It's far healthier to live below the overweight line (I shudder to think how many hours I've spent on a treadmill or jogging just to stay at an acceptable "overweight" level). You can encourage healthiness in your household in different ways. But it might not be a priority for either of you, and that's okay. We all have limited time and resources. Maybe you're *not* the CrossFit couple who likes to run up mountains at 5:00 a.m. for fun—Ginger and I certainly aren't!

The trouble comes when one person wants their significant other to appear a certain way, but they don't regularly reach that standard. This issue is like any other we could discuss, except that it needs to be handled with extra care because it could send your wife (or husband) into a spiral of feeling objectified. Beauty *is* important to most women's sense of identity, whereas for most men, "handsomeness" is a tertiary quality at most. This is one area where you must apply the "start with me" principle and the sleuthing principle. In starting this conversation, ask your spouse what they look for. There is (or at least used to be) a prevalent double standard: men could have the "dad bod," but women had to look like some kind of swimsuit model. Such an idea sounds old-fashioned, but the media still promotes it.

So where does that leave this problem of attractiveness? One place to leave it is to charge each spouse. Women, just like you want him to smell good and have decent hygiene, your man might have preferences about your appearance (preferences that aren't essential to his attraction and love). For example, certain clothes or makeup. You can't change your body type, but you could see if your weight is even a concern—it might not be!

Husbands, check in with your wives about their preferences. Husbands, your wives may *not* like the dad bod. Others might not care about your physique as long as you win as a dad. Ask her: does she care? If she does, consider putting in those extra few hours a week for both your health and her pleasure.

If it's a concern, consider consulting each other on a ballpark goal. For example, "Let's exercise together twice a week," or, "What if we both aimed for 'not overweight?'" or, "Let's try eating clean for two months."

Wives, at least, reflect on whether he cares. If he's a God-fearing, wonderful husband, then he'll hopefully be able to communicate your beauty, making you feel comfortable in your body, and simultaneously talk honestly about healthiness.

Work together toward that goal, knowing that it's far from essential to arousal and lovemaking. It doesn't bear on whether he finds you beautiful—there are countless factors to your beauty. Your relative fitness might be a preference of his, like hygiene. While hygiene may be important to you, you (probably) don't think less of him as a person for not trimming his unibrow as often as you'd like. In a similar way, your husband may find physical health more important than you find hygiene, but it doesn't need to reflect negatively on your *identity*. Again, you might be surprised at his lack of care about your weight. Whether or not *you* want to "let yourself go" a bit is another matter. You might care about your fitness more than he does.

Here's where expectations can become dangerous again. If he predicts you will stay skinny, or God forbid it, creates a boundary that you *must* stay skinny, it will create a conflict. This is why I'm carefully saying "want" rather than "expects," because you, husband, said, "for better or worse, in sickness and health." Extrapolated a bit, that includes "skinny or with love handles."

Of course, while weight is one issue, "objective attractiveness" is fairly mute in marriages. If things go according to plan, you will be with each other *until you die*. In case you haven't noticed, people start to look like raisins after a few decades. So-called objective attractiveness fluctuates and pretty quickly declines. A loving heart, charitable spirit, willingness to grow, and maturity (in other words, character) will make you more lovely than all the Botox or steroids in the world. Character plus *what you mean to your spouse* and your relationship's depth creates more arousal than any ripped muscles or a flat stomach. There's nothing wrong with preferences for your spouse, their makeup or facial hair, but if those things come at the expense of sacrificial love, something's gone amiss.

Above all, do away with *expectations*. There's nothing more poisonous to a marriage than expecting your spouse to keep up an unrealistic routine of Kardashian levels (they make themselves look attractive as a full-time job with millions of dollars to pour into it). Find a reasonable ground and discuss it, free of expectation but brimming with hope and togetherness.

Prayer

I probably should've brought prayer into the picture many chapters ago. Here seems like a good place for the reminder, where I see so many marriages get stuck. Arousal, or lack thereof, can feel like ground zero for sexual dissatisfaction and conflict. This can feel existential, like an incredibly difficult moment where you both feel stuck—hopeless.

In times of barrenness, in dry and difficult seasons, sometimes only the Spirit's movement can shift us to the point of repentance. If arousal seems faltering, fleeting, and contentious, pray for renewal and sex pleasing to God in your mutual conjugal enjoyment. It's a gift of God in the first place, and He is a generous father. As the apostle John writes, "And this is the confidence that we have toward him, that if we ask anything according to his will he hears us. And if we know that he hears us in whatever we ask, we know that we have the requests that we have asked of him" (1 John 5:14–15).

Having intimate, fulfilling sex is part of His will for us—even if consistency in erotic attraction comes and goes. No matter how resentful, hurt, or stuck we feel, prayer is always a vital step to real change. If you cannot find hope in yourself or your partner, you may be looking in the wrong place for hope. If you have come to the point of saying that nothing you do seems to make things better, then I would encourage you to step back and, like David, strengthen yourself in the LORD your God (1 Sam. 30:6).

Pray for arousal, pray for the fulfillment of God's gift to marriage, for He loves to "give good things to those who ask him" (Matt. 7:11)!

---

1. Marcus C. Thomlinson, "Stop It—Bob Newhart," The Mindset Revolution, November 16, 2022, video, 6:17, https://www.youtube.com/watch?v=jvujypVVBAY.

2. François Giuliano and Olivier Rampin, "Neural Control of Erection," *Physiology & Behavior* 83, no. 2 (November 2004): 189–201, https://doi.org/10.1016/j.physbeh.2004.08.014.

3. C. S. Lewis, chap. 7 in *The Screwtape Letters*.

4. Malone and Harris, *Battles of the Sexes*, v-vi.

5. Malone and Harris, *Battles of the Sexes*, 17.

6. Malone and Harris, *Battles of the Sexes*, 19.

7. Gottman et al., *The Man's Guide to Women*, 28.

8. Matthew Solan, "Working around Health Issues and Sex," Harvard Health, March 1, 2022, accessed January 5, 2024, https://www.health.harvard.edu/mens-health/working-around-health-issues-and-sex; Giulia Rastrelli, Giovanni Corona, and Mario Maggi, "Testosterone and Sexual Function in Men," *Maturitas* 112, no. 1 (June 2018): 46–52, https://doi.org/10.1016/j.maturitas.2018.04.004.

9. Vi Nguyen, Austin Leonard, and Tung-Chin Hsieh, "Testosterone and Sexual Desire: A Review of the Evidence," *Androgens* 3, no. 1 (October 2022): 85–90, https://doi.org/10.1089/andro.2021.0034.

10. Tasha Seiter, "Spontaneous vs. Responsive (and Libido vs. Stress)," *Psychology Today*, February 20, 2023, accessed January 5, 2024, https://www.psychologytoday.com/us/blog/mindful-relationships/202302/the-truth-about-female-sexual-desire-every-one-should-know.

11. Snyder, *Love Worth Making*, 121.

12. Malone and Harris, *Battles of the Sexes,* 42.

13. Feldhahn, *For Women Only*, 103.

14. Another aside, the worldview of viewing humanity purely as a result of evolution *does* contradict the biblical view. I've got a nuanced perspective on evolution that I won't delve into in this book.

15. Nicola De Pisapia et al., "Sex Differences in Directional Brain Responses to Infant Hunger Cries," *NeuroReport* 24, no. 3 (February 13, 2013): 142–46, https://doi.org/10.1097/wnr.0b013e32835df4fa.

16. Shan Gao et al., "Oxytocin, the Peptide That Bonds the Sexes Also Divides Them," *Proceedings of the National Academy of Sciences of the United States of America* 113, no. 27 (June 20, 2016): 7650–54, https://doi.org/10.1073/pnas.1602620113.

17. Elliot Dorff, *Love Your Neighbor and Yourself: A Jewish Approach to Modern Personal Ethics* (Philadelphia, PA: Jewish Publication Society, 2006), 74.

18. Brad Walker, *Get Her in the Mood: Seventeen Easy Steps to Seduce Your Wife Tonight* (2015), 98, 104, 108, 115, 133, 153.

19. Paget, *How to Give Her Absolute Pleasure*, 75.

20. Feldhahn and Sytsma, *Secrets of Sex and Marriage*, 168.

21. Funny Or Die, "Hot Dads," YouTube, video, 3:58, June 15, 2018, https://www.youtube.com/watch?v=AhDoZzSF1pQ.

22. Malone and Harris, *The Battles of the Sexes*, 84.

Ten

BARRIERS TO AROUSAL

Over the years, many wives have explained to me the disconnect she feels when her husband wants to mess around but her most recent thoughts about him were "I wish he would just pick up his socks and underwear off of the floor!" Either spouse can feel this ("I asked her to run one errand for me, and while she got five other things done, she didn't get that one thing I asked done?"). But I see it block arousal most often when the husband is so unhelpful around the house or with the kids that he is essentially like another child to take care of. Of course, he may work hard and make money in the business world, but her job at home (whether she works outside of the home or not) is made more difficult by his presence—not easier!

I had a wife explain that jumping from having to tend to her husband like a son and then trying to engage with him as his lover was too big a hurdle. This provides an excellent (terrible?) example of a barrier to arousal.

I want to toss out a few things I have read or heard from men and women (especially women) that are examples of things that can reduce a sense of arousal. These are in no particular order, and they are intended to be general examples that you and your spouse might want to discuss as arousal door locks.

You might think it's strange that I want to spend more time on barriers to arousal than investments, but it makes sense. This man or woman married you. Apparently, it's not unnatural for them to feel arousal for you. They knew marriage meant sex (among so many other things, of course), so they are *able* to feel arousal about you. At least they did, however many years ago, when you got married. That door has been unlocked and opened in the past—it can be unlocked and opened again.

The following barriers focus on men because men usually find less inhibition to arousal. But if you're a man in a marriage where your wife is dissatisfied with sex and wishes you had sex more, I've included a couple of possibilities about barriers.

A Failure of Gentleness and Chivalry

One of the most common words in all of the books I read to men about engaging sexually with their wives was "gentle." It is common for authors to remind men to speak, touch, and act "gently" dozens of times in each book. In my view, a failure of gentleness is a failure of chivalry and masculinity.

Gentleness, as a character trait, is defined as "using the least force necessary." A new mother handing you their child will want you to be gentle—not too harsh but also not too weak. If a nurse is setting your bone, you want them to be perfectly gentle. They need to use just enough force to set the bone (even though it will hurt), but not any more than is necessary.

Often, when wives talk with me about what makes them feel disconnected from their husbands, it's his lack of gentleness. He is too demanding, insecure, impatient, and very often too angry. He creates more pressure than he needs to for the task. He is too harsh with his words or judgments, and not just of her. His lack of gentleness and care with the kids is just as big a turn-off. Of course, a lack of gentleness during the act of sex will be a turn-off as well. Notice I didn't say gentleness was maximally soft, but as using the least force necessary. Passionate sex can become a bit "rough," but even then, gentleness must apply. Use the least force necessary to create the desired effect.

This potential barrier can apply when the man is more adventurous about sex. Obviously, this preference can rest with either spouse, and the pressure can go both ways. One spouse's preference for more experiences and diversity can come across as lacking in gentleness. Imagine a wife not comfortable with flirty or sexual texts, but her husband sends them or pushes (or demands or cajoles or pressures) anyway. The husband's "ungentle" and "ungentlemanly" treatment of her, which will likely create a sense of division, will only worsen if she gives in to his pressure.

Unfortunately, many men express their anger or frustration physically. Since anger leads to a lack of control, anger hinders people from regulating their gentleness. Sometimes, men corner their spouse or tower over a child, using their size and strength to intimidate. Except in the case, maybe, of defending against direct physical attack, there is never a good time for this use of force. Yes, our families need to know that we can be dangerous, but they must know we'll never turn our dangerous power against them! Our physical strength should always protect—*never* threaten our kids or spouse.

Abuse from men or women should never be tolerated. Never slap, hit, punch, or shove in anger—*ever*.

If a man loses his temper and uses physical force in his anger *once*, his wife and kids will expect it every time he gets angry. They'll cringe away. That may be painful to hear, but it's true. How could they not? They have to assume that he might do it again. Men, if you have ever been physically ungentle, it can take months or years of self-control before your family truly believes that you aren't going there again next time. Ungentleness breaches trust and security, which are necessary for intimacy. If this has happened, I recommend that the husband get counseling and accountability about his anger and that the couple get help to seek to heal the rift it creates.

However, the lack of gentleness does not have to degrade all the way to physical abuse to create a rift. A pattern of grumpy, unkind, or cruel words can do it. Men, just know that the ugliest expression of your anger or childishness is always a part of your wife's consideration of you.

Seek gentleness. Here is a way I encourage husbands especially: never say anything to your wife that you would want to hurt another man for saying to her. Dr. Gary Smalley has several references to gentleness in his book, *If Only He Knew*, addressed to married men. My favorite was an insight gained by a specific man: "George has finally realized that his wife is a special person who needs tender treatment, almost as if her forehead were stamped 'Very Important—Handle with Care.'"[1] This may overstate the issue in some ways. Of course, women aren't fragile like a China teapot, ready to shatter at any second. But George needed a reminder to be aware that his words and actions can have a damaging effect, and somehow, many men seem to live as though this weren't the case.

What is considered "gentlemanly" differs in various cultures. But, no matter the culture, I suspect women prefer men to act according to said customs. In his famous list defining the principles of true love, Paul says that love is not rude (1 Cor. 13:5). Women, in particular, would appreciate less crassness and rudeness.

Imagine an aroused woman in the mood for sex who suddenly gets nervous about a strange sound in the house. She asks her husband to check on it and see that everything is locked up. Impatient, he responds, "You are the one who wants it checked, so you should go check it!" Or, more plausibly, "Couldn't it wait?" To say that this is going to cool off her arousal feelings is an understatement. Women want to feel safe and cherished. The biblically minded man needs to seek to show his wife's willingness to sacrifice.

In addition, men will have probably grown up joking about sex in crass ways. This may have been somewhat innocent and naive. But now you need to burn that out of your tongue. You won't be perfect at first, but trust me, it's a demeaning, harmful habit. Now you can probably understand why. Sexual jokes separate sex from the person and make sex about something harsh, crude, or dirty. Your wife is not naive, simple, arrogant, or squeamish for wanting you to cut out vulgar language about sex. You'll notice I carefully avoid making such jokes. Maybe some humor about men and women, but not about sex. Why? Because sex is *sacred*. Joking treats it as coarse or common. Remember, sex is about her, so being flippant about sex communicates that you do not take her seriously as your lover.

Sex can be fun and even funny sometimes, but I'm confident that no one wants to have their sexuality belittled. Having a private laugh about sex with your spouse is not a problem, but negative, crass jokes or humor treating sex as commonplace is wrong. Is sex enjoyable? Absolutely. Should we be squeamish about it? Most definitely not! Should we joke about it in a crude, uncomfortable way? I say be very, very careful. When we cheapen sex or make our spouse feel uncomfortable, we do ourselves no favors in the bedroom.

Would anything under this heading apply to couples with roles reversed from the norm? You bet! In those cases within counseling, I've heard men say their wives' perfectionism, critical nature, and anger can lock their arousal up tight. Naturally, wives who abuse, speak impatiently and harshly, and neglect their hygiene will also throw up barriers to their husband's arousal.

Unrestfulness

Imagine if I said I want you to create feelings of "restfulness" in your bedroom. What would you change? Notice that you cannot decide to feel rested, but you can influence whether you feel more or less restful. Can you just feel tranquil by deciding to? Most people can't, but you *can* create an environment where it naturally feels tranquil. Now consider what feelings and environment you want to create in your bedroom. Peaceful? Restful? Playful? Warm? Safe? Special? Intimate? Those are common answers I would get from women with the same question.

Do you want to know what declares war on those feelings? Media. Screens. I think TVs should not be in your master bedroom. Also, set guidelines about mobile phones, computers, or iPads. Quickly set them aside in the bedroom if either of you is interested in arousal. Better yet, limit their time or just don't use your screens in bed, full stop.

So, firstly, a major source for creating arousal is focus. It is arousing, or at least affirming, to be focused on. How well do you focus on your spouse in your bedroom? It's arousing to feel like someone else wants you to be aroused, but you can't give off that energy if you're glued to a screen.

Second, bad smells. Of course, what smells people consider "bad" differs from person to person, but typically, avoiding bad hygiene is helpful for arousing feelings. Cigar smoke may be an instant turn-off or a turn-on for others. Wine breath may kill arousal or increase it.

Third, discomfort is also really tough on arousal. Pain, cold, and hunger are common complaints I hear. It is great to help your spouse feel comfortable in bed. Plus, these often lead to fantastic gift ideas that can make you a hero.

Take time to figure out your spouse. Ginger easily worries about our children, which can create a massive psychological drain. Over the years, I've learned that for romantic weekends away, just the two of us, the kids need to be relatively close by and in safe hands. We won't travel halfway across the world because, to her, "What if an emergency happens?" Instead of fighting or staying stubborn about barriers like this, sacrifice for the one with the barriers. There are chances to meet in the middle here—some wives need to hear that not every chore that could possibly be done can be done before sex. The point stands: Team up *together* to help remove each other's barriers.

All these center around creating the *space* for arousal, and setting is key. Stay sensitive to each other's ideal setting for sex, which may be different for each of you. As homework, ask each other what their perfect setting for sex is. Don't let it create expectations, but let the information lead you in how to serve them when you can.

Lack of Margin

We've covered margin at length already, but I'd be amiss not to mention it here. Specifically, I want to charge whichever spouse has the lower sex drive (usually wives): create margin. Create whatever emotional, psychological, or scheduling margin to allow for sex. So often, wives don't have the psychological energy to start lovemaking. Wives, you need to communicate with your husband what is draining that energy to create margin. Husbands, you need to step up and help take care of that load. It's possible (though not likely) that you don't have the time margin. If you don't have time for sex (which usually doesn't take terribly long), something definitely needs to change. More often, we need to create margin for our spouses' psychological energy.

This was one of the turning points for Ginger and me. We started figuring out *together* how to create an energy margin for Ginger so we could be regularly aroused and ready to make love.

Embarrassment

Embarrassment often blocks feelings of arousal. Sometimes, feelings of guilt from past teachings about sex or from past sexual behavior create embarrassment or shame. Gently helping your spouse move past these feelings or helping them get counseling to work through them is a great idea.

For both men and women, embarrassment about their bodies is a major barrier to arousal. Especially as people age and have children, our bodies naturally have less of the same erotic appeal as they once did. Helping someone understand what you find attractive about them and working to stay healthy can create less embarrassment for the person making the adjustments (even small improvements in decisions about exercise and eating can make a big difference in how we feel about our bodies).

To counteract embarrassment in your spouse, shower them with affection, affirmation, and encouragement. It's hard to overdo it! Let it flow from the heart and constantly remind you of how much you treasure each other.

There could be hundreds of items on this list, but a better use of your time at this point would be to reach out to your spouse and invite them to let you know what you do or don't do that is accidentally locking the door for them. Be gentle, and *do not* take their preferences personally. No matter what it is, if you really want to know and to make simple adjustments toward some progress, don't take offense. If there is something about your presentation or style or whatever that is a turn-off and you want to know, it doesn't need to mean that your spouse doesn't love or choose you; all of us can improve, and all of us need to.

Pressure to Perform

Performance anxiety can affect anyone, but research suggests men feel it more prominently.[2] This often contributes to men's barrier to arousal. As I've stated over and over, around 30 percent of marriages have women wanting more sex than they have. In those marriages, countless things could be going on (FAQs 1 and 2), but for many, I suspect something like performance anxiety could have something to do with it.

Some Christian men have received a masculine image to live up to, whose expression of masculinity is rough, tough, and sexually hungry. Sometimes our church men's conferences can overdo this side of things. Men often don't fit this stereotype but may subliminally (or explicitly) think that biblical manhood means nothing more than chopping down trees; being emotionally deficient; having big muscles, a stout beard, a gruff voice; and, of course, being a sex machine who can never get enough sex. This either becomes a self-fulfilling prophecy, which causes men and boys to sin, or makes men with low libido feel like freaks.

In either case, it is normal for men's libido to rise and fall as well throughout life or based on circumstances. Sometimes, when a man faces some "failure" in sex, like being unable to maintain an erection or have an orgasm, it gets into his thinking, and he can't easily shake it. In these cases, I encourage men to remember that having sex is not about having "sex" but about having another person. I advise them to focus on the pleasure of their spouse and not worry about their own. Often, this alone can get his mind back on the right track.

However, at other times, mental or physical issues can create long-term effects. In those cases, talk to a professional for psychological or medical options, too. Also, sometimes a man's "inability to perform" is actually linked to our next topic:

Pornography and Arousal

We examine this some more in FAQ 7, but I feel like it is worth making a point here at the end of Chapter 10. Recently, it's become popular to deal with pornography in a "smart" way, using porn to try and invest the arousal created into their own relationship. I recall a few years ago when a fan fiction about a dominant/submissive sexual relationship was turned into a published gold mine. People were reading this erotic fiction unashamedly and openly. Some Christian women thought that they could read this material, get aroused, and then invest that arousal in their husbands. Perhaps it worked for a while, but there are consequences. In *The Fantasy Fallacy*, Shannon Etheridge lays out the dangers of this thinking, and I will not duplicate her work here.[3]

Dangers apply to all kinds of pornographic or unbiblical efforts to spice up the sex life (remember the section on illicit sexuality in Chapter 7). Yes, these can create a lot of "hot" feelings, but so does a house fire. The short-term gain is not worth the long-term consequences. Arousal at the cost of intimacy is not a good long-term trade. Why? Well, depersonalization is not sexy for healthy people. Thinking that you are just a replaceable person in your spouse's sex life is typically not going to be arousing at all. Pornography works to make the real person in your life merely a place to deposit your personal pleasure and arousal, not an intimate partner. It is a terrible idea, and for Christians, it's clearly sinful.[4] Fight the battle of lust and against the draw of masturbation. Everyone stumbles in some ways, but you should never make the mistake of excusing, justifying, or embracing broken sexuality to create healthy arousal.

Once Again, Investing in Arousal

Arousal is a wonderful gift that God has given us that allows us to bond certain feelings to our lover for life. If we shepherd these emotions well, investing in creating these feelings in our spouse, we will unlock and open the door to open, free, intimate sex. Arousal is a big part of why manipulation, emotional blackmail, and browbeating are terrible ideas. Those may result in a sexual encounter, but it becomes a sexual encounter not set free by arousal. To elaborate on the metaphor, it's taking a sledgehammer to the door of arousal and stepping through before your spouse is ready to open the door for you. Instead of walking through the threshold together, you're dragging them along.

As mentioned, we cannot always just choose to feel something, but we can create the conditions for feelings and allow ourselves to be open to them. If you know your spouse well and you're willing to risk a little, you probably know what gets them aroused, turned on, and in the mood. If your spouse knows you well, they likely know those buttons for you, too.

Are we willing to let them get us aroused even if we aren't already? Are we willing to try to seduce them sometimes, too?

Stressors and arousal do not go well together. The relational failures listed above, plus all of the things that may be demanding our psychological energy, can make feelings of arousal kind of uninspiring. Knowing what works for us and works for our lovers has been the key to this entire book. The principle of stocking the fridge for your spouse lives on.

Sometimes, you are serving Christ to give your spouse a few moments to try to get you aroused. If you get there, great. If you do not, maybe you need to try something else or figure out what is in the way of those feelings, then communicate about those roadblocks. Firework-like sex will follow if both of you commit to setting them alight—sometimes, it's just a slow burn to set them off.

Whoever has less sex drive, commit to your spouse *trying* and *prioritizing* finding your barriers and discovering what turns you on—for their sake and yours. Both of you commit to communicating more. "Hey, when you do this when we have sex, it really bothers me." Or "Would you mind doing more of this? I love it when you do this . . ." These should be ongoing insider trading conversations. How fun could it be to tell your spouse, "You know, I am not sure, but I think _____ might really feel arousing to me right now. You game to try?"

I have a final few thoughts on specifically investing in the pleasure of sex before we wrap up.

---

1. Gary Smalley, *If Only He Knew: A Valuable Guide to Knowing, Understanding, and Loving Your Wife* (Grand Rapids, MI: Zondervan, 2010), 4.

2. Marita P. McCabe, "The Role of Performance Anxiety in the Development and Maintenance of Sexual Dysfunction in Men and Women," *International Journal of Stress Management* 12, no. 4 (2005): 379–88, https://doi.org/10.1037/1072-5245.12.4.379.

3. Shannon Ethridge, *The Fantasy Fallacy: Exposing the Deeper Meaning Behind Sexual Thoughts* (Nashville: Thomas Nelson, 2012).

4. Mark Legg, "What Does the Bible Say about Pornography? Can You Break Free from Sexual Temptation?" *Denison Forum*, 2023 https://www.denisonforum.org/resources/what-does-the-bible-say-about-pornography-can-you-break-free-from-sexual-temptation.

Eleven

INVEST IN PLEASURE

There are quite literally thousands of books that offer insight and advice about sexual skill development. Some of the most ancient literature in existence are shockingly explicit how-to sex guides. For example, many ancient Hindu writings, sculptures, and reliefs include sexual techniques intended to guide practitioners toward integration with the divine. These can date back to a few hundred years BC. The *Kama Sutra* is probably the most famous, at least in the West. We didn't recently invent sexual pleasure. Efforts at improving sexual experiences have been an obsession for humans for a very, very long time.

So I am going to make very little effort to create some kind of master class for sexual prowess. I will, however, go over the essentials.

You'll never guess—communicate!

I'm always shocked how often couples tell me they don't talk sex. They do not talk during sex. Sometimes, they do not talk before or after sex either. In some rare cases, they have almost never talked *about* sex. Here's a shocking fact: You are only directly aware of what *you* feel. If I touch a table, I only know what my finger experiences. I do not know what the table experiences.

There is a wonderful exchange in Douglas Adams's comedic masterpiece, *The Hitchhiker's Guide to the Galaxy*, which exhibits this.

A well-traveled space alien warns his earthling friend, "You'd better be prepared for the jump into hyperspace. It's unpleasantly like being drunk."

His friend naturally asks, "What's so unpleasant about being drunk?"

The alien replies, "You ask a glass of water."[1]

What makes this a funny pun is, of course, that we have never wondered what it feels like for a glass of water to get drunk (Drunken? Drank? I never know for sure).

When I touch my wife in an effort to give her sexual pleasure, of course, I can look for all of the signs and indications of arousal. That's good. However, it would also be just as good or even better for her to let me know with her words. Counselors often joke that the most important sex organ is the mouth. That isn't about oral sex. It's about communication! After all, I can actually only experience what my hand feels, not what her body feels. I need her to tell me about that part.

This is proven over and over. Long-term commitment leads to better sex, not worse. Among other reasons, in my interpretation, this is because couples get to learn about one another's bodies and get to practice sex safely without the pressure to perform.

Talk about sex like this author suggests talking about kissing. "You may want to ask her to 'kiss me the way you want me to kiss you.' So if she nibbles around the side of your mouth or sucks on your lower lip, definitely ask, 'Do you want me to do that to you?'"[2]

We must be willing to serve as teachers and pupils when it comes to mastering sex with another person. Sure, learning basic anatomy can help, but even so, each person is unique, and every single sexual encounter is unique with that person. Something that felt rapturous one time can feel overwhelming and uncomfortable the next time. We have to speak, and we have to listen in order to be great intimate lovers. We can listen and speak with our bodies too, but words are a sure bet. To reiterate the "start with me" principle, we should work to instill curiosity about our spouse's desires. Sadly, in Feldhahn and Sytsma's new research, "only about half (52 percent) of our survey-takers viewed their spouse as generally 'open, inviting, and curious' about what they enjoyed sexually."[3] Let's commit to being open, inviting, and curious about our spouses!

Arousal and Pleasure

As the sexual relationship in a marriage becomes more dependent on intimacy and less on eroticism (novelty or raw attraction), the relationship between arousal and pleasure may change.

Here's what I mean: Early on, two people may be aroused just because they are in the presence of the one they love. The slightest contact draws sparks. This represents the novelty phase of the relationship. These emotions can reappear at any time in a healthy marriage. However, the novelty will tend to wear off.

This is not a loss of love, merely a loss of novelty. This lack of novelty can make people look for illicit love to fill the gap. Watch out for such vicious temptations and instead invest more and more in intimacy and your spouse's experiences.

During your honeymoon, you might have gone to the theater and been aroused the entire movie, barely able to wait until you got back home to make love.

So how do healthy couples integrate pleasure and arousal when they don't feel this way as automatically or frequently? Is there an idea we humans commonly experience that would help us get past our momentary hesitation? You bet!

Often, arousal kicks in during lovemaking rather than before.

This is especially true when psychological energy is low. Arousal may actually increase substantially in the first moments of sexual pleasure. The husband's erection may not fully kick in until the couple is engaging in foreplay; the wife's arousal may not truly kick off until her husband begins to touch or kiss her toward orgasm. This is not a failure. Rather, making love in anticipation of arousal rather than based on it shows wisdom. This practice reveals that the two people know each other well enough to know when arousal, pleasure, and connection are there for the having.

Orgasms are a good gift from a good Creator. God was not obliged to hardwire such potential for pleasure into sex and procreation, but He did. I give Him full credit! Especially when you consider that secular evolutionary scientists still struggle to come up with any strictly secular explanation for the existence of the female orgasm, though it is fun to watch them try.[4]

The bond of sexual pleasure and orgasm is a powerful act of cleaving. It floods our bodies with some of the most powerful hormones for safety and attachment.[5] Remember that females often enjoy sex without orgasm. While sex is not only about orgasming, it's a healthy ambition to improve the giving and receiving of orgasms. The goal is especially relevant to men since women orgasm less frequently on average. Around 31 percent of women report that they never, almost never, rarely, or occasionally orgasm during sex, as opposed to nine percent of males who say the same.[6]

In my effort to relieve you of the pressure, some of you may feel the pressure from another direction: the need to improve. Some will take my charge and overtalk about sex. They might overanalyze every act to try to get better and better, taking furious mental notes and doing everything in their power to improve.

Relax.

You and your spouse are in this together, and you have decades ahead. *Carpe diem* when it comes to sex with your spouse, but even *carpe diem* can create its own kind of sinister pressure. Plan for fun lovemaking? Yes. Prioritize intimate arousal? Absolutely. But don't idolize sexual pleasure—sex is a gift and, at its best, is enjoyed freely!

The Anatomy of Orgasm

I am impressed (and quite concerned) at how often I ask couples, premarital or married for decades, whether they can correctly draw or label sex organs. The majority cannot. So, like every other book about marriage and sex, we will include a simple artist's rendering of the male and female genitals.

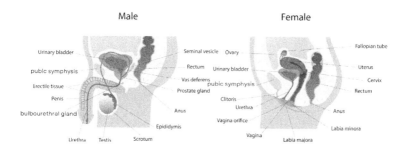

For the first several weeks of a baby's development, the sex organs look the same for both sexes. When the cells form a ball known as a blastocyst about a week after conception, the sphere develops with just a few holes for the digestive system's input and output. "In a male embryo, androgens secreted by the testes cause the phallus to elongate into the penis and the urogenital folds to fuse and form the spongy urethra [. . .]. [In female embryos,] the phallus becomes the clitoris."[7] This development leaves behind a kind of seam. It is clearly evident in most men running the underside of the penis, down the middle of the scrotum, and then to the anus. In women, it is most clear in the perineum (the space between the vulva and the anus), but it also runs through the bisection of the vulva.[8]

This "seam" houses most of the more sexually intense erogenous zones in most people. For most men to experience orgasm, the place where the seam is found nearest the head of the penis will have to be stimulated. For most women to experience orgasm, that same spot has developed into an organ called the clitoris, which is largely hidden but comes to the surface near the top of the vulva in the form of a small bump. People who are familiar with the clitoris are only aware of this button or pearl-shaped aspect. In truth, the clitoris is a much larger organ (often described as shaped like a butterfly) that kind of wraps around the vagina and can be stimulated in many different ways.

Vulva

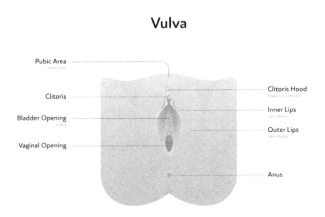

This means that for the majority of women, penetrative sex will not be sufficient to give them the gift of an orgasm. Husbands have the awesome opportunity to learn to stimulate their wife's clitoris (and for many women, this is new to them as well) by gently, carefully, considerately touching her in a way that she likes, under her guidance.

Keep in mind, as we have noted before, there are essentially no restrictions for a married couple when it comes to sexual behavior. I can see no biblical teaching that restricts married couples from exploring manual sex (using hands and fingers), oral sex (using mouth and tongue), or "mechanical" touches (vibrators, massagers, etc.). Based on how they were raised or taught, I'm sure some people will be troubled by this idea. Our life rules and upbringings can be why we experience shame when thinking about creating sexual pleasure in creative ways.

I see it differently. I believe God wants us to enjoy each other.

> Drink water from your own cistern, flowing water from
> your own well. Should your springs be scattered abroad,
> streams of water in the streets? Let them be for yourself
> alone, and not for strangers with you. Let your fountain
> be blessed, and rejoice in the wife of your youth, a lovely
> deer, a graceful doe. Let her breasts fill you at all times with
> delight; be intoxicated always in her love (Prov. 5:15–19).

I do not think Solomon was trying to be subtle with passages like that.

Unfortunately, there is an "orgasm gap" between men and women that
implies that men are missing out on a golden and godly opportunity to
invest in the intimate pleasure of their wives. That said, I don't want
to overreach the evidence. There's research to suggest that committed,
faithful evangelicals do better than the average marriage at engaging with
sexual satisfaction. Crucially, they have to be *committed* evangelicals, not
in name only.[9] In more religiously committed marriages, women tend
to have higher sexual satisfaction than nonreligious married women![10]
Once again, we see that if the culture teaches us something about sex,
they are almost always either wrong or lying.

Obviously, there are biological reasons why it's easier for men to orgasm.
I'm not saying it's practically feasible to close that gap completely, but
we can do quite a bit more to help. Remember, we're not trying to think
through the lens of expectation (for men or women), but we certainly
should take the knowledge of how our wife's body works and add to
it the insight from our wives on how to give her an orgasm. Then, we

practice. As a reminder, many women can (sometimes!) feel completely satisfied and content with lovemaking that doesn't involve their orgasm, so communication is once again key.

Wives, be open about what you like and what you want. You have permission to gently, kindly, and graciously give him pointers. I'm confident he'll love to hear it. When you communicate tips for him, it also communicates that you're interested in sex and want to get better and actually enjoy it more. Enjoying sex more will be a huge win for your husband (as well as a win for you, obviously!)

The Mechanics of Sex

What follows is a practical explanation of how sex works, in case your parents never told you, you skipped sex-ed class (probably for the better), or it's completely new to you. Even if you have been married for decades and have several children, I strongly encourage you to read this. If nothing else, it should inspire worship for the God who designed sex, and we can see how He intended for it to bond us.

The goal of any given sexual encounter is to serve your spouse in a sexually pleasurable way (in addition to possibly conceiving, of course). Given our examination of orgasms and the anatomy of our sex organs, the rest of the mechanics are pretty simple.

In premarital counseling, I prepare the couple to have great sexual encounters in their marriage. We usually start with some very pragmatic basics.

For example, I talk about lubrication, which you can get from the pharmacy section at any store. Lubrication is important for several reasons, no matter how many times a couple has had sex. Lube can make the experience more fun for the woman since skin-on-skin friction can become uncomfortable for her in intercourse (the part of sex when the penis penetrates the vagina). Friction also brings guys to an orgasm, so if a couple uses lube, he's more likely to enjoy intercourse for longer. Many couples use lubrication every time they have sex. When aroused, most women produce natural lubrication, but more doesn't hurt! Using extra lube is not some kind of failure.

Sex is typically pretty messy (something they leave out of the sexual encounters in most movies). You'll likely want a handcloth or towel or something. OB-GYNs encourage the woman to urinate soon after intercourse in order to flush out her urethra (because the potential for a urinary tract infection is increased from intercourse). When talking to engaged couples, I also, of course, go over birth control, from hormonal varieties to condoms to natural methods.

Usually, I find people have many false ideas about intercourse. I could create a list and go through them one after the other, but what matters isn't what others experience but what your spouse wants! What do they enjoy? What do they prefer?

We note that many women I have worked with report being unable to have an orgasm merely through penetration. Of course, this isn't what movies, romance books, or pornography present, but in my experience in sex counseling, it's almost universal. According to the National Library of Medicine, less than 30 percent of women can experience an orgasm without direct stimulation of the clitoris.[11] This should be no surprise! Notice in the graphic where the clitoris comes to the surface about an inch above her vagina. It's not likely to be given much contact during penetrative intercourse. There are some positions, like the woman-on-top in which the couple faces each other, which give her more control over the clitoris, getting the kind of pressure that can bring her to orgasm.

Typically, sexual encounters are going to move into the after stage (cleaning up, snuggling, whatever) soon after the husband has an orgasm (though it doesn't have to). So it's important they work to give, or at least prepare to give, the wife an orgasm so that she is right on the edge when they engage in penetration (which is not required every time you have sex by any stretch). It can take several days to several weeks for an inexperienced newlywed couple to find what works best to give her an orgasm, but I encourage them to have fun with it and not feel pressured. As we mentioned earlier in the "no holds barred" section, I think the sexual acts shared by a married couple are not immoral, so long as it includes only the two of them.

So I think it's an expression of great freedom and grace for them to experiment with using fingers, mouths, and mechanical stimulation to help her experience an orgasm with him. I don't think it's an accident of creation that the small centimeter of intense pleasure on the man's body and the matching centimeter of intense pleasure on the woman's body seldom come into contact during sex. It is almost like God hardwired sacrificial love into sex, isn't it?

I coach couples to take their time on their honeymoon night. I encourage them to bathe together, have him brush her hair or massage her shoulders, and generally get used to being naked together. I encourage them to then maybe give her a chance to try on some of the lingerie from her lingerie shower. The concept of lingerie showers is beautiful. I always encourage brides to invite their grandmothers if any are alive. They often understand the importance of sex in a healthy marriage and proudly give the nicest and sexiest lingerie.

Of course, not every night for the next sixty years is going to be another honeymoon. Sometimes, a sexual encounter will be a "quickie." Sometimes, sex will be an intensely planned out romantic seduction. Sometimes, you will fall into one another's arms without warning.

For people who have moved out of the novelty phase of sex together, remember to invest in the intimacy of knowing your spouse sexually. It's such a high to know what pleasures your spouse even better than they do! When you know what touch or what word or what movement is going to push them over the edge, and you grow in this knowledge more specifically during every encounter—that's a PhD level sexual intimacy.

Also, for those not in the novelty phase, keep in mind what we noted under the "Arousal and Pleasure" heading: "Often, arousal kicks in during lovemaking rather than before." Sometimes the arousal won't show up until the first touches do. When we allow our spouse to begin the process of pleasuring us, it often doesn't take long. Intimate sex (experiencing another person) may not always have the shock of a brand-new outfit, but instead, the perfection of your favorite sweatshirt. And, now, to mix metaphors a little, when we tend the garden, no matter how long we are married, sometimes the fruit of crazy eros can surprise us!

Most of the time, you can prioritize her orgasm and then move on to whatever seems good next for bringing him to orgasm. You will likely move through phases of favorites over the years—favorite sexual actions, positions, clothing, lighting, music, all of it. However, listening, feeling, and adapting to your spouse's pleasure is a powerful bonding agent.

Orgasms are a good gift from a loving God. He surely meant to give them as an advantage to married couples. Share orgasms exclusively with one a nother!

For many of you, all of this may be old news. If not, I am glad we mentioned it here. Keep in mind that sexual encounters aren't scripted or directed in real life; things don't always go perfectly. For that reason, once again, sacrifice and grace are keys to good sex.

Room to Fail

Dr. Marty Klein summarizes this sentiment well: "One of the wonderful things about sex is that we can make it a place where mistakes are simply not possible, and where virtually nothing can go wrong—not because we become sexually perfect, but because we radically redefine sexual 'success.'"[12]

Sometimes couples get distracted by trying to create "good" sex rather than just enjoying their spouse sexually.

Avoid making sex about whether you each reach climax every time, much less both of you climaxing at the exact same time. Instead, listen to one another. It may especially take time to get back where it becomes mutually enjoyable if you've been traumatized or hurt or are just stale and out of practice. But if you can move that needle so that it's more pleasurable for both of you, it makes the end satisfaction higher and the investment of energy less risky—especially for women.

Wives, you get the same opportunity to love your husband. Hearing him and his suggestions may make a lot of difference, too. Work on receiving satisfaction from providing that pleasure for him. Remember that it affirms him in who he is. Consider sex an opportunity to build intimacy since it's incredibly important to his sense of intimacy. And it *is* incredibly important to intimacy since it's the unique kind of intimacy you share with only each other.

Klein makes the powerful case that focusing on "normal sex" is detrimental to *joyful* sex. In this section, he reviews a discussion he once had with a couple.

> "Rather than try to create a certain kind of sex, why don't you just make love the way you do other things?" I continued: "How would you characterize the way you do other things together—you know, house projects, going out to dinner?" They easily generated and agreed on a half-dozen words: cooperative, fun, respectful, friendly, capable, relaxed. "And sometimes lazy," Thomas added, and they both laughed. "Great," I said. "You know, not every couple is like this. But since you are, why don't you just make love the way you do everything else?"

An overemphasis on performance does nothing but steal from the wonder of lovemaking. Let's help each other chip away at the pressure to perform in sex so that what's left is free, fun, and brings us closer together.

Feldhahn and Sytsma remind us of what we've already hammered home: "Sex is ultimately designed to bring you and your spouse together in oneness. When that is the focus, the climaxes are put in the right perspective: They are great, but they aren't the goal."[13]

Sex Positions

It's difficult to guide people through sex positions without being pornographic—especially while using drawings. A few, like Ethridge's *Sexually Confident Wife*, include a few classy sketches to give some ideas. While I don't recommend the *Kama Sutra*, I do suggest checking out the website "Christian Friendly Sex Positions."[14] While it sounds prudish, the explanations are far from it. There are illustrations and descriptive how-tos, which include all varieties that may or may not be right for you. These include inspirations for oral sex, manual stimulation, and even safe ways of having anal sex. Of their over three hundred ideas, some are positions almost anyone could use, while others require years of yoga or a miracle—they have the whole spectrum. Each position and motion are explained in purely descriptive terms and the site uses blocky figures instead of nudity or realistic drawings. Exploring sex positions this way may not be for everyone, but it's great for couples who want to branch out and try new things. Most couples seem to find a few favorite positions that allow for the most mutual pleasure, but sometimes you transition to a new favorite. Body changes, age, and other influences can greatly impact what feels good over time.

Perusing Christian Friendly Sex Positions with your spouse can feel overwhelming, so just have fun with it. Hopefully, this book has hammered into your heads that none of this is necessary or expected—it's an adventurous, exciting resource if you want to pursue it together, but don't feel ashamed about limiting yourselves to a couple of tried-and-true ways. As long as both partners are content, that's what matters most. I'll repeat once more, and finally, the Bible does not morally prohibit sexual acts between a man and a woman, as long as they don't bring anyone else into the bedroom and thus defile the marriage bed.

This whole book, and I've spent only a couple of paragraphs on sex positions?

Yes. And hopefully, after reading this far, you understand why.

Sometimes, when I teach, I tell the audience that I'm going to buy flowers for my wife on my way home. I ask them for advice—what kind of flowers should I get her?

People call out all kinds of answers: breeds of flowers, arrangements, colors, and more. After I get sufficient responses, I ask them what value I should give to their opinions. They all admit that I should give little. Why? Because there is only one person whose opinion matters in the circumstances, my wife's opinion! I use this to distinguish between what many people think religion is. Instead of everyone worshiping God in the way they prefer, it's seeking to understand how God wants to be worshiped.

That's why I see little value in going into more detail about engaging in the act of sex. My opinion isn't the one that you should value when it comes to engaging sexually and intimately with your spouse. I am still working on my second PhD with my own wife, and it is time to make good use of what you have learned here.

You've made it to the end of the book. I'm proud of you. So many people start marriage books (or any other self-improvement books) but never complete them! I want to close our time with one final look at our Bride and Groom.

1. Douglas Adams, chap. 6 in *The Hitchhiker's Guide to the Galaxy* (New York: DelRey, 1995).

2. Paget, 75.

3. Feldhahn and Sytsma, *Secrets of Sex and Marriage*, 158.

4. Elizabeth Pennisi, "New Theory Suggests Female Orgasms Are an Evolutionary Leftover," *Science*, August 1, 2016, accessed December 29, 2023, https://www.science.org/content/article/new-theory-suggests-female-orgasms-are-evolutionary-leftover.

5. Sophia Mitrokostas, "Here's What Happens to Your Body and Brain When You Orgasm," *Science Alert*, January 25, 2019, https://www.sciencealert.com/here-s-what-happens-to-your-brain-when-you-orgasm.

6. Feldhahn and Sytsma, *Secrets of Sex and Marriage*, 44.

7. University of Michigan Medical School, "Reproductive System," *Anatomy*, 1999, accessed, December 29, 2023, https://www.med.umich.edu/lrc/coursepages/m1/embryology/embryo/12reproductivesystem.htm; Richard J. Harrison, "Human Reproductive System | Definition, Diagram & Facts," *Encyclopedia Britannica*, last updated December 23, 2023, https://www.britannica.com/science/human-reproductive-system.

8. Visible Body, "Reproductive Process," 2023, accessed November 28, 2023, https://www.visiblebody.com/learn/reproductive/reproductive-process.

9. The sociologist Dr. Brad Wilcox delves into this: W. Bradford Wilcox, Jason S. Carroll, and Laurie DeRose, "Religious Men Can Be Devoted Dads, Too," *The New York Times*, May 18, 2019, https://www.nytimes.com/2019/05/18/opinion/sunday/happy-marriages.html; W. Bradford Wilcox, *Soft Patriarchs, New Men: How Christianity Shapes Fathers and Husbands* (Chicago: University of Chicago Press, 2004).

10. Nitzan Peri-Rotem and Vegard Skirbekk, "Religiosity, Sex Frequency, and Sexual Satisfaction in Britain: Evidence from the Third National Survey of Sexual Attitudes and Lifestyles (Natsal)," *Journal of Sex Research* 60, no. 1 (August 26, 2022): 13–35, https://doi.org/10.1080/00224499.2022.2108745.

11. James G. Pfaus et al., "The Whole versus the Sum of Some of the Parts: Toward Resolving the Apparent Controversy of Clitoral versus Vaginal Orgasms," *Socioaffective Neuroscience & Psychology* 6, no. 1 (October 2016): 32578, https://doi.org/10.3402/snp.v6.32578.

12. Marty Klein, *Sexual Intelligence: What We Really Want from Sex—and How to Get It* (New York: Harper Collins, 2012), 20.

13. Shaunti Feldhahn and Michael Sytsma, *Secrets of Sex and Marriage: 8 Surprises That Make All the Difference* (Ada, MI: Baker Books, 2023).

14. Christian Friendly Sex Positions (website), https://www.christianfriendlysexpositions.com

Twelve

THE BRIDE AND GROOM
AGAIN

What if Bride and Groom applied these lessons to the potential crisis of disunity from earlier on? What if they stayed strong to these principles, even in the toughest moments? How would the conversation change and could they avoid the spiral?

While we're not pretending things will always work out so poetically, life isn't that scripted, we do think the effort to understand one another, as the research has revealed, can be, well, kind of poetic after all. So here it goes: Bride and Groom one last time.

Read This Last (For Now)

Here's the scenario, verbatim, from the introduction:

It's one of those days. You and your spouse can't seem to get on the same page. You're together but never in sync. Miscommunication abounds. Both of you feel misunderstood. Throughout the day, you get snappier and more short-tempered. A few times, one of you attempts something more harmonious, but it doesn't play.

Man, days like that are exhausting, emotionally and spiritually. In situations like these, neither spouse feels loved or even like you like each other very much.

Now, imagine that at the end of a day like this, the husband sidles up to his wife and says, conspiratorially, "Hey . . . you wanna mess around?"

This time, after reading this book, husband, you know what to do, and you have a better idea of what to say. You understand the risk of her intuiting that you're pursuing sex rather than her.

Ladies, imagine that instead of "Hey, you wanna mess around?" your husband stopped you at the end of that rotten day, looked you in the eyes (maybe even taking your hands), and said, "I know that today has been a rough day. I know that we have not been on the same page. Days like today are really hard, but at the end of a day like this, I want you to know something very clearly: I choose you. Even on a day like today, I still choose you, and I still only want to be chosen by you. Even when things are hard, that never changes."

That would be a different experience, wouldn't it, ladies?

The amazing and mind-boggling thing: That is *exactly* what the guy thought he had said when he said, "Hey . . . you wanna mess around?" Guys, let's learn to say it in a way so that she experiences the fullness of our intentions.

When I conclude a talk like that, telling wives to imagine their husbands saying, "Even after a day like today, I choose you, and I only want to be chosen by you," I look out at a room full of women with tears in their eyes.

The difference is profound. From angry hurt to receptive warmth. Why? You, Mr. Groom, understood how she would interpret your words, and you chose the ones that would seduce her soul in your effort to love her better.

So this time, with these new words that make sense to her, what is her response? "What the—he chooses me? Even after today?" She is shocked that even though it has been a tough day—both of them are at fault. He doesn't blame her or ignore the problems. Instead, he actively chooses her over and above their tension. His response to her appreciation? He can see that his words hit home. She clearly wants to be chosen by him, and her moist eyes looking at him make that clear enough.

At the end of a tension-fraught day, she is not *devastated* by him asking; she is *restored* by his understanding; he is not *crushed* by her dismissal; he is *empowered* by how significant he clearly is to her.

Or, on the flip side, imagine when he asks conspiratorially, "Hey . . . you wanna mess around?" his wife hears what he thinks he's saying. She knows he is choosing her; she can see that he wants to communicate his connection to her in the most powerful way he knows how.

Guys, imagine your wife looks you in the eyes, kisses you, and says, "I'm hurting from today. I feel like you don't really like me. It's confusing to me that you want to have sex when I feel like you don't enjoy my company. I love that you want me, and I love that you choose me, even after a day like today. But I would feel your love more powerfully right now if we could talk a little, maybe shower together, maybe you can brush my hair, and then we'll see . . ."

Would you be inspired to connect in all of those ways? Are you ready to invest in what will bless and encourage her most? You may not have tears, but I bet your touch is gentle, and you're ready to hold her and listen. Why?

Because you, Mrs. Bride, understood what he meant in his question. Because of your agape love for him, you choose to understand him through his eyes. You know that he wants to love you well, so you gently guide him to accomplish what he wants—to seduce you. Not just your body, but your whole person choosing his whole person and being chosen by his whole person.

Do they both limp away emotionally like wounded soldiers? No, likely they hug, and maybe he gets to wipe away tears as they clean up after this busy day or take turns with the kids. They end up more bonded than before. I can confidently say that the chances of those feelings of intimacy ending up in *sexual* intimacy—the kind they *both* desire—are much higher than before, even if it's not guaranteed.

Why? Because you, Bride and Groom, are determined to transform this tough moment into a taste of the Garden. You chose vulnerability and grace. You decided to live out a living parable of His love. You chose to love intimately and sacrificially, just as Christ did for us.

FAQs

Within our research, we uncovered several issues and ideas that didn't work within the format of this book but were some of the common questions that I get whenever I teach this material or implement it in counseling. All too often, these are the main themes of marriage books or are integrated in unhealthy ways, and that is part of why they are often the issues for people. Here, we will handle them carefully; many of these questions are about patterns and tendencies that comedians and speakers make fortunes from implying they're universal. This is funny to the majority, but they can make the minority feel like circus freaks. Tread carefully.

1. What if the wife has a higher sex drive?

2. Do men have a higher "sex drive" than women?

3. Are men more "visual"?

4. Is sex a "need"?

5. What about pornography?

6. Why do I—why does he (or she)—seem too childish about sex sometimes?

7. Does personality and temperament play a role in psychological energy?

8. What about mixed-orientation marriages?

9. How often should couples have sex?

10. How can I have a right relationship with this God you talk about so much?

1. Question: What if the wife has a higher sex drive?

Answer: It might be for many reasons, but it's not uncommon. Worry not!

In many marriages, it's the woman who is pining for more frequent sexual engagement—about one in four to one in three, according to FAQ 2. So, if you're in that situation, you're not alone.

Men, it may be that you're naturally wired differently. No man perfectly fits the John Wayne stereotype, nor should they. Jesus wasn't weak (actually, he was omnipotent), but he wasn't the quiet, gruff, lumberjack type either. He preached about peace and strength submitted to a higher authority. He wept openly. The point is you must detach secular masculinity from biblical masculinity.

Your libido may naturally be lower than your spouse's—full stop. There is nothing more to interpret, no hidden, suppressed reason; you're just built that way. Maybe you actually have lower testosterone than your wife! This might feel shameful, but you should take peace in it. Sometimes we're simply wired differently. The goal is still to try to create the sexually intimate life that she desires. Maybe you have a more reactive sexual energy, and once you get started, the engine will rev. Regardless, there are certainly ways to give her sexual stimulation even if you aren't interested in it for yourself.

It's also possible you've had a nuclear reactor meltdown of psychological energy. You've overstretched yourself so much that you're at negative psychological energy every night. You're therefore at the point of physical or mental exhaustion, such that even though it costs you zero points to start sex, your body forces you straight into sleep. The mornings don't work either because you're up early to take the kids to school and go to work.

We've talked elsewhere about pornography, but pornography and masturbation will direct your libido away from the healthy place—in bed with your wife—and toward places of sin. This won't allow leftover arousal for sex. You're stealing the joy of intimacy from your spouse and robbing yourself of fulfilling sex—in addition to outright sinning. Cut it out of your life straight away; don't wait!

In FAQ 8, we talk about mixed-orientation marriages. This is where one spouse is more or only attracted to the same sex but married to someone of the opposite sex. If this is you, turn there.

I've considered various reasons why women separate out their identity from sex. I talk about it more in Chapter 9, under "Hormones and Arousal." Some of these reasons might apply to you, husband. For example, you may have been in an abusive relationship where a girlfriend or ex-wife physically or emotionally abused you, and this abuse seeped into sex. Perhaps you were sexually abused in even more sinister ways as a child, and incest trauma made you put up a wall to sex. Besides miraculous healing by Jesus's hand, which I believe you should pray for, seek aid from a counselor, a pastor, strong friends, and spiritual mentors to walk you through this. You're not alone!

Finally, it's possible that you feel pressure to perform. You feel the pressure of false church teaching, which assumes that men will always be hungering for sex like animals, but you simply don't feel that way. You may feel the double pressure to "be a man" and feel like a failure of a man for not being a sex-driven machine. This, in turn, makes you doubt yourself, which lowers your sex drive, which lowers your confidence, and so forth. Or, in some healthier but still dangerous church cultures, maybe you feel the pressure to be hyper-intentional, pleasing her perfectly in every way every time, beating yourself up if she doesn't have an orgasm. If you're generally prone to perfectionism or self-flagellation, this could backfire and create more pressure than necessary. Through these barriers, your libido might lower, or sex takes psychological energy points from you as an investment.

In either case, I'd recommend taking this concern to your spouse. Her gracious reassurance and affection will hopefully win you over and assuage your fears. She can lovingly remind you, over and over, not to put pressure on yourself.

Wives, this also doesn't mean there is something broken in you. It doesn't mean that you're some kind of sex fiend or that you are just not attractive enough to inspire your husband. As noted above, he may be dealing with pornography (see FAQ 5), a health issue, or just a reduced drive. You can help guide him in ways to give you sexual satisfaction even if he isn't as interested in being a recipient. We all like it when someone works to remove our barriers. Are there any you could remove for him?

Pay special attention to the "Room to Fail" section in Chapter 11 and "Pressure to Perform" in Chapter 10.

This FAQ assumes the lower sex drive in the husband is a problem, but it doesn't need to be problematic in itself. If both the husband and wife have low drives or exceedingly *high* drives, they likely won't experience much conflict—so they're probably not reading this book. As I mentioned before in the introduction, your intuitions about sex and identity might be flipped—the wife might intuit sex as affirming her at a core level, and the husband does not. In that case, great! Apply the principles of this book in those terms.

This FAQ is directed to men who experience shame because of their lower sex drive, but some women feel shame because of their higher sex drive. These women likely intuit things in the best way—that sex is about affirmation of *them*. This is no cause for shame; that intuition is a cause for celebration! At church conferences on marriage, you might feel left out in that 30 percent minority, but remember your aim is to grow and enjoy *your* marriage, not fit in. And, at those white foldout tables with four other couples in a breakout session, *be honest*! The more we recognize the minority of marriages, the more those couples will feel welcomed, and the more honest and healing the community can become. Hopefully, throughout the book, I've broken down enough of the damaging stereotypes to undermine the same that comes with living with the minority experience or struggle.

Ultimately, take this issue to the Lord in prayer and to your Christian community for support. But if the Christian community burns you, lean on each other. Sex is for you and your spouse to share alone, after all.

2. Question: Do men have a higher "sex drive" than women?

Answer: Yes, but that discrepancy is probably less than you think and for different reasons.

Around 70 percent of men have a higher sex drive than women. That is substantial, but most of us subconsciously think of the discrepancy as higher. "What? Isn't it 100 percent of men have a higher sex drive?" No. It's not. I'll now delve into some of the research into the 70–30 I've claimed, which I've seen in my practice and in the data.

In a review, Baumeister et al. write, "A majority of husbands (60 percent) but only a minority of wives (32 percent) said they would prefer to have sex more often."[1] While this split is 60–30, with 10 percent in the middle, other results suggest a slightly higher discrepancy. For example, one study found, "Nearly all the men (91 percent) but only half the women (52 percent) experienced sexual desire several times a week or more."[2] This suggests a 40 percent disparity, similar to my prediction.

There are some interesting nuances here that are drawn in studies on sex drive. First, "sex drive" is difficult to define and control in academic research, so analysts look at more specific things. One meta-analysis summarized everything:

> In spontaneous thoughts about sex, frequency and variety of sexual fantasies, desired frequency of intercourse, desired number of partners, masturbation, liking for various sexual practices, willingness to forego sex, initiating versus refusing sex, making sacrifices for sex, and other measures.

No contrary findings (indicating stronger sexual motivation among women) were found. Hence we conclude that the male sex drive is stronger than the female sex drive.[3]

Another self-reported study conducted online surveyed two hundred thousand people across the entire world, and men consistently had a higher sex drive than women. "The current research identified two additional sex differences that were remarkably consistent across cultures. In all nations, men reported having higher sex drives than women [. . .] and in all nations, women had more variable sex drives than men did."[4]

Feldhahn and Sytsma's survey found that "79 percent of couples the spouses have different levels of desire. The husband has the higher desire in 54 percent of marriages, and the wife has the higher desire in 24 percent of marriages. (Due to rounding, those percentages don't quite total 79 percent.)"[5] So twice as many husbands have a higher sex drive than their spouses, according to their cutting-edge research.

Men's sex drive is also more consistent over time and more consistent over contexts. Another way to measure sex drive is how often men think about sex.

It does seem to be an established fact that men think about sex more often than women. Fifty-four percent of men compared to 19 percent of women think about sex every day or several times a day.[6]

Another study of seven hundred people in 2006 found that men report having specific instances of sexual desire around thirty-seven times a week, whereas women tend to desire it around eight times per week. As far as thinking about it, men thought about sex sixty times a week, whereas women thought about it fourteen times.[7]

To summarize, in my own practice, I have found that around 70 percent of men have a higher sex drive than their spouses, which leaves 30 percent of women who have a higher drive. This is especially true for those who struggle with sex. That overlaps with the research pretty well.

I say all that to say, *yes*, men, on average, have a higher sex drive and think differently about sex than women. This inherent higher sex drive seems to somewhat transcend cultures. Though, again, it's lower than you might think.

Some research shows that the "hot and sexy" hormones drop for a married man, yet they rise, along with oxytocin, for a married woman in a good relationship. "The picture becomes even bleaker when looked at from a basic chemical level. The 'hot and sexy' chemicals (like dopamine) drop for a married man, yet they rise, along with oxytocin, for a married woman in a good relationship. Bluntly put, the chemicals that result in a high reward need to be stoked up within marriages."[8]

So, even for men, long-term sexual intimacy requires intentional investment in the other person as your lover. Men naturally unite these emotions of sexuality and intimacy more than most women do (which is kind of the theme of this whole book).

3. Question: Are men more "visual"?

Answer: Maybe. Sort of? Tentatively, yes.

Once again, we are talking in generalities here (I'm personally not nearly as visually driven as most men), but yes. If women wear something revealing, it normally gets guys' minds racing.[9] Guys, the next step in this process, lusting, is on you. You make the mental action or decide not to dwell on the spark of lust. Ladies, you don't *cause* guys to sin by wearing something revealing, but the Christian life is about more than not causing someone to sin (see Romans 14). It is about helping, encouraging, and loving.

Guys can look away, but it's nearly impossible for men not to at least take notice when women wear something exposing. Consider wearing more modest clothing in the godly effort to encourage the boys, boyfriends, and husbands of other women. You are also being a better sister to those other wives and girlfriends. But, of course, the final responsibility of sin rests squarely on the sinner's shoulders.

That aside, most often, men apparently do think more "visually." Marketers, social media algorithms, and the pornography industry exploit this. Men may be aroused more easily by visual stimuli because their brains tend to operate differently in their attention in general.[10] More research is being done into why this is, but the main reason seems to be because it takes less imagination to fantasize about sex playing out.

Well, where does this "visual" attraction and potential lust go? Lust means desiring something you cannot or should not have. If you could have it without being caught, you would; that is lust (see Matt. 5:28). This idea also connects with "fantasies," which is imagining what sex or a fling would be like with some person. This is a dangerous, dangerous feeling to give any rope to—flee from these men and women!

Unfortunately, in recent decades, pornography has given access to these fantasies in the most destructive ways. Now, all of what I said can be true of women too, but we're speaking in generalities, and men tend to be more moved by visual stimuli (I'm not in the majority).

4. Question: Is sex a "need"?

Answer: It depends on what you mean by "need," but in the sense we often use it, no.

I see this word in books, hear it from speakers, and read it in articles all the time: sex is a "need" for men. Although most men are simply trying to get across the importance of sex, and it helps communicate the strength of their psychological desire, I *need* to clarify and limit that word.

Men indeed have a stronger hormonal desire for sex, and the physical buildup of sperm does physically accumulate for release. But the problem with "need" is that it equates having sex to something like eating food or drinking water. That can be dangerous. If sex is a need for food or water, then it justifies quite a bit for men.

If a man has been away from his wife for a week, he finds himself in a hotel room, and he "needs" sexual release . . . Do you see how this language is a problem?

Men will not starve to death if they don't have sex. Living in sexual purity is difficult, but it's not impossible. That's why I caution against "need."

However, women, you would very likely describe your own desires for romantic dates, time with your girlfriends, or emotional affirmation as "needs." Because, in truth, you do need those things for a healthy relationship. And I would say the same about sex.

If you guys don't go on romantic dates, you, wife, cannot use that as an excuse for infidelity. Neither can men use a thin sex life as an excuse for infidelity. Both of you should strive for a full, rich relationship that includes time spent in sexual intimacy and romantic dates.

You need to go on romantic dates and you need to make love for a healthy marriage.

You don't need either of those things like you need food and water.

Remember the "start with me" principle.

5. Question: What about pornography?

Answer: You can survive this.

First things first, if you still struggle with pornography at all, you need to seek help from others to destroy the cancer in your life. You will not be able to do it all; you'll need to pull together with other men or women and take it one day at a time. Lean on your church and depend on the strength of the Spirit—and you must also get rid of your access to it. Put a filter on your phone. On my devices, I have Covenant Eyes, an internet browser and filter that checks my activity. It sends a weekly report to one of my accountability partners, who checks it and talks to me about anything suspicious.

It forces me to think, "What I'm about to do will be seen by my friend who's going to confront me."

I also don't have access to my Apple ID password because I know in my flesh I'll eventually download something sketchy. Other people have access to my Kindle account and see what I get on there. If you get access through Instagram, delete it. If you find a backdoor around your blockers, find a way to shut those doors. Do whatever you need to do, even if it's just temporary.

It's worth noting that more and more women are, unfortunately, also struggling with porn. Researchers in 2018 found that 25 percent of young women had looked at porn in the last week.[11] If you include books like *Fifty Shades of Grey* or other explicit romance novels, the discrepancy between men's and women's porn engagement almost disappears.[12]

Jesus once taught: "You have heard that it was said, 'You shall not commit adultery.' But I say to you that everyone who looks at a woman with lustful intent has already committed adultery with her in his heart. If your right eye causes you to sin, tear it out and throw it away. For it is better that you lose one of your members than that your whole body be thrown into hell. And if your right hand causes you to sin, cut it off and throw it away. For it is better that you lose one of your members than that your whole body go into hell" (Matt. 5:27–30). There's so much I could unpack here, but the main message is clear: sin is serious stuff, especially lust. God knows how powerful sex is to instill lust.

If you've never confessed these things to your spouse in any way, shape, or form, you *need* to confess it to them, as difficult as it is. This is a delicate process because it will probably hurt badly. You will want a therapist or your pastor or another godly, mature Christian leader to help walk you through this difficult process. It doesn't mean updating them on how your progress is going—that's normally just going to crush them with inadequacy and sadness if you ever mess up again.

But confess at least a one-time "Honey, I've struggled with this for years now, but I'm ready to be done with it. I'm putting blockers in place, I'm calling Joe every day to check in with him, and I'm taking it one step at a time. Please forgive me. I love you and want to cherish you more than anything else." Add whatever else you need to add.

If your spouse comes to you with this, I implore you to treat them graciously. You have every right to feel angry and sad, confused and hurt. They don't turn to pornography because you're inadequate. They turn to it because *they're* addicted and in sin. This can be especially difficult for women to hear about—so wives, respond with sadness, anger, and whatever else you need to, but also grace.

If your spouse is getting help, they're on their way to overcoming it. You must support them in this struggle. Be on their team, not against them. You've committed to being on their team, just like they've committed to being on your team. Understand that if they confess this to you, it's good news because almost all men and many women have, at the very least, been exposed to it.

If you've never talked about it at all, you should. If they're free from the addiction, then they probably have talked to you about it. Cry if you need to, be angry, but do not sin. Forgive them when you can, and help them in their journey to healing so that you can both experience freedom. If you *and* their addiction are against them, it makes something that feels impossible all the more.

Men and women, once you've started the process of becoming unaddicted and breaking free from it, you'll have to continue to unlearn expectations from those books or videos. Zimmerman said in her book that "watching porn is a prevalent way people think they are learning about sex. Except porn isn't sex; it's entertainment."[13]

Something that trains us to be self-centered, lustful, exploitative, or abusive is "entertainment" that will steal God's best from us.

Remember that those are fantasies; they aren't real. Those porn stars often struggle more than anyone else with sexual dysfunction. The "professionals" can have the worst, most broken, horrendous sexuality. Many of them are effectively slaves in the sex trading industry. You must constantly remember that it is fake, but you have access to the real deal. Those images and videos are tricking your brain into releasing the chemicals that produce sexual gratification, but those women or men don't actually want you at all. Your wife or husband actually wants you.

Yes, your spouse will be imperfect, and they're definitely not going to fulfill all of your fantasies. Instead, you need to remember that they *are* your fantasy. However he or she approaches sex with you must *become* your fantasy.

Wives and husbands, this is the time to redouble your efforts to show your struggling spouse how much you love them. Don't pull away. Press in and show them your affection through sex. If you're unreasonably close-handed and pulling away, it will make things harder. Don't think to remove sex as a punishment. It will breed greater insecurity and send them back to their temptations.

I cannot stress enough the importance of seeking help from a psychologist at this point. I would add that you should try to find one that's a strong Christian—some progressive psychologists have gotten the notion that pornography isn't all that bad, contrary to all available evidence.

6. Question: Why do I—why does he (or she)—seem so childish about sex sometimes?

Answer: It may have to do with when he (or she) was introduced it.

Maybe you feel childish when you're turned down sexually. You have your feelings hurt and start to pout and mope like a five-year-old. Maybe you even lash out and throw a fit. Then, when you reflect on it, you feel stupid for acting out of such a childish mindset. I went through this in my life, and began wondering why, then it hit me: I was exposed to adult sexuality when I was five years old. Surely it's not a coincidence I started acting like a five-year-old when something frustrated me sexually.

So for those struggling with this, ask yourself: When were you exposed? This could be through walking in on sex, hearing about sex, sexual abuse, or even being taught in school. For many, their first exposure was through pornography. If you were exposed to porn or other expressions of sex around nine years old, then you may default to acting/feeling a little like a nine-year-old when you feel things about sex.

I have not been able to uncover any good research that speaks directly to this (though there are many studies that report on the dangers of early sexualization in general). Still, something must be triggered in the brain chemistry that has some lasting effect so that later in life, there is what feels like a default setting to that maturity stage. Once you grow aware of this, you can consciously choose different actions, of course, but the instinctive feelings can be intense.

A child in a man's body with his responsibility is dangerous, so we need to tackle it, fast. If you were exposed to sex early on in your life, that's not an excuse, but those childish feelings make sense now, don't they? As I mentioned, I can relate. I was exposed to sex via pornography when I was five. I wish that were uncommon, but it was nearly ubiquitous in my generation for boys to be exposed in exactly the way I was—somebody had snuck Dad's *Playboy* into the woods.

Decades later and married, in a moment of doing a "nobody on the playground likes me" kind of tantrum alone one night after feeling rejected, I wrote my feelings in a journal. A few minutes later, when I read back over it, I was struck by how childish my words seemed! I started chuckling, and when my wife came out to check on me, I asked her if I was pouting. She said yes. I asked her if I ever pouted about anything else. She said she couldn't think of anything. At that moment, I realized that I had psychologically reverted back to that five-year-old!

It was a battle to mature my views about sex and start thinking about it like a man and not a boy. It's possible to do; there is no controlling puppeteer making you act like a foolish child, though it feels like it. If you rely on the strength of the Holy Spirit, you have the ability to cut those strings and make your life better.

However, there is a much more serious version of this as well. More harmful than early introduction of pornography: Sexual abuse. Childhood sex play is also tragically common. It may progress from "playing house/married/doctor" to "show me yours, and I will show you mine," to actual sex acts that one kid in a neighborhood teaches to the other kids. Often, these experiences can create a strong and lifelong sense of shame impacting adult sexuality!

This venue is not appropriate to engage in either of these topics. Abuse is too complex to be covered in an FAQ section. But, of course, childhood abuse can have a powerful influence on your feelings about and experience of sex. Instead, let me strongly recommend professional counseling with a licensed counselor who is a Bible-believing Christian and has experience working with people through trauma. You can experience freedom from the trauma, pain, lies and abuses that haunt you. You can find closure and recovery. There is no close second for receiving trauma recovery.

I would also recommend some books that can offer some insights. They include *The Wounded Heart* by Dan Allender and *The Body Keeps the Score* by Bessel van der Kolk. I've also had *The Courage to Heal* by Ellen Bass and Laura Davis strongly recommended to me, though I haven't worked through it myself yet. Much like how we responded to mental illness in Chapter 8, try to become a mini-expert on abuse to walk with your spouse in healing.

7. Question: Does personality and temperament play a role in psychological energy?

Answer: Of course it does.

In many ways, temperament is best understood as nothing more than an inventory of what comes naturally to you (costs little or no psychological energy).

So, as an example to illustrate my point, let's follow Jill through her day. Jill is an introvert, but she spends the whole day in meetings that go in circles. On top of that, she went to her sister's house for a party. At the end of the day, she's mentally exhausted. To clear her mind and recharge a little before bed, she continues one of her canvas paintings. It's spending physical energy but really recharging her psych tank. She hits the hay, spent physically but not completely drained mentally, ready for sleep.

Now, what's close to the center of your identity is motivating. It means that, for the most part, you receive psychological points from doing it. If someone is passionate, and it's in their niche for their personality and temperament, they'll recharge their batteries. Jill is a painter. She loves to paint because it brings her satisfaction, a sense of completion, and expressiveness. When something like that is fairly central to you, painting isn't hard to do. It doesn't take many psych points to get started, and it returns points.

Let's say Jill starts with forty. Those pointless meetings cost twenty-five. She left her sister's party early, so it only cost her ten points. She's at the end of the day with only five psych points to spend. Painting costs zero up front, maybe three or four at most. Luckily, painting recharges her, so it returns thirty after she's done. Sleep will catch her up to full by the next day.

Obviously, I'm just making up the point system to get a message across, but you get the idea.

Some things have a high cost but a high reward. When you're single, going out on a date is a high-risk, high-reward scenario. It takes some psych points to get ready, plan where to go, and think ahead about questions, but the reward is big. Getting into a good book may be another one. It takes psych points to invest in the characters of the book and actually sit down to read, but the payoff can be awesome. Maybe the date crashes and burns, or maybe the book has a terrible ending. Low payoff.

If you're exhausted and just want to crash in bed, you won't be able to muster the psych points to start a book, even if you know it will pay off with more down the line. One of the driving factors in her low tank is her introversion, but there are countless such character traits.

8. Question: What about mixed-orientation marriages?

Answer: Find support from others! You're not in this alone.

If you are older than forty, you may wonder about including an FAQ like this one. If you're younger than thirty, you probably don't. Mark thought it was a must, and I agreed. Like the other FAQs, this isn't an easy topic, but many young couples especially are facing confusion here, and with the changes in the culture, more older couples are asking tough questions as well. "Mixed orientation" refers to those situations in which either the husband is primarily attracted to other men or the bride is primarily attracted to other women or both.

I've counseled and been friends with a few people in marriages like this, but in no way do I consider this my expertise. Many churches are coming to grips with the reality that some in our congregations will not be called to abstinence/singleness but still find themselves attracted to the same sex. Opinions vary on whether sexual orientation can change over time, but according even to the utterly secular APA, sexual orientation is probably a complex mixture of both nature and nurture.[14]

It's a contentious point of study in psychology for obvious reasons, but even secular publications usually admit the mixed bag. Some will be more strongly influenced by nature, others more strongly influenced by nurture. In heterosexual marriages, nurture can be faithfully submitted to God such that, hopefully, attraction turns to their spouse.

I'd say to couples struggling with sex in a relationship like this something similar to other couples: *Learn to love your spouse.* Make sex not broadly about what kind of people you're interested in, but making love to one person only—your husband or wife.

Sometimes, after years of faithful obedience and prayer, people will find their same-sex attraction diminishing. Praise God when that happens. Jackie Hill Perry, a theologian and poet, reflects on this joyful occurrence. She married her husband and has a blossoming family of several children after years of being lesbian before becoming a Christian.[15] But her story is not everyone's.

The beautiful thing about marriage in God's sight is that erotic sex is not essential for marriages. *Intimate* sex, where you get to know the other person, is pretty essential. As long as your marriage looks like a living parable of God's love for His people, you're pretty much set theologically.

As far as practically, I would suggest counsel from a Bible-affirming therapist, pastoral insight, and finding other couples who are in your boat. As isolated as you may feel, you're not alone. Trust this information to close friends and mentors, but since shame and embarrassment probably come easily with this burden, there's no need to be vocal unless you're called to it. While I may not necessarily affirm everything on the Center of Faith, Gender, and Sexuality website,[16] they do an excellent job of providing resources and blogs on mixed-orientation marriages—and they hold to a Christian, orthodox view of marriage and sex.

Trust the Lord throughout; lean on Him who knows your heart better than even your spouse. Remember, there's no need to put pressure on yourself—work with each other in graciousness toward what God wants: a sacred marriage with intimate, if not erotic, love.

9. Question: How often should couples have sex?

Answer: You already know there isn't one answer to this, don't you?

This is one particular area where some well-intentioned Christian teaching can cause damage by talking about expectations like a good thing. In particular, Christian speakers and writers have a nasty habit of prescribing expectations on the frequency of sex.

Let me clarify. I firmly believe that sex should be a regular engagement of married couples. Some neglect it, and that's unhealthy, don't get me wrong. But saying *as a rule* "you should do it *X* number of times a week," is extremely damaging. This is something *you* have to discuss. I have rarely met couples who naturally desire sex just as often as the other. Many just give up, and one spouse will say, "Fine, we'll do it your way." One "wins," but then both are unsatisfied. So, really, no one wins.

I've written on my website, "They cannot consider them both being able to win, so one of them just bears the brunt of the frequency or infrequency. What was once a source of strength, energy, and encouragement for them both has become a taboo topic filled with silence or long lectures, misunderstanding and resentment."[17]

As is the truth for *every* application of this book, the answer will not be easy. It takes both spouses' self-sacrifice and love to figure it out.

This is as good a time as any to remind you of an important fact: 30 percent of women reading this will statistically want sex more than their husbands. If that's the case, don't worry! If these are reversed, then they're reversed. Work from there.

What I say is this: As long as both parties are truly satisfied with their frequency, there's an open means of communication, and both of you regularly have intimate sex, then you're in the clear. When I say satisfied or content, I'm not implying *easy*. It's okay if it's hard work to keep up with regular sex. It's a worthy, essential sacrifice.

It may take time for the habit to bear fruit. That's okay. Push through.

One couple I counseled told me they had sex two to three times a day (they were in their forties). Another satisfied couple I counseled told me they happily had sex once a month. This certainly brushes against my qualifier that sex is "regular," but okay.

There's a range. Anywhere in between isn't necessarily bad. It depends on the couple.

The rule of thumb: Make room for sex in your lives however you can, however often you can. Yet, as mentioned in Chapter 8, avoid expectations, and enjoy the freer, more gratifying sex for the rest of your lives.

10. Question: How can I have a right relationship with this God you talk about so much?

Answer: You have an open invitation.

You can find all of these concepts in the Holy Bible in Romans 3:10–27, Ephesians 2:1–10, Romans 10:9–13, and John 3:1–21. Please don't take my word for it—go read them yourself.

I'm a donut guy. I know different people are tempted, food-wise, by various things, but donuts are a pretty easy sell to me. There have been many, many times when I've said to myself, "I am only going to have one donut." I mean it when I say it. However, later, when someone offers me another, I often (okay, usually) say yes. I'll bet there's something like this in your life as well.

Knowing that we are like this, how can we possibly think we could depend on ourselves and our good behavior for eternal salvation? How could we save ourselves from death or the consequences of our selfish choices? How could we doubt we need a savior? If I'm too weak to say "no" to a second donut, then how could I possibly be strong enough for stuff like defining my own value, creating my own purpose, or saving my own soul? I doubt in myself because, though I may be weak, I am not stupid enough to trust myself.

I need someone else to offer to save me, someone who would stand in for me, who might actually have the chops to pull off saving me. I've considered a lot of different options and opinions in my life, but most of them said that the whole thing depended mostly, largely, or entirely on me. We went over why that won't work.

Fortunately, a person exists who did all the heavy lifting for us. He did it according to His plan because He loved us. They called Him Jesus, and He came to save His own. I've put my faith in Him. All the eggs are in His basket. If He could live the way He did, die the way He did, and conquer death the way He did, then I know my chances with Him are good. I believe I'm secure in His hands just as surely as I know I'm *not* secure in mine.

If you've never asked Jesus to save you or have never put your faith in Him, I hope you will today. Someone challenged me that one more section needed to be in the book, and this is it. It's something we all need to know. All you have to do is talk to God about it—there aren't magic words, just a confession of needing Him and calling on Him to save you. That's *the* good news (the "gospel"), and it is good news indeed.

---

1. Roy F. Baumeister, Kathleen R. Catanese, and Kathleen D. Vohs, "Is There a Gender Difference in Strength of Sex Drive? Theoretical Views, Conceptual Distinctions, and a Review of Relevant Evidence," *Personality and Social Psychology Review* 5, no. 3 (August 2001): 242–73, https://doi.org/10.1207/s15327957pspr0503_5.

2. M. Brown and A. Auerback, "Communication Patterns in Initiation of Marital Sex," *Medical Aspects of Human Sexuality* 15, no. 1 (1981): 105–17.

3. Baumeister et al., "Is There a Gender Difference in Strength of Sex Drive?", 242.

4. Richard A. Lippa, "Sex Differences in Sex Drive, Sociosexuality, and Height across 53 Nations: Testing Evolutionary and Social Structural Theories," *Archives of Sexual Behavior* 38, no. 5 (November 2, 2007): 631–51, https://doi.org/10.1007/s10508-007-9242-8.

5. Feldhahn and Sytsma, *Secrets of Sex and Marriage*, 110.

6. Gottman et al., *The Man's Guide to Women*, 94.

7. Pamela C. Regan and Leah Atkins, "Sex Differences and Similarities in Frequency and Intensity of Sexual Desire," *Social Behavior and Personality* 34, no. 1 (January 2006): 95–102, https://doi.org/10.2224/sbp.2006.34.1.95.

8. Malone and Harris, *Battles of the Sexes*, 67.

9. Sharron J. Lennon et al., "Dress and Sex: A Review of Empirical Research Involving Human Participants and Published in Refereed Journals," *Fashion and Textiles* 4, no. 14 (July 28, 2017), https://doi.org/10.1186/s40691-017-0101-5.

10. Heather A. Rupp and Kim Wallen, "Sex Differences in Response to Visual Sexual Stimuli: A Review," *Archives of Sexual Behavior* 37, no. 2 (August 1, 2007): 206–18, https://doi.org/10.1007/s10508-007-9217-9.

11. Marie-Ève Daspe et al., "When Pornography Use Feels Out of Control: The Moderation Effect of Relationship and Sexual Satisfaction," *Journal of Sex & Marital Therapy* 44, no. 4 (February 15, 2018): 343–53, https://doi.org/10.1080/0092623x.2017.1405301.

12. Stuart O'Brien, "Half of Women Reading More Erotic Literature during Lockdown," PA Life, March 10, 2021, https://palife.co.uk/news/half-of-women-reading-more-erotic-literature-during-lockdown/.

13. Zimmerman, *Sex Without Stress*, 26.

14. "Many think that nature and nurture both play complex roles; most people experience little or no sense of choice about their sexual orientation." From "Understanding Sexual Orientation and Homosexuality," APA, October 29, 2008, https://www.apa.org/topics/lgbtq/orientation.

15. Jackie Hill Perry, *Gay Girl, Good God: The Story of Who I Was, and Who God Has Always Been* (Nashville: B&H Publishing Group, 2018).

16. The Center for Faith, Sexuality & Gender (website), https://www.centerforfaith.com.

17. Chris Legg, "How Often Should a Married Couple Have Sex? Part I," March 19, 2015, Alethia Counseling, https://chrismlegg.com/2015/03/19/how-often-should-a-married-couple-have-sex-part-i/.

ACKNOWLEDGMENTS

From Chris:

To all my friends, family, audiences, clients, and others who let me practice and develop these ideas, I'm thankful. I'm also indebted to those innovators, like the Feldhahns, who changed the course of Christian marriage publishing.

Thank you, Christi Martin, for proofreading in such a timely, excellent manner. This book leveled up when we took you on.

And thanks to Mark, my beloved son, for helping me finally make this a reality.

From Mark:

Thanks to Dad for supporting me and believing in me throughout this project, even as I learned how to write a book alongside you. Thanks to Blake Atwood, my mentor in all things writing and editing. You invested in my potential early on as my boss, and I'm deeply grateful to you. Thanks, Mom, for homeschooling and raising me in the Bible so well.

Thank you Shannon, my beloved, best friend. I'm grateful for our year of marriage so far and can't wait for a lifetime of love with you.

Printed in Great Britain
by Amazon

37879203R00195